MILLENNIAL CINEMA

MILLENNIAL CINEMA
MEMORY IN GLOBAL FILM

Edited by
Amresh Sinha and Terence McSweeney

WALLFLOWER PRESS
LONDON & NEW YORK

A Wallflower Book
Published by
Columbia University Press
Publishers Since 1893
New York • Chichester, West Sussex
cup.columbia.edu

A complete CIP record is available from the Library of Congress

ISBN 978-0-231-16192-3 (cloth : alk. paper)
ISBN 978-0-231-16193-0 (pbk. : alk. paper)
ISBN 978-0-231-85001-8 (e-book)

Design by Elsa Mathern

Columbia University Press books are printed on permanent
and durable acid-free paper.
This book is printed on paper with recycled content.
Printed in the United States of America

c 10 9 8 7 6 5 4 3 2 1
p 10 9 8 7 6 5 4 3 2 1

CONTENTS

In the loving memory of my father, Dr. B. P. Sinha (1919–2002).
– Amresh Sinha

This volume is dedicated to the memory of my late brother-in-law Dima, a great lover of film; and to my sons Harrison and Wyatt.
– Terence McSweeney

ACKNOWLEDGEMENTS

It is with great pleasure we acknowledge the contributions of all those who participated at the initial stage of production of the book, especially Gillian Harkins and Mary Savigar. Together we sincerely thank Yoram Allon, Jodie Lee Taylor and Jackie Downs of Wallflower Press for their infrastructural support and help in making this volume come to life. We would also like to express our deep gratitude to all our esteemed scholars whose contributions here have added further significance to the contemporary discourse of memory in global cinema.

An ambitious project of this size and scope would not be possible without the help and support of a huge number of people.

Terence would like to thank Alistair Harvey for his role in the early evolution of the project, Jeff Geiger for his continued assistance and support of his academic career, Jason Moran and George Greenhalgh for their input and feedback on his *Oldboy* article, and above all his family, especially his father, who introduced him to film, and his loving and always patient wife, proofreader and inspiration, Olga McSweeney, who always offered wise council.

Amresh would like to thank his teachers, colleagues and friends at JNU, SUNY, Buffalo, York University, New York University, The School of Visual Arts, College of Staten Island, Brooklyn College and The New School. He also thanks Ian Balfour, Reeves Lehmann, Sal Petrosino, Amit Das, Anil Pal for their invaluable friendship and Liz Helfgott for her diligent editing, advice and helpful suggestions on his article, but most of all for being his loving and joyful partner.

NOTES ON CONTRIBUTORS

PAUL ATKINSON teaches in the Communications and Writing programme at Monash University, Melbourne. His early research focuses on the relationship between materiality and corporeality in Henri Bergson's writings on science, with particular emphasis on the relationship between immanent change and extended movement. He is currently working on a series of articles that explore the relationship between processual theories of time, aesthetics and narrative. Published articles explore a range of topics including Bergson's vitalism, cinema and foreseeability, the relationship between animation and comic books, time and recognition, the durational limits of affect and the implied movement in still images.

LYNDA CHAPPLE has taught widely in the areas of film studies, literature, cultural studies and language in Hong Kong, Macao and Australia. She has published articles in the areas of film studies, literature and pedagogical practice, and is working on a book on the intersections between costume, femininity and cinema. She currently teaches at Monash University, Melbourne.

JONATHAN ELLIS is Senior Lecturer in American Literature at Sheffield University. He is the author of *Art and Memory in the Work of Elizabeth Bishop* (2006), as well as articles and essays on Woody Allen, Paul Muldoon, Sylvia Plath, Anne Stevenson and Jeanette Winterson. He has been the recipient of a Leverhulme Early Career Fellowship and a British Academy Research Development Award. His next book is on twentieth-century letter writing.

JEHANNE-MARIE GAVARINI is a visual artist whose work has been exhibited extensively. In addition to her artistic work, she writes about art and visual culture. She is the co-translator of *Tomboy* (2007), an autobiographical novel by acclaimed Franco-Algerian writer Nina Bouraoui. Recent publications include 'Permeable Borders in *Notre Musique*' in *Zoom in, Zoom out: Crossing Borders in Contemporary European Cinema* (2007).

Gavarini is currently Professor of Art at the University of Massachusetts Lowell and Resident Scholar at the Women's Studies Research Center at Brandeis University.

RUSSELL J. A. KILBOURN is Associate Professor in Wilfrid Laurier University's Department of English and Film Studies, specialising in film theory. His current research interest is the representation of memory in film, which is the focus of his book *Cinema, Memory, Modernity* (2010). He has published on film, cultural studies and comparative literature, as well as contributions to three book collections on German author W. G. Sebald. Dr. Kilbourn is also a series editor for the *Film and Media Studies* series at Wilfrid Laurier University Press.

TERENCE McSWEENEY is Lecturer in Film Studies at Southampton Solent University. His most recent publications include 'Apocalypto Now: A New Millennial Pax Americana in Crisis?' in *Media and the Apocalypse Anthology* (2009) and 'Land of the Dead: George Romero's Vision of a Post 9/11 America' in *Re-Framing 9/11: Popular Culture and The War on Terror* (2010), and is the author of *Contemporary American Cinema: 9/11 Frames per Second* (forthcoming, 2012).

BELINDA MORRISSEY is currently an independent scholar. She is the author of *When Women Kill: Questions of Agency and Subjectivity* (2003) and has published in journals including *Social Semiotics*, *Continuum* and *Australian Feminist Studies*. She has also contributed chapters to *When Women Kill: Questions of Agency and Subjectivity* (2006) and *The Reinvention of Everyday Life* (2006).

DAVID MURPHY is Professor of French and Postcolonial Studies at the University of Stirling, UK. He has published widely on African cinema, and is the author of *Sembene: Imagining Alternatives in Film and Fiction* (2000) and co-author of *Postcolonial African Cinema: Ten Directors* (2007). He is also co-editor of several collections of essays, including: *Francophone Postcolonial Studies* (2003) and *Postcolonial Thought in the French-Speaking World* (2009).

WARWICK MULES teaches in the School of English, Media Studies and Art History at University of Queensland. He is co-author of *Introducing Cultural and Media Studies: a Semiotic Approach* (2002) and author of numerous articles on film and visual culture. He is also the founding editor of peer-reviewed online journal *Transformations*.

STEVEN RAWLE is Lecturer in Film Studies at York St John University, UK. He is the co-author of *Basic Filmmaking: The Language of Film* (2010) and author of *Performance in the Cinema of Hal Hartley* (2011). Other published work has appeared in the *Journal of Japanese and Korean Cinema*, *Film Criticism* and *Asian Cinema*, and book chapters on subjects including *Battlestar Galactica*, the *Ring* films, the work of Takashi Miike and cult indie film stars.

ANA MARÍA SÁNCHEZ-ARCE is Lecturer in Twentieth and Twenty-First Century Literature and Critical Theory at Sheffield Hallam University, UK. She is co-editor of *European Intertexts: A Study of Women's Writing in English as Part of a European Fabric* (2005). She has published on contemporary literature and is currently finishing a monograph on Pedro Almodóvar and editing a collection of essays on identity and form.

AMRESH SINHA teaches film and media theory at New York University, the School of Visual Arts and the College of Staten Island. His articles have appeared in *In Practice: Adorno, Critical Theory and Cultural Studies* (2001), *Lost in the Archives* (2002) and *Subtitles: On the Foreignness of Film* (2004) as well as in *Transformations*; *Scope: An Online Journal of Film Studies*; *Colloquy: Text, Theory, Critique*; *Film-Philosophy*; and the *Connecticut Review*.

ALANNA THAIN is Assistant Professor of Film and Cultural Studies in the Department of English at McGill University, Montreal. She has published on David Lynch, *Battlestar Galactica*, David Cronenberg, contemporary intermedial dance performance and the animations of William Kentridge in journals such as *differences*, *Invisible Culture*, *Parallax* and *Nouvelles Vues sur le Cinéma Québécois*. She is also an editor of *Inflexions: A Journal of Research-Creation* and a researcher at the Moving Image Research Laboratory (MIRL) at McGill University.

PREFACE

Millennial Cinema: Memory in Global Film argues that the turn of the twenty-first century obsession with memory has had a particular impact on the production and reception of contemporary film. As an anthology it seeks to make a significant contribution to a growing area of teaching and research in memory studies. Demand for research and teaching on the topic of memory has proven inexhaustible; there is a huge appetite for this subject in the intellectual world today, as can be seen in the multitude of conferences organised and books or journals published in the last few years. But there are also significant gaps in this research, which *Millennial Cinema* is designed to fill, including studies of films treating memory in the era of the so-called 'memory boom'. In its single focus on the intersection of memory and film at century's end/beginning, *Millennial Cinema* meets a demonstrable need and opens up exciting new lines of scholarly inquiry.

Indeed, this volume is the first anthology to treat this particular nexus of film, memory, globalisation and contemporary history. In the last ten years or so, several studies have begun to explore memory in cinema more broadly, but none with such sustained contemporaneity or global focus. Recent anthologies on memory and visuality include Ana Douglass and Thomas A. Vogler's collection *Witness and Memory: The Discourse of Trauma* (2003) and Lisa Saltzman and Eric Rosenberg's anthology *Trauma and Visuality in Modernity* (2006). Both these texts explore trauma and visual culture, but neither explores problems of memory more broadly or pursues an international scope. Paul Grainge's edited collection *Memory and Popular Film* (2003) is more broadly focused on film and memory, but is not contemporary and focuses almost exclusively on Hollywood cinema. Pam Cook's *Screening the Past: Memory and Nostalgia in Cinema* (2004) is thematically closer to *Millennial Cinema*, but Cook's monograph provides a very broad overview of cinematic developments rather than a detailed focus on individual texts. While she discusses some contemporary films, many of the most interesting and challenging films of the new millennium have been produced since her study. Annette Kuhn's *An Everyday Magic: Cinema and Cultural Memory* (2002), another relevant volume, studies the activity of cinema-going and spectatorship more than the cinematic texts themselves. While *Millennial Cinema* also addresses issues of spectatorship and phenomenology, it does so from the perspective of the films rather than the audiences.

Several additional volumes do not treat film specifically, but they do highlight a growing interest in visual studies of memory across disciplines. Two texts exploring the subject of memory in the media include Marcia Landy's edited collection *The Historical Film: History and Memory in Media* (2000) and Gary R. Edgerton and Peter C. Rollins' anthology *Television Histories: Shaping Collective Memory in the Media Age* (2001). Loosely related as well is Vivian Sobchack's anthology *The Persistence of Vision: Cinema, Television, and the Modern Event* (1996), which deals with the history of modernity's representation in the mass media. Robert A. Rosentone's interesting volume *Visions of the Past: The Challenge of Film to Our Idea of History* (1995) explores how ideas of history are transformed when translated into images, a companion project but one quite different from the focus here on memory as a trope of the contemporary politics in recent films.

To our knowledge, there are no comparable texts available. What makes this volume unique is its interdisciplinary treatment of memory as a core component of films over the past twenty years. This interdisciplinary scholarship develops a new archive for enquiry into one of the central, as yet unexplored, problematics of cinema and culture at the turn of the twenty-first century.

Finally, *Millennial Cinema* demonstrates that memory is at the heart of film theory, technology, form and history of this period. Combining individual readings and interdisciplinary methodologies, our anthology thus offers some new analyses of the most discussed and debated films of the late twentieth and early twenty-first century.

INTRODUCTION
MILLENNIAL CINEMA: MEMORY IN GLOBAL FILM
AMRESH SINHA AND TERENCE McSWEENEY

Millennial Cinema: Memory in Global Film is the first anthology devoted exclusively to the study of memory, in its multiple forms, in twenty-first-century cinema, across films as diverse as *In the Mood for Love* (Wong Kar-wai, 2000), *Memento* (Christopher Nolan, 2000), *Mulholland Drive* (David Lynch, 2001), *City of God* (Fernando Meirelles, 2002), *Irreversible* (Gaspar Noé, 2002), *Oldboy* (Chan-wook Park, 2003), *Eternal Sunshine of the Spotless Mind* (Michel Gondry, 2004), *Moolaadé* (Ousmane Sembene, 2004), *Caché* (Michael Haneke, 2005), *Pan's Labyrinth* (Guillermo del Toro, 2006) and *The Namesake* (Mira Nair, 2006). The fascination with memory, which spans the globe, crossing ideological and cultural boundaries, is the central theme of this volume which interrogates films by some of the most well-known, interesting, challenging and talked-about directors working in cinema today around the globe.

Starting in the 1980s, memory became a significant topic across diverse humanities and social science disciplines. By the 1990s it was quite apparent that the technologies of globalism had affected the public discourse of memory in a thoroughly unprecedented manner all across the varied economic, political and cultural spectrum of the globe. One might trace this 'memory boom' to Yosef Hayim Yerushalmi's first publication of *Zakhor: Jewish History and Jewish Memory* in 1982. In the same year, Paul de Man published his famous paper on memory in *Yale French Studies*. A new edition of Yerushalmi's book was published in 1989, the same year that the English translation of an excerpt of Pierre Nora's epochal 'Between Memory and History: *Les Lieux de Memoire*' appeared in the spring issue of the now defunct journal, *Representations*. The work of Yerushalmi, de Man, Nora and, later, Derrida, Blanchot and the renaissance in Benjamin studies mark the beginning of the 'global memory culture' across the disciplinary boundaries of many North American universities. What started as an anxiety-prone discourse of the Jewish 'collective memory' (borrowed from Maurice Halbwachs) that Yerushalmi feared (a sentiment also shared by Nora and Jacques Le Goff, the French historian) would be 'eradicated by the conquering force of history' not only proved to be erroneous but launched a memory discourse that has proliferated in so many different areas of academic discourse that it is hard to imagine that memory as a subject matter prior to the turn of the century was mostly applied to the fields of classical philology, behavioural and/or applied psychology and neurobiology (see Nora 1996: 2).

Historically speaking, the rapidly growing phenomenon of memory studies at the intersection of local/global in the millennium is deeply indebted to Holocaust Studies and to the emergent discourse of national memory in postmodern and postcolonial studies of literature and films in the 1980s and 1990s. A number of conferences, journal articles, special collections and monographs quickly followed, making the 1990s the decade of memory across a number of research disciplines. Commenting on the world-wide popularity of the topic of memory in the millennium, Andreas Huyssen, states that 'since the epochal change of 1989/90, we observed the emergence of a transnational or global memory culture of astonishing proportions, and we have come to ask ourselves what the intense focus on the past and on traumatic memory might mean for the history of the present' (2007: 81–2). This 'astonishing' growth of memory studies has much to do with the changing constellation of time and space with regard to the intensification of globalising process in the turn of the twenty-first century. Perhaps therefore, the best way to examine how the emergence of this new phenomenon, the 'memory boom', has impacted upon the cultural productions of films around the globe is by asking scholars in the field of Philosophy, Literature, Humanities, Cultural Studies, Cinema Studies and the Arts, to consider particular works produced in different parts of the world during the beginning of the new millennium.

It is fitting that memory has become part of the cinematic zeitgeist. Since its invention film has had an almost symbiotic interaction with memory. The intertwining of memory and writing is underscored by both Plato and Aristotle and most notably in our times by Derrida. The presence of writing, as mechanical or prosthetic memory, has altered the very nature of memory and its reproduction. Although both Plato and Aristotle associate writing with the decline of memory (see the myth of Theuth, the inventor of writing, in the *Phaedrus*), we, on the other hand, following Proust and Derrida, believe that the existence of writing has transformed the nature of memory by releasing it from the confines of interiority of the soul into the exteriority of things/signs (see Plato 1998: 85, 274c–275a). It is equally the case that the invention of the photographic medium and then cinema also changed memory, in even as powerful and compelling ways. Perhaps the memory auteur *sui generis*, Andrei Tarkovsky, asserted that it was with the invention of the cinema in the last decade of the nineteenth century that man had created the means to effectively capture and replicate time: 'And simultaneously the possibility of reproducing that time on screen as often as he wanted, to repeat it and go back to it. He acquired a matrix for *actual time*' (Tarkovsky 1989: 62; emphasis in original). This 'impression of time' that Tarkovsky described shares the functions of memory in its ability to create a replica of a moment from the past and store it for later 'use'. For film this moment is captured and projected onto a screen; in the realm of the mind a memory is recreated through thought; for what more is memory other than an 'impression of time'?

This anthology seeks to raise important questions about the relationship between film and memory in the twenty-first century. It focuses on cinematic representation – situated within broader technologies of representation across the twentieth century – illuminating key elements of memory studies. What precisely is the relationship between memory and film? Is cinema the technology of memory *par excellence*, as so often asserted in its early emergence into popular culture? Or are the tensions between cinema and memory such that filmic representation is always already 'traumatic', in Freud's sense of the term, a retroaction that can only be realised in its future manifestations, such as the dimly-lit world of film reception? What do theories, technologies (virtual and prosthetic) and histories as well as social and cultural forms of memory tell us about how the past is remembered or forgotten? In other words, how does memory *become* cinematic, and has this process changed in the era of so-called globalisation? Moments recorded on film have become part of an indelible sense of cultural memory, touchstones of experience even for those not there to witness the events firsthand. Consider the lingering presence of the famous 26 seconds of the Zapruder footage, the moon landings or more recently the destruction of the Twin Towers in New York by two hijacked commercial airliners on 11 September 2001.

Here we address these questions through an interrogation of the complementary and at times contradictory relation between film and memory across dominant and emergent cultures of the late twentieth/early twenty-first centuries, and so the volume concentrates on films that captured

Fig. 1 The reverse chronological structure of *Memento* forces the viewer to experience a form of the protagonist's anterograde amnesia.

public attention and created a media spectacle since the late 1990s. Christopher Nolan's ground-breaking and critically acclaimed *Memento*, which unfolds in a reverse direction (like Gaspar Noé's *Irreversible*) in which the protagonist suffers from a condition of anterograde (short-term) memory loss, or Michel Gondry's dizzying *Eternal Sunshine of the Spotless Mind* in which a heartbroken man seeks to undergo a procedure which will literally erase the memories of a former girlfriend from his mind before ultimately discovering how integral these memories, both good and bad, are to his personality. Films like *Oldboy*, *In the Mood for Love* and *Pan's Labyrinth* deal with memory in more cultural and historical ways, but each tell intriguingly personal stories concerned with the role of memory in the formation of identity. Collectively these films represent, interrogate and participate in an archive of the recent past, a cultural synthesis and disjunction in film historiography worth interrogating as an epochal fragment of collective consciousness.

It is our hope that this volume will make a unique contribution, connecting considerations of memory to studies of film theory, culture, history and globalisation. It explores, from multi-faceted perspectives, the 'screening' of memory during the period of its alleged historical apotheosis: the turn of the twenty-first century. The following pages examine questions of amnesia, virtual memory, cultural and historical memory, episodic memory, collective memory, prosthetic memories, nostalgic experience and notions of (diasporic) identity in relation to memory by opening them up to the mnemonic discourses of theorists such as Hegel, Kant, Freud, Benjamin, Husserl, Proust, Bazin, Deleuze, Bergson, Ricoeur, Derrida, Foucault and others. More specifically, this book offers twelve chapters written exclusively for the volume that reflect a wide range of critical perspectives on discourses of memory in contemporary global cinema. These chapters focus in particular on diverse discourses of memory as they emerge through as well as opposed to the dominant narrative structures of Hollywood and global cinema.

This recent scholarship is split between studies of memory and trauma. While these areas overlap, there are also significant differences between them. Studies of memory have frequently undertaken broader historical and cultural critique. Explorations of the rise of memory as a concept have focused on the long nineteenth century and its generation of new theories and technologies of the self. For Pierre Nora 'the historical transformation of memory marks a decisive shift from the historical to psychological, from the social to the individual, from concrete … to subjective, from repetition to remembrance' (1996: 11). At the turn of last century, memory not only becomes 'a private affair', but it also finds itself deeply implicated in the Freudian discourse of trauma of the primal scene. Yet, despite this over-whelming interest in the study of memory and trauma, no single volume has yet explored the centrality of memory to films of this era in a global context. Existing work focuses almost entirely on broad, interdisciplinary approaches to individual and collective memory, either in its normative or its distorted forms. This anthology thus fills a substantial gap in film scholarship and is designed to reach audiences across Film Studies, to those interested in Cultural Studies, Feminism, Critical Theory, globalisa-tion and contemporary politics. The volume is also specifically designed for teaching, intended for students and tutors in the fields of Film Studies, Cultural Studies, Philosophy and Communication Theory. It makes a vital contribution to a growing area of teaching and research in memory studies, and gathers essays from a range of perspectives that interrogate the historical privileging of print media over other genres of representa-tion, while also questioning the turn to visual media as the *sine qua non* of memory, particularly as it figures crises of the twentieth century.

The growing influence of Henri Bergson and Gilles Deleuze on recent studies of both memory and film are evident in the first section of the book which is entitled Virtual and Prosthetic Memory. The explosion of Deleuze-related volumes can be partially attributed to the expanding interest and research on memory and identity. David Rodowick's account in the 'Preface' of his brilliant book on Deleuze suggests that the publica-tion of Deleuze's two influential cinema books 'had comparatively little impact on contemporary Anglophone film theory' (1997: ix). Judging from the articles in this anthology, Rodowick's account seems rather premature, or simply incorrect. Out of twelve chapters in this volume, almost all share a strong critical and interpretive reading of Deleuze's cinema philosophy, especially in relation to memory. Another strong current that permeates through various articles in this volume is the cultural and historical rep-resentation of memory in our contemporary global cinema. We have also designed the structure of the volume to include trauma and allegory; the latter signifies the art of storytelling in the memory discourse. A set of articles is devoted to precisely the allegorical and traumatic reconstruction of memory in films, namely those by Amresh Sinha (*The Namesake*), Belinda Morrisey (*Memento* and *Mulholland Drive*), Warwick Mules (*Tom White*) and Alanna Thain (*Caché*).

Thematically and structurally, the chapters are grouped under three sub-headings engaging with both topical and emerging memory debates which have appeared in the first decade of the new millennium: (1) Virtual and Prosthetic Memory; (2) Traumatic and Allegorical Memory; (3) Historical and Cultural Memory. The volume begins with an analysis of one of most controversial and compelling films of recent years, *Irreversible*. In 'Time, Memory and Movement in Gaspar Noé's *Irreversible* (2002)', Paul Atkinson considers the relationship between memory and film experience in Noé's shocking film. Atkinson's starting point is the Bergsonian concept of *durée*, or Bergson's claim that time is irreversible due to the interpolation of memory in perception. This idea is intriguingly explored in relation to *Irreversible* where the future is shown before its past, with the narrative revealed in the form of a succession of continuous flashbacks. Atkinson's analysis involves an examination of reversibility and irreversibility in the film; in particular, the relationship between phenomenological and narrative aspects of film form. *Irreversible* highlights the implied role of memory in narrative and audience reception through the inversion of its plot. This inversion foregrounds the theoretical connection between the occurrent memory of the viewer and the visible memory of the film.

The Academy Award-winning and hugely successful *Eternal Sunshine of the Spotless Mind* is one of the most 'theoretical' films to come out of Hollywood since the turn of the century. In 'Reconstructing Memory: Visual Virtuality in *Eternal Sunshine of the Spotless Mind*', Steven Rawle proposes that the film revolves around the relationship between images of memory and more concrete 'real' objects. Drawing on Deleuze's theory of 'the crystal image' and corresponding notions of virtuality, Rawle explores how the film depicts images of the recollected past, which coalesce with actual experiences in the perception of present moments. Gondry's use of repetitive stylistic and narrative schema manifests the past in the 'present' moments of narration throughout the film, especially during its memory-located sequences. By engaging with questions of spectatorship Rawle also contemplates the viewers' own experience of watching the film, arguing that Gondry's cinematic reconstruction of memory as theory engages the audience as an experiential force.

In 'Death Every Sunday Afternoon: The Virtual Memories of Hirokazu Kore-Eda's *Afterlife*', Alanna Thain's reading of this highly sensitive and nuanced Japanese film in the millennium is also deeply inflected by the works of Deleuze and Bergson. She is interested in exploring the question of cinematic specificity and its relation to memory through Bazin's seminal essay 'Death Every Afternoon'. Thain suggests that we often think of memory and memorialisation as a kind of fidelity to the past, remembrance as an act of love. If cinema has altered this, it might be in the sense that memory has become linked to a kind of infidelity through the force of cinematic repetition, a repetition that Bazin's essay describes as both the ultimate form of cinematic specificity and at the same time its greatest obscenity. By developing the notion of love as the infidelity of the filmic self, Thain argues that film itself functions as a memory machine. Love becomes the hinge between cinema and memory in *Afterlife*, with each of the main characters trying to come to terms with their memories of having been loved. Thain's reading of the film provocatively explores film's technological mediation of reality, memory and the role of the spectator.

We move in this section from the virtual to transnational memory, to cinema as memory machine, as prosthetic memory. We have included three chapters in this section representing Brazilian, Indian diasporic and African cinema. The emphasis here is on the treatment of memory in global culture, the intergenerational conflicts of transnational memory in the diaspora, and the memory of personalised and historicised trauma of female genital mutilation in a remote Senegalese village. We begin with Russell J. A. Kilbourn, in ''Prosthetic Memory' and Transnational Cinema: Globalised Identity and Narrative Recursivity in *City of God*', who takes on Alison Landsberg's idea of 'prosthetic memory' in application to the critically acclaimed Brazilian film *City of God* (2002) by Fernando Meirelles. 'Cinema as "cultural memory" is not a new idea', Kilbourn concurs, 'but what does it really mean to think of cinema as a kind of global memory system; as both source of and storehouse for our collectively most cherished memories?' What 'we' consider as our 'own' memory is to a large extent constituted in this day and age of globalisation by the discourse of visual representations in news media, film and photography. By conforming to the generic cinematic code of Hollywood cinema, *City of God*, as an example of transnational postmodern cinema, invokes both nostalgia (*à la*

Jameson) and a sense of an artificial collective memory system in the global consumption of these cinematic codes. *City of God* is thus at once intensely local, i.e. Brazilian, both in cultural and political terms, but also global in the sense that it lends itself to the commodification of visual matrix across transnational spaces. Kilbourn's focus in this chapter is to theorise the intertextual aspects of 'prosthetic memory' – 'the eminently cinematic nature of postmodern memory' – in *City of God*, within the context of global consumption of popular culture produced in America.

Amresh Sinha, in 'Memories of a Catastrophe: Trauma and the Name in Mira Nair's *The Namesake*', explores the complex nexus between memory, trauma, desire and the name in the Indian diaspora in the United States. According to him, the significance of the relationship between the name and memory cannot be 'exaggerated' in the context of this film. Through a complex analysis of the significance of Gogol's name as the *sine qua non* of remembering, Sinha introduces us to a trajectory in film and cultural studies that has been rarely traversed. The inseparability of the name from its identity is the crux of Sinha's thesis which he mediates through the works of Hegel, Benjamin and Derrida. The name 'Gogol' responds, answers to, in the memory of the name, in the absence of the self. It is in that sense, in its 'essence', that the name signifies an exteriority, an outside, which resists being dialectically absorbed by the interiority of recollection. 'Gogol' becomes an exterior sign, *tekhné*, of remembering the trauma, both inside and outside of its textual significance, in the allegory of a father/son relationship, exemplified in the context of literary geneal-ogy between Gogol and Dostoyevsky, the latter acknowledging the debt of his literary father by declaring the often repeated mantra in the film: 'We all came out of Gogol's Overcoat'. It is Sinha's contention that a film like *The Namesake* must also be interrogated from a political – the politics of diaspora and transnationalism, the intergenerational conflict – as well as a philosophical and ethical perspective, focusing on the bond between name and memory, between memory and trauma.

David Murphy addresses the politics of memory and tradition in the final film of the enigmatic Senegalese auteur Ousmane Sembene in 'Filming the Past, Present and Future of an African Village: Ousmane Sembene's *Moolaadé*'. Throughout his long and prestigious career Sembene was one of many African directors to reject what the anthropologist Johannes Fabian called, in his landmark text, *Time and the Other* (1983), the 'denial of coevalness' to which Africa has been subjected by the West, consistently relegated to a less 'developed' moment of human existence. *Moolaadé* reveals a rural Africa in a struggle with its ancestral past in which a remote village wrestles with the issue of female genital mutilation (or excision), at the turn of the twenty-first century, which allows the director to explore competing notions of time, place and memory. The unchanging mythical framework that village elders (male and female) locate the village within is challenged by a rival memory of the past, at once both personal and historicised, revealed through the character of Collé whose recollection of her own traumatic experience of excision motivates her to protect her daughter and other girls from the hands of the Salindana (the women who carry out excision). In one of the film's most striking images, one which offers an ambiguous commentary on the potential of a technologised future for rural Africa, a shot of the ostrich egg atop the village mosque is replaced by the image of a television aerial. This is no timeless village, living out an eternal repetition of the past: on the contrary, it is a place locked in a struggle to determine its relationship to the past and the nature of its evolving present.

Following explorations of Global Memory, the anthology considers the emergence of concepts of Traumatic Memory on film and questions how memory takes 'form' through various discourses of trauma. Cathy Caruth, in the 'Introduction' to *Trauma: Explorations in Memory*, suggests that 'the phenomenon of trauma has seemed to become all-inclusive, but it has done so precisely because it brings us to the limits of our understanding: if psychoanalysis, psychiatry, sociology and even literature are beginning to hear each other anew in the study of trauma, it is because they are listening through the radical disruption and gaps of traumatic experience' (1995: 4). We might add that film, given its visceral and kinetic properties of narrative, visual and sound has the potency to reflect on the nature of trauma with considerable force.

Film has frequently been drawn to memory trauma even before the likes of *Citizen Kane* (Welles, 1941), *Random Harvest* (LeRoy, 1943) and *Spellbound* (Hitchcock, 1945). In the last ten years traumatic memory has become more and more of a recurring motif in the cinema across a diverse variety of genres exploring the 'disruption and gaps' afforded by memory trauma narratives: see dramas like *Memento*, *Mulholland Drive* and *The English Patient* (Minghella, 1996), thrillers such as *Memories of Murder* (Joon Ho-Bong, 2003), and even action films such as *The Bourne Identity* (Liman, 2002), science fiction as in *Paycheck* (Woo, 2003), *Dark*

City (Proyas, 1998) and *Southland Tales* (Kelly, 2006) or comedy as in *Clean Slate* (Jackson, 1994) and *50 First Dates* (Segal, 2004). Many of these films conduct experimentation with film form as a way to comment on the nature of trauma and engage in complicated debates concerning identity and truth in both the personal and the cultural spheres.

In 'Impossible Memory: Traumatic Narratives in *Memento* and *Mulholland Drive*', Belinda Morrissey compares the ways in which narrative memory and traumatic memory are portrayed in two of the most intriguing Hollywood films of the decade, Christopher Nolan's *Memento* and David Lynch's *Mulholland Drive*. Both feature protagonists who experience traumatic events which affects their memory in different ways. Morrissey astutely analyses how psychological theories of traumatic memory correspond to modern aesthetic forms: where narrative memory is analogous to realism, and traumatic memory is expressed in postmodern structures. However, Morrissey casts doubt on such unproblematic assertions in her readings of *Memento* and *Mulholland Drive*. In *Memento*, when Leonard Shelby, a prototypical traumatic subject in search of narrative memory manages to recreate his narrative, the audience is not certain whether the 'truth' has been reached, or whether Shelby's whole search has been some sort of simulation or fantasy. By recreating Shelby's troubled memory in the narrative structure and stylistic presentation of the film, Nolan facilitates a sense of shared and fragmented understanding on the part of the audience. A similar effect is achieved by Lynch in the surrealistic, neo-noir *Mulholland Drive*, when the protagonist Betty Elms (and the various aliases she may or may not have throughout the film) encounters a beautiful, mysterious woman living in her apartment whose only memory is that someone is trying to kill her. Like many of Lynch's texts the Möbius-strip-like narrative reflects Betty's fragmented psyche and memory by creating alternative scenarios, dreams, events and multiple identities to cover whatever the 'truth' actually might be. Ultimately the conclusions of both *Mulholland Drive* and *Memento* prove as unstable and unambiguous as their protagonists and, according to Morrissey, in doing so they present a sustained challenge to memory forms and reveal how traumatic memory is effectively dramatised by the cinematic medium.

Terence McSweeney also explores the impact of a traumatic event on the protagonist of *Oldboy*, reading the film as a cultural artifact and symptomatic of a personal, historical, national and cultural identity crisis in 'Memory as Cultural Battleground in Park Chan-wook's *Oldboy*'. Like many contemporary South Korean films *Oldboy* both reflects and provides a commentary on the anxiety and lingering identity trauma caused by the turbulent social and political events of the twentieth century in Korea. *Oldboy*, the second part in the Park's 'Vengeance Trilogy', is arguably the emblematic text in the emergence of the New Wave of South Korean Cinema. McSweeney explores the ability of film to recreate traumatic memories on screen with a visceral potency as the protagonist is forced to participate in the reconstruction of his own memories as if they were a decidedly palpable present. The hero of the film, Oh Dae Su, can persuasively be seen as an interrogation of the traumatic history undergone by the divided peninsula and the attempt of South Koreans to reconcile themselves with their past and the possibility of unification in the future.

Warwick Mules, in 'The Future at Odds with the Past: Journey Through the Ruins of Memory in Alkinos Tsilimodos's *Tom White*', discusses the Australian film *Tom White* (2004) which portrays a very different Australia to the one audiences have become familiar with in populist works such as *Crocodile Dundee* (Faiman, 1986), *Muriel's Wedding* (Hogan, 2004) and *Australia* (Luhrman, 2008). Mules reads the film as an allegory that reflects on the condition of global, corporatised capital and the people whose lives are affected by it in modern advanced economies. The eponymous Tom White suffers a mental breakdown, traumatised by his disillusionment with the aims of life under corporate capitalism. In this essay, Mules also explores this potential in *Tom White* (and by implication in all film) as film's deconstruction of its own materiality as a Deleuzian time-image: the figural tracing of its own event as an appearing or disappearing, as becoming. Drawing on ideas from Benjamin ('dialectical images'), Barthes (Photographic Image), Deleuze (Movement and Time-Image) and Derrida (Archive), Mules' essay shows how it is possible to recover the figural dimensions of film through 'destructive forgetting', the exposure of the structure of forgetting enacted in film as the very affirmation of a 'yet to come' in absolute openness — a positive affirmation of life in the ruins of self-forgetting.

This anthology concludes with an exploration of a more historical and cultural approach to memory which raises questions crucial to the understanding of the connection between memory and history. It considers the relationship between the collective and the personal, and how cultural experience and memory is passed on to succeeding generations. Jonathan Ellis and Ana María Sánchez-Arce, in ''The Unquiet Dead': Memories

Fig. 2 Ofelia's transformation into Princess Moanna in *Pan's Labyrinth*.

of the Spanish Civil War in Guillermo del Toro's *Pan's Labyrinth*', analyse *Pan's Labyrinth* as a film not so much about memory *per se*, but about the individual and collective memory of not being able to remember. Ellis and Sánchez-Arce argue that the film is a representation of memory loss on three significant levels: Ofelia's role as a princess who forgot where she was and where she came from; her mother's erasure of the memory of her first husband; and Captain Vidal's attempts to live up to other people's memories of his own father's heroic death. Ellis and Sánchez-Arce read these three personal memory losses as a comment on the enforced forgetting of the Spanish Civil War during General Franco's dictatorship. In a more conventional historical film, each buried memory is brought painfully to light. But Del Toro focuses on the act of repression rather than what is actually being repressed. In so doing, Ellis and Sánchez-Arce argue that Del Toro shows the corrosive effect of the failure to remember alongside the trauma of the memory itself. Ellis and Sánchez-Arce demonstrate how Del Toro uses his filmic text to remember repression as much as that which has been repressed, including those repressions enacted through cinema in Victor Erice's *The Spirit of the Beehive* (1973) as well as Del Toro's own previous work in *Cronos* (1993) and *The Devil's Backbone* (2001).

Lynda Chapple's 'Memory, Nostalgia and the Feminine: *In the Mood for Love* and Those *Qipaos*' examines Hong Kong director Wong Kar-wai's most famous and arguably most intriguing work, from 2000. Beginning with the film's temporal and spatial ambiguities and its rich visual and aural textures, Chapple addresses its evocative sense of longing and desire through the lens of subjective memory. Reading the film's nostalgia for a long-vanished past, she critically examines the more disturbing aspects of its excessive representation of the *qipao* – the central costume worn by the female protagonist – which screens the female body in troubling, often highly fetishised ways. The garment provides a central link between the enunciation of the feminine and the film's nostalgia: it is a highly gendered relic from the past, yet intimately related to the female body. Chapple reads this relationship of nostalgia to the feminine in socio-historical and psychoanalytic terms, arguing that the dress enacts a theoretical nostalgia for the female body and its supposedly tactile relationship to historical experience.

Jehanne-Marie Gavarini's chapter, 'Rewind: The Will to Remember, The Will to Forget in Michael Haneke's *Caché*', examines the opposite forces of remembering and forgetting within the film, exploring its theoretical parallels between personal and collective memory. Although the 17 October 1961 massacre is mentioned only in passing in the film, Gavarini argues that there is an undeniable relationship between Georges' repressed memories and France's will to forget its colonial past along with the horrors of the Algerian War of Independence. *Caché* reveals how Georges' ability to forget his own past is intimately intertwined with the nation's ability to forget its legacies of colonialism. But as Gavarini points out, Georges' obsessive need to forget is offset by his compulsion to record. Georges has become 'his own historian'; his drive to record the present is the means by which his past remains '*caché*'. This paradox of memory and forgetting becomes the central dynamic of history itself, unravelling the relation between national and personal history as a public record of visible loss and lost visibility. To explore this dynamic, Gavarini reads *Caché* in relation to recent philosophical research on memory and history, in particular focusing on Paul Ricoeur's *Memory, History, Forgetting* and W. James Booth's *Communities of Memory: On Witness, Identity and Justice*.

We conclude this 'Introduction' by once again reiterating that there are no comparable texts available which discuss representations of memory in contemporary film matching the scope of this anthology. What makes this volume unique is its interdisciplinary treatment of memory as a core component of films in the past twenty years. *Millennial Cinema* thus demonstrates that memory is at the heart of film theory, technology, form and history in contemporary global popular culture. Combining individual readings and interdisciplinary methodologies, our anthology offers new analyses of the most discussed and debated films of late twentieth and early twenty-first century.

WORKS CITED

Booth, James W. (2006) *Communities of Memory: On Witness, Identity and Justice*. Ithaca: Cornell University Press.

Caruth, C. (ed.) (1995) *Trauma: Explorations in Memory*. Baltimore: Johns Hopkins University

Press.

De Man, P. (1985) '"Conclusions": Walter Benjamin's "The Task of the Translator"', *Yale French Studies*, 69, 25–46.

Fabian, J. (1983) *Time and the Other: How Anthropology Makes its Object*. New York: Columbia University Press.

Huyssen, A. (2007) 'Diaspora and Nation: Migration into Other Pasts', in M.-A. Baronian, S. Besser and Y. Jansen (eds) *Diaspora and Memory: Figures of Displacement in Contemporary Literature, Arts, and Politics*. Amsterdam: Rodolphi, 81–96.

Nora, P. (1989) 'Between Memory and History: *Les Lieux de Memoire*', *Representations*, 26, 7–25.

_____ (1996) *Realms of Memory: Rethinking the French Past, Vol. 1 – Conflicts and Divisions*, ed. L. D. Kritzman, trans. A. Goldhammer. New York: Columbia University Press.

Plato (1998) *Phaedrus*, trans. James H Nichols, Jr. Ithaca: Cornell University Press.

Ricoeur, P. (2004) *Memory, History, Forgetting*, trans. K. Blamey and D. Pellauer. Chicago: University of Chicago Press.

Rodowick, D. N. (1997) *Gilles Deleuze's Time Machine*. Durham and London: Duke University Press.

Tarkovsky, A. (1989) *Sculpting in Time: Reflections on the Cinema*, trans. K. Hunter-Blair. Austin: University of Texas Press.

Yerushalmi, Y. H. (1982) *Zakhor: Jewish History and Jewish Memory*. New York: Schocken.

VIRTUAL AND PROSTHETIC MEMORY

1. TIME, MEMORY AND MOVEMENT IN GASPAR NOÉ'S *IRREVERSIBLE*

PAUL ATKINSON

Gaspar Noé's *Irreversible* received significant attention upon its release in 2002 with audience members walking out of screenings due to its depiction of violence and use of disorientating stylistic devices, including spiralling camera movement and nauseating sound effects. This was followed by a debate in the media on the appropriateness, or otherwise, of the notorious rape scene. This debate placed greater emphasis on the length of the take (nine minutes in length) rather than the specific actions of the characters. It also overshadowed other features of the film, in particular the retelling of the story in reverse, where the final scene is presented first but not in the usual form of a prelude to a retelling of the story in the correct order, as is common in classic Hollywood tales such as *Sunset Boulevard* (1950). Instead each scene finds its place in an inverted chronological order with the dénouement placed equally among the other events.[1] The film remains intelligible despite the reversal of the order of scenes because the action in each scene unfolds chronologically and each scene is of long duration. This gives the viewer sufficient time to understand the relationship between the characters and the motives underlying their actions. On one level the plot is experimental and gives rise to many metafictional questions, but unlike other films directly addressing the issue of time – such as *Last Year at Marienbad* (1961), *La Jetée* (1962), *Memento* (2000), *Eternal Sunshine of the Spotless Mind* (2004) – there is no undermining of the ontology of memory. The reversal is restricted to the presentation of the action in what is a reasonably straightforward revenge narrative.

The film has three main characters: Alex (Monica Belluci), her partner Marcus (played by her offscreen partner Vincent Cassel) and her ex-partner Pierre (Albert DuPontel). There are few scenes that do not contain at least one of the three characters, which gives the viewer both a visual and a narrative reference point and reduces the level of incoherence that could arise due to the reversal of the plot. The use of three main characters also suggests a *ménage à trois* because Pierre still desires Alex and constantly parades this desire during a trip on the metro. However, she is happy in her relationship with Marcus, which is clearly adumbrated in a number of domestic scenes where the couple find pleasure in each other's company, including a playful sex scene. The relationship is likely to be further affirmed with Alex's pregnancy. The pregnancy and domestic harmony is underscored by the closing scene (the first scene if the film was arranged chronologically) where Alex relaxes in a park reading an English edition of J. W. Dunne's *An Experiment with Time* surrounded by families and children on a summer's day. If the film was told in chronological order, Pierre's continued attraction to Alex would be the main source of tension in the plot, which would most likely reach its apotheosis at the party all three attend. In the inversion of the plot, the sexual tension is barely visible at the party because the trio has not yet been united in a scene and because it follows two violent events which render unrequited desire trivial.

Fig. 3 Alex (Monica Bellucci) relaxes in a park reading J. W. Dunne's *An Experiment with Time.*

The trio take the Metro to the party after learning that Pierre's car has broken down and, on the train, Pierre's insecurity is expressed in a series of taunts about Marcus's sexual prowess, which are blithely ignored by the couple. At the party, Marcus introduces Pierre to other women in order to divert his attention from Alex but he ends up taking drugs and in a compromised state flirts with the same women in view of Alex. Alex is disconcerted by the behaviour of both men and decides to leave the party early without her companions. She is stranded on one side of a busy street and to reach a taxi ramp on the other side of the road she takes an underpass. In the isolation of the underpass, she sees a man harassing a woman but decides to walk past, at which point his attention turns to her and she is raped. This is a particularly brutal scene not only due to the actions of the rapist but because the camera does not move throughout the nine-minute take and due to the use of a low camera angle which shows Alex's face and her suffering.

Marcus and Pierre leave the party sometime later only to see Alex badly beaten and unconscious entering an ambulance on a stretcher. Rather than following Alex to the hospital, Marcus, fuelled by drugs, has a burgeoning desire for revenge and is given the opportunity when two men, in exchange for cash, indicate they will help. Marcus accepts their offer and takes the reluctant Pierre on a trip across the city in search of the assailant, which is also a trip into the underworld of crime and prostitution. It also marks a contrast with the bourgeois lives of the two men, who gradually lose their civilised inhibitions in their course of their revenge. After a series of confrontations, Pierre and Marcus are eventually given the name of the rapist 'Le Ténia' ('Tapeworm') and the place where he can most likely be found, the hardcore gay club 'Rectum'.[2] They enter the club where, after a long and violent search, Marcus attacks a man who he believes is the Tapeworm. This man breaks Marcus's arm and then attempts to rape him as a crowd, which contains the actual rapist, cheers him on. This leads to arguably the most confronting and violent scene in the film as Pierre steps in and hits the man over the head with a fire extinguisher and continues to bash him until there is little left of his face. The excessiveness of Pierre's response, the unbridled desire to kill, is ironically juxtaposed later in the film, earlier in the story, with his criticisms of Marcus's animality. The story of the two men ends with Marcus, like Alex, taken away in an ambulance and Pierre arrested.

There are many other details interwoven in this narrative but this short summary demonstrates the ease with which the plot can be returned to the chronology of the story. Furthermore, it seems to contradict the film's titular claim to irreversibility because the characters are not, at any stage, forced to confront questions of irreversibility *in medias res*. The reflection on the themes of irreversibility does not occur within the diegesis because even the most regrettable act, the killing of an innocent man, is not acknowledged by the characters at the time of the film's chronological ending – its actual beginning. It is the viewer, instead, who is asked to ponder the questions of irreversibility through imagining the relationship between time and consequence. This in turn invokes questions on the nature of film time itself because the consequences of each character's actions are only made visible by the framework of presentation.

Before addressing the phenomenological and narrative limits of reversibility in film, it is worth outlining the concept of time implied in the word 'irreversible' and how this concept differs from the popular use of the term.[3] The word irreversible is often grouped with other terms such as unchangeable or irrevocable to refer to those events that lead to an unalterable change in the status of an object – with death the clearest example. The inverse, reversibility, indicates that there is a capacity for an object to be returned to an earlier state, which could refer to a range of events including the change in psychological states, the movement of objects in space or indeed the revocation or repeal of an existing statement. Reversibility and irreversibility are bound together in a broader concept of time, for to state that events or states are irreversible is to assume that there is a background of reversibility against which they are distinguished. To state that a plot element is irreversible is to distinguish this event from a general field of events that are reversible. Irreversibility often refers to the actions of the living, in which there is a general path from birth until death, which is contrasted with the inanimate world of objects that might change their position but in themselves are unalterable. The idea of reversibility was a product of the laws of motion in nineteenth-century physics which were not dependent on and did not recognise the division between past, present and future: 'All physical laws known by the middle of the nineteenth century were symmetrical for both directions of time, for the past and the future' (Szumilewicz 1971: 181). This symmetry is grounded in a model which assumes that the movement from future to past is not qualitatively different from the movement from past to future. One could imagine the world as a clockwork mechanism which could operate either in forward or reverse motion depending on only one variable, the negative or positive value of t (time).[4]

If the term irreversibility is to have any value and specificity in the analysis of film it must also retain this scientific lineage, that is, there must be some idea of the regularity of time, managed by a single variable, that passes irrespective of the various perspectives on time. This notion of the inviolable and invariable movement of absolute time serves as a canvas for the rare moments of irreversibility, those acts of the living that are destined to occur only once. This temporal regularity is found in the physical processes of film production and can be contrasted with the acts of characters within the film. In analogue modes, such as the recording of film, there is symmetry between the movement of the film through the camera and the eventual playing back of the film in the projector. This regular movement can also be found in digital media, where the collected still images are placed in a strict and regular order of inscription. Time must be regular if the world is to remain intelligible. Of course, this is not to say that an object recorded in the camera is the same as the one projected, as production and post-production significantly shape the time of the final film, but that they both take as their ground absolute, uniform time. The regularity of movement is implied in the transcription of the visible world and any variation in the speed of projection and recording will only take place against the normality of regular movement.

This notion of a regular time of recording is taken as a given but one could imagine a different film ontology where the film speed is automatically altered to suit the objects or events recorded. There would be different rates of recording according to the different rhythms of the object, and there is already some adoption of this method in nature documentaries with their consistent use of time-lapse photography to represent the natural movement of the plant. Even in this case, there is still regularity in the succession of images, despite the fact that they are replayed at a rate greater than that at which they were recorded. In most cases, the relationship of the camera to the visual field is underpinned by a single, homogenous time and it is only after it is recorded that the speed is varied. The various filmic machines (editing suites, film projectors, etc) can speed up and slow down the film without regard to the particular temporal qualities of the reproduced visual or sonic field. The time of the image can be unhinged from the 'real' – there can be a change in direction and speed – and reversibility can easily be imagined in the projection of the image backwards at a speed roughly equal to its forward movement. In physics it does not matter in which direction matter moves; it is the relationship between the parts that is important and the image of the most famous of physical models – the planets of our solar system – is just as intelligible as a forward or reverse movement. The complete reversal of film certainly makes sense when examined on the level of the projector but does not apply so easily to the narrated image – what is visible on the screen – because the reversed image, and more importantly reversed sound, lose their intelligibility because they are not conceived as part of an abstract cinematic whole but as immanent moments thoroughly tied to the present of the viewer.

The conception of time as a single variable that coordinates static snapshots of reality is the source of the *fin de siècle* French philosopher Henri Bergson's celebrated critique of the cinematograph.[5] He examines the assumptions underpinning cinema's claim to inscribe the real and argues that the cinematograph is emblematic of both science's and philosophy's rejection of time as becoming because it focuses on the general framework of becoming – the homogenous time that subtends it – rather than articulating the variability and particularity of the experience of time. He states in *Creative Evolution* that in the notion of the cinematograph we are only interested in the 'the unmovable plan of the movement rather than the movement itself' (1944: 329). Bergson, along with phenomenology and process philosophy, argues that time cannot be conceptualised as an instantaneous section, a knife-edged present cut off from a substantial past and future. It is always of a definite duration (*durée*) and this is most clearly understood in the experience of time passing, which involves the retention of the past – the interpenetration of memory with the present and a directedness toward the future in the form of expectation.

Bergson's theory of duration is one of radical continuity where the difference between past and present cannot be separated from perception and memory, with the latter the driving force of becoming. He argues that memory, like the past, continues to accumulate and in doing so integrates the past and present. This argument is first posited as a psychological principle in *Matter and Memory*, in order to explain how apparently lost words and images in aphasia and agnosia can be retrieved at a later date. He argues that in forgetting there is no actual erasure or deformation of memory but rather an inability to access particular memories, and that depending on the conditions, these memories can reappear in consciousness. Memory is not a passive repository because recollections and habits exert pressure as they strive for conscious realisation. Bergson develops a series of arguments from this principle of which the most important is that memory as a whole, or 'pure memory' unhinged from its application to a perception, always coexists with the present (1991: 102–4).

This psychological theory of the continual accumulation of memory is given ontological expression in the same text and it is this which serves as the foundation for the theory of cinematic time articulated by Deleuze. Film seems to be ideally suited to Bergson's theory of memory because there is no loss of the past in the accumulation of individual frames (images, recollections) and also in the broader sense that all films coexist with each other in cinematic history, and this is why Hollis Frampton argues that film is the 'last machine' due to its capacity to incorporate all other machines in its ever expanding memory (1983: 112–13). Furthermore, films recognise the division between past and present, with each frame allied to a particular time and, like Bergson's recollections (*souvenirs*), all are equal with respect to the whole. However, the analogy between Bergson's theory of pure memory and film should not be pushed too far for there is a difference between the material collection of images, the sequenced set of images and sounds that constitutes a film, and the dynamic relationship between the past and the present in Bergson's ontology. In film, there is no contraction of the past with respect to a present perception for this only occurs at the intersection of film time and the viewer's duration. It is a function of the film's relationship to other systems (viewers), who bring film memory into play, rather than a feature of the film in itself.

Positing irreversibility is dependent on the conceptualisation of the whole, whether this is a film or any other physical system. For Gilles Deleuze, one of Bergson's foremost proponents, science makes the mistake of assuming that the 'whole is given' and can be differentiated into parts that exhaustively describe it (1986: 9). This is to imagine that any event can be described as a set and as such we need only note the type of objects and their number, and in the case of film, we need only count the number of cells and the temporal rule governing their organisation. It is within this framework that reversibility is easily conceived because it only requires knowledge of the composition of the set and the reversal of the rule governing its organisation. It also assumes that all questions of time in film are reducible to knowledge of the film stock, the time of recording and playback. In contrast, Deleuze argues that film remains unfinished and open despite this obvious material boundary: firstly, because it is always immanent to the movement of time in its broadest sense as duration,[6] and secondly, because it is open to the multiplicity of all other open wholes – there is a thread connecting each whole to every other whole such that a change in one leads to a change in all the others. To deny this interconnection and interpenetration is to 'artificially close' the set (1986: 10) as is the case with the construction of reversibility in film. A film delimits rather than 'closes' movement, in that it contains movement within partially closed sets (the shot, the scene, the frame), but it also sets the conditions for each movement's relation to other interrelated and open wholes (*Ibid.*: 11). Film draws boundaries around each movement but these boundaries are permeable because time is not a quality that is restricted to a single object or whole.

In *Irreversible*, the direct inversion of the chronological order of scenes, the reversal of the order of the end credits and the mirrored letters in the titles, mimic the reversibility of time as envisioned in classical physics. The film suggests that reversibility is possible and invoked by these various signs of mechanical inversion. Time is simply rolled backwards and the credit sequence is the most readily accessible image of such a change because the viewer is familiar with its structure and does not expect the full description of the film's participants to appear at the beginning. However, it is a false image because the credit sequence is outside the diegesis; it is a purely formal list that can be inverted without a substantial change to its content. The list is a closed whole that is thoroughly defined by the objects contained within it. The film teases the viewer in the title and end credits with the possibility of a truly inverted and reversed film but this invocation of reversibility only serves to highlight the impossibility of a mechanical model applied to the film as a whole. *Irreversible* attests to the impossibility of film as a closed set and each reversal actually accentuates the qualitative difference between time and its inverted image. The film, like all films, is open to a range of other times; in particular, the time of the viewer and the common means of organising time in film through montage and plot. In the film's reversal, the temporal flow of the viewer serves as a variable and directional gauge by which to understand each of the particular temporal wholes in the film: the duration of the take, the movement of the camera relative to the frame, and the narrative interconnection between scenes.

The rejection of true reversibility, where the system (film) moving in reverse is substantially the same as one moving forward, does not necessarily lead to a belief in unchangeability where nothing changes and nothing can be reversed, for the latter is founded on the acceptance that time is located in particular objects rather than the interconnection of open wholes. Instead, film can be understood as a multiplicity of different times each overlapping and conditioning the other. For Bergson time is variable with all forms, living or otherwise, distinguished by their temporality such that a plant growing from a seed, the morphogenesis of an insect or the qualitative change of a colour are all different species of movement (1944: 330). Therefore an examination of becoming is always a process of differentiating the species of movement while recognising their ultimate interconnection.

In his critique of the scientific notion of simultaneity, Bergson argues that time should be conceived as interlocking flows that advance into the foreground or retreat into the background depending on the attention that is given to them:

We stated that it is the very essence of our attention to be able to be divided without being split up. When we are seated on the bank of a river, the flowing of the water, the gliding of a boat or the flight of a bird, the ceaseless murmur in our life's deeps are for us three separate things or only one, as we choose. We can interiorise the whole, dealing with a single perception that carries along the three flows, mingled, in its course; or we can leave the first two outside and then divide our attention between the inner and the outer; or, better yet, we can do both at one and the same time, our attention uniting and yet differentiating the three flows, thanks to the singular privilege of being one and several. Such is the primary idea of simultaneity. We there- fore call two external flows that occupy the same duration 'simultaneous' because they both depend upon the duration of a like third, our own; this duration is ours only when our consciousness is concerned with us alone, but it becomes equally theirs when our attention embraces the three flows in a single indivisible act. (1965: 52)

For Bergson, there is an oscillation in attention between the flows but they are always held together in the 'unfolding of duration', which is at once differentiable into a series of movements which remain genetically tied to the whole. In film, there obtains in the division of any one move- ment the history of this division including the prior connection to other species of movement (the bird and boat were once connected and, at one level, will remain connected in our attention). Our attention varies and is conditioned by the film frame, which delineates a field of contemporane- ity, but the frame can never fully determine the movements it contains. These movements are continually divided and recombined according to the specific focus of our attention. Deleuze uses Bergson's example of contemporaneity in *Cinema 1* but bypasses the issue of attention when he argues that the camera forms a cinematographic consciousness that is not tied to the constraints of human consciousness (1986: 20). Deleuze is keen to separate the ontology of cinema from the temporal conditions of specta- torship, unlike Bergson who often grounds duration in consciousness. In either case, film time cannot be defined by any one movement if we accept that time is the concrete interpenetration of a range of movements. Even the movement of the cells through the projector is an abstraction that can- not be used to understand the quality of particular movements in much the same way that the movement of the earth cannot sufficiently explain the multiplicity of times on the earth.

Time is raised as a concept in *Irreversible* through the invocation of dif- ferent species of time and their intersection and comparison, which are framed by a general notion of reversibility and irreversibility implied in the title. In Gaspar Noé's epitextual notes on the film – printed on a publicity brochure and the DVD cover – he raises the issue of the multiplicity of time with statements referring to particular species of time. There are multiple references to the particular human and biological renderings of time: an 'arrow invented by our brain,' the pluralistic 'each to his own arrow' and the corporeal 'Time exists only in our reptilian perception. Pain, pleasure, past or future too.' This animal/human irreversibility is played out against an overall indifference of universal time. In the refrain 'time destroys everything' – a written statement which also closes the film – there are echoes of the second law of thermodynamics and this is further accentuated when time is presented as a force indifferent to human suffering, 'a multi-dimensional chaos that couldn't care less about us'. This intersection of broader physical notion of becoming with the particularity of the human action is also explored in the film's plot. In the penultimate scene, we see Alex receive a positive result on a pregnancy test as she walks past a poster on the wall showing an image of the foetus from *2001: A Space Odyssey* (1968).

This image of cosmic creation is redoubled in the closing scene where the spiralling camera segues into an image of a spiralling universe, metonymic of the ultimate creative act, the Big Bang. The vastly different timescales of the two forms of creation are held together in the 'contemporaneity' of the shot and the importance of Alex's pregnancy – an 'irreversible premise'[7] – is amplified by its connection to the *longue durée* of evolutionary and planetary notions of time. This displacement of the quality of time also works in the other direction as the forward movement of Alex's life, given meaning in her expectation of a child, is displaced onto the spiralling movement of the stars and planets. The spiral movement that is usually so divorced from the sphere of our own action could move in any direction – there is no automatic judgement as to whether the spiral should move clockwise or counter clockwise – but when two forms of time are combined in a single shot, the directionality of one form of movement must obtain to all movements. The frame forces the admixture of different regimes of time because it combines them in a single act of attention. However, the cinema's capacity to combine the different rates of temporal flow does not allow for a true coexistence of irreversibility and reversibility, as regardless of the devices employed to indicate reversibility there is always movement in a particular direction.

If there is always a forward movement in film, a confluence of different times, then the notion of irreversibility can only be invoked through abstraction, that is, by separating the image from the continuity of other times and thus creating a closed system. For example, when *Irreversible* closes with the spiral movement of the galaxy, this movement is partially unhinged from the broader temporal movement of the film. It is more readily abstracted from its physical context, and the overall temporal flow, by the conceptual void of space manifest onscreen as a dark border surrounding the moving objects.[8] The movement is only deemed reversible because it lacks a definite connection to a broader network of other events. It is a closed movement similar to that of the film reel because there is no suggestion of exchange with the broader universe and, as such, the movement appears thoroughly determinable. This conceptually reversible movement is always an abstraction, insofar as there is a reduction in the level of interconnectedness, and can be contrasted with most movements onscreen which when reversed are qualitatively changed. Furthermore, there is no strict division of the past and present or interplay, within Bergson's ontology, between memory and perception as all is devolved into an ever-repeatable circular movement. In this repetition, there are no moments which can be located in a particular past as a particular recollection.

In contrast, the penultimate scene of the film, immediately preceding the shot of the rotating galaxy, functions as a utopian recollection, distilled in a particular time, that must precede the violent murder and rape. Alex lies on the grass in a park reading the English philosopher J. W. Dunne's *An Experiment with Time*, unaware of what is to come. This is certainly an incongruous image as the book is not suitable for a light Sunday read and it is not clear why Alex, a French woman, has chosen to read an English book on the nature of time. However, the prosaic style of the book belies its extraordinary premise, for Dunne claims that he is having dreams of the future and uses elements from Einstein's General Theory of Relativity to explain this phenomenon.[9] This suits the film's purpose in that it describes how the future can be imagined before it has actually happened. In the film, we see the consequence of various actions before the events leading up to those actions are revealed. We are presented with the dream of the future before we are presented with the conditions of its appearance. The viewer bears these future dreams as they follow the plot back to its beginning because they have already seen what will happen to each of the main characters. They have already seen the rape of Alex while watching her read calmly on the grass. There is a doubling in the diegesis of the temporal structure of the film, that of an already prescribed future, when Alex tells Marcus and Pierre on the way to the party that she is reading a book about a 'future that is already written' in the form of premonitions. She also tells Marcus in a subsequent scene that she had a dream of a red tunnel, before the rape, which is presented to the viewer in the form of a spiralling image of the red tunnel identical to the one in which the rape occurred. The effect of this narrative prevision is that, in watching *Irreversible*, the viewer is constantly confronted with the question, 'what if they had acted otherwise?' and it is easy to imagine as the film undoes each of its narrative threads that the future events did not have to happen. This is the main premise of the film and the reason why the scenes are presented in reverse.

There is, however, a tension between the inevitability of the future, grounded in the diegesis, and the constant imagining that it could be otherwise on the part of the viewer. The absolute terrifying nature of the future events, the murder and rape, act as a *telos* that the viewer imagines could be avoided and gives rise to a number of 'if only' questions. Early in the film, we see Marcus and Pierre involved in a bloody fight with a man at a nightclub of whom we know nothing about except that he is angry and aggressive. Pierre kills the man brutally with a fire extinguisher but the reason for his action is not given and the viewer must speculate on the cause. We find out later, in the subway scene, that they killed the wrong man and as we watch the rape, we have an accompanying feeling of 'if only' they had killed the right man. In a later scene, Marcus largely ignores Alex at the party and she leaves early without her two male companions. She is alone when she decides to walk through the tunnel but she wouldn't have been if the group of friends had left together. We find out one of the reasons for Marcus' erratic behaviour, he has taken drugs at the party, and this

Fig. 4 Alex walks through the underpass after leaving the party.

probably leads both to his flippancy with Alex and the mood with which he seeks revenge. As these questions abound, it is worth asking if the same questions would have arisen if the plot followed a chronological order.

The reversal of the plot means that the effect of an action is always given before the cause which is qualitatively different to the other direction from the point of view of an observer. In the theories of reversible time in science, it is assumed that the whole universe is reversed which does not present a logical problem, in that it is similar to turning back a projector. However, when there is an observer/viewer who stands outside the reversal and reconstructs the proper path of the narrative, the film is no longer a closed system. The viewer opens the film up to the notion of time, experienced in consciousness, where there is an interpenetration of time and memory. The viewer's memory serves as an intermediary between plot and story, constantly integrating plot elements into a continuous temporal movement but also maintaining the distinction between particular scenes, which retain their specificity like recollections.

To understand how different types of memory are deployed in the viewer's integration of filmic elements into a cohesive present moment, it is useful to turn to the work of Edmund Husserl. He argues that memory is central to the directedness of time and establishes continuity, but in doing so he makes a firm distinction between 'primary' and 'secondary' memory. 'Primary memory' is fully implicated in perception and provides what Husserl calls the 'comet's tail' of perception manifest either as 'retention' or 'protention'. In any present perception, there is a retention of a past event and the protention into an expected future. Husserl uses the example of hearing a tone, and more broadly a melody, which cannot be apprehended in the immediacy of the present but as a conglomerate of the 'just past' and the immediate future:

> Primary memory of the tones that, as it were, I have just heard and expectation (protention) of the tones that are yet to come fuse with the apprehension of the tone that is now appearing and that, as it were, I am now hearing. (1991: 37)

It is impossible to hear any sound, or a melody, in an absolute present because sound is always formed over time and to hear the sound memory must articulate a general form of the sound that stretches from the past into the future. 'Secondary memory' is quite different in that it is a recollection of what has happened rather than the continuous experience of the present moment; the memory is recalled and bracketed in a new present. In film, the fusion of cells into a single continuous movement involves 'primary memory' but the remembrance of an earlier scene and its place within the plot is always 'secondary memory'. In the latter, the memory is distinctly attached to a past that has disappeared.

This distinction can also be used to understand how memory is utilised differently depending on the structure of the plot. In a chronological plot, where the emphasis is on continuity, the memory of past events folds seamlessly into the causal structure of the narrative. The past is not visible *as past* but forms a continuity with the present moment as in the hearing of a melody or sound in 'primary memory'. Each present action is the necessary consequence of a previous action and in a truly predictable plot, the viewer finds each of their expectations confirmed. Here memory supports expectation, that is, it gives it a certain force and continuity in the same way that primary memory shapes and confirms a sound. The whole weight of the remembered film past is fulfilled in each subsequent action and it is not actively distinguished from the present. If *Irreversible* was told chronologically, our memory of what happened to Alex in the tunnel would offer a context and a motivation for each of Pierre's and Marcus's actions and explain these actions as the quest for revenge. To kill on behalf of a raped lover is understandable and within the realm of the viewer's expectations, for whom the memory of the earlier events could well coalesce into a general feeling that revenge is necessary. However, in the reversed film, the memory of the past does not support or fulfil expectation because the viewer has to recollect the past and place in relation to its proper cause. This is secondary memory because the past retains its distinctiveness and is part of a distinctly remembered or formulated sequence. For example, when at the end of the film the viewer is made aware of Alex's pregnancy, the earlier scenes are put in relief and recalled and we ask why did Marcus act so irresponsibly at the party when he knew that Alex was probably pregnant? When we find out that Pierre's car is not working, we remember the rape and this leads to speculation as to what could have happened if they had driven to the party rather than taken the Metro. In each case the past is recollected and placed side by side with a present event and as such leads the viewer to imagine the plot as a range of abstract possibilities. In short, the relationship between a viewer's memory of a film and the film itself is dependent on the structure of expectation which is largely coordinated by the plot and its relationship to a viewer's memory. The plot cannot be inverted without a substantial change in the form and expression of expectation. If the film confirms its own premises in each successive theme, memory invisibly fills the channels of expectation but if expectation is not directly met, as in a reversed plot, then there is a constant recollection of past events and speculation of what could have been.

It was stated above that the reversibility or non-reversibility of the visual and sonic fields should be examined separately to the reversibility of the plot because what is in the frame at any one moment is a plenitude. The plot, in comparison, is always a framework or skeleton that describes the sequence of events rather than describing the precise visual and auditory context in which they appeared. Plot is always an abstraction and as such changes in the plot are much more easily imagined than what will appear in the frame at any one time. To give a facile example, if someone who has not seen the film is asked what would Pierre and Marcus do after Alex is raped it is quite conceivable that they would predict that the pair would seek revenge. This does not take any great prescience because the structure of a plot is so removed from the actuality of film representation that the various permutations are easily imaginable. However, it is very unlikely that a viewer could predict the exact pictorial or visual qualities of an upcoming scene, that is, describe what will occupy the frame. There is no simple line that can describe the actual future of the film image; it is always elusive because it speaks of the complexity of the plenitude. Bergson states that we cannot separate an object from the complete circumstances of its creation and uses artistic production as an example. It might be possible to imagine that Shakespeare will write another text but it is impossible to predict the actual text. To predict Hamlet is to predict the complete perceptual, intentional and experiential framework of the author, that is, to actually be Shakespeare (1944: 121). The broad idea of a text or a future plot element is always a generality whereas the actual text or what will actually appear in the frame of an upcoming scene is a specificity. When Dunne argues that we can see the future in our dreams and that to do so we must describe the dreams in as much detail as possible, he is not so much talking about the predictability of the future as the capacity to extract a general plot element from the complexity of a dream. In any dream there is always something that can be derived that could, provided there is the right context, come to resemble an event in the future.

It is much more difficult to imagine a visual sequence in reverse than it is to imagine a reversal of the plot. Seymour Chatman argues that there is an 'over-specification' of description in film due to the plenitude of the visual image, although in the practice of film viewing we do not attend to all the details but instead focus on those elements that further our understanding of the narrative (1980: 125–6). In verbal description there is much greater attention to the object in the act of describing and each element is drawn into the narrative structure – although there is a difference between incidental and highlighted features (*Ibid.*: 128). The reversal of the verbal description is often nothing more than a change of one word, for example, 'Alex walks forwards through the tunnel' becomes 'Alex walked backwards through the tunnel'. The literary object is directly isolated in the form of the description and due to this isolation, the event has an inherent capacity for reversibility. In the reversal of a section of film, however, every detail of the image must be reversed – which can be easily performed through the reversal of the projector – but the visual form is much more

Fig. 5 In the film's pivotal scene Alex is threatened by Le Ténia (Jo Prestia) after entering the underpass.

complex because each of the objects in the frame must also be reversed and must be contained within the specific attention of the viewer. The reversed image is entropic in that the viewer looks at each of the movements and with this there is a significant degree of indetermination which appears disarticulated as Alex walks backwards. The narrative is also disarticulated as each of the movements does not follow an expected course, that is, they no longer conform to the expectation of primary memory. The greater the number of parts of an image that the eye must take into account, that occupy a single period of contemporaneity, the more resistant the image is to reversibility. This principle gives greater force to the horror of watching Pierre smash the man's face with a fire extinguisher in the nightclub. The face is fragmented with each blow and it becomes increasingly more difficult to imagine a reversal of his action and a recreation of the body that is broken.

Reversibility is visually conceivable when movement can be abstracted from the objects it coordinates and/or is appended to. The movement must form a stable gestalt that functions as a pivot upon which the image can move backwards and forwards. Deleuze calls this a movement-image because the movement of the whole – the movement of the camera – is not limited to any one of the objects in the frame. The multiplicity of movements in the shot serves as a field indicating the movement of the camera and becomes a type of movement without a vehicle (1986: 23). In *Irreversible*, there is a long sequence in the club 'Rectum', which begins just over eleven minutes into the film, where the viewer is given a tour of the passageways of the club before Marcus's and Pierre's misdirected act of revenge is shown. The handheld camera moves up the stairs and the passageway and we only get fleeting shots of the people that Marcus and Pierre will encounter in the subsequent scene. There are only glimpses because the emphasis is on the movement of the camera, which moves constantly in wide arcs and spirals, and not on individual participants in the narrative. It is only in the subsequent scene, when the camera retraces the same path but this time with consistent shots of Marcus as he questions the clientele of the club, that the movement is subordinate to the narrative.

The relationship between the content of each shot to the narrative is tenuous but the movement of the camera acquires a consistency in the balance between its upward movement and the spiralling downward movement. This movement is not entirely random because any disequilibrium, when the viewer loses a sense of points of reference, is always followed by a downward movement and a return to equilibrium. The camera moves up with a type of visual exertion before falling back to a state of rest, only to again lose its equilibrium. So although it is a movement-image, the viewer's sense of equilibrium serves as an anchor for the qualitative difference between up and down. The viewer looks for points of rest and order in what is seen and this, for Merleau-Ponty, is a primary type of organisation of the visible world which is integrally linked to the body because visuality is always a combination of what the eye sees in relation to the general articulation of the body's movement; the body is the 'zero point or zero degree of spatiality' where spatiality is constituted in movement rather than copied, read or transcribed from the world (1964: 178). In the movement up the stairs, with the camera moving from one side to the other, it is the fact that we have some reference point in the visible world (the wall, door, light) that serves to orientate the viewer with respect to the difference between upward and downward movement but numerous points of reference are not needed because the eye soon follows the pattern of the extracted movement.

This type of movement is reversible because it is not linked to objects fixed in time or to narrative progression. The camera moves like a pendulum, which might generate the time on a clock, but in itself is abstracted from any true notion of change through its repetition. The pendulum could just as easily be swinging forwards and backwards rather than backwards and forwards. The viewer certainly serves as an anchor point but only for a general indicator of position and movement, much like gravity, in what is a relatively closed movement. This can be contrasted to the nine-minute rape scene where the camera stays in a fixed low-angle shot. Movement here is thoroughly linked to the characters and a fundamental transformation of each character with respect to the narrative as a whole. One of the reasons it is so difficult to watch this scene is because the abasement of Alex does not end quickly and becomes increasingly violent – time here is always an augmentation rather than a repetition. The movement is not reversible because it is so thoroughly linked to the transformation of the character and the irreversible premises that underpin the plot.

Understanding irreversibility in film is a means of understanding the relationship between different types of movement and how they relate to the position of the viewer. There is a tendency to accept that films are reversible due to our familiarity with images shown in reverse but the idea of irreversibility is not exhausted by the capacity to reverse the movement of film through a projector or on a computer. We have to look instead to how each movement is reversed rather than the abstract reversal of the whole. In *Irreversible*, there is experimentation with the idea of reversibility on the level of the plot and in the production of credit sequences. There is certainly no complete reversal because the reversal of every shot and sequence would undermine the notion of character, fundamental to plot development. The viewer would overwhelmingly focus on the peculiarity of each of the reversed movements in the *mise-en-scène*, including a reversed soundtrack, and as such the image would become an abstract field of movement that does not entirely resemble the movement of the plot. For in the plot, we look into the image as through a transparent screen at a sequence of events which organise the visual field and reduce our attention to the visual detail. In the reversed image, however, the details of the image are foregrounded and as such they are disarticulated from common and expected movements. It is only in the abstraction of movement from the visual field, where there is no absolute difference in the direction of the movement, that the idea of reversibility can truly be considered in the *mise-en-scène*. This essay speculates on these ideas to further delineate the boundaries of film time but to also demonstrate the various points of resistance in a film to models of reversibility.

NOTES

1   The same device was used by François Ozon in *5 X 2* (2004), which tells the story of marriage breakdown in reverse. *Irreversible*, however, is a much more interesting film because it directly addresses issues of time and irreversibility rather than remaining content with the unveiling of its plot.

2   There is an obvious connection between the name of the club, the fact that Alex was anally raped and the name 'tapeworm'. This connection is further accentuated in the spiralling movement of the camera which reveals the dark interior walls of the club like a colonoscopy.

3   As there are no significant differences between the French *irréversible* and its English counterpart, the French title of the film is not subjected to separate analysis.

4   This model of reversibility is only applicable to those perfect, closed systems where there is no waste, or loss of energy (in the form of friction or heat), or wear on the mechanism (see Schlegel 1968: 24).

5   This argument is revisited by Gilles Deleuze in *Cinema 1* (1986) where he argues that Bergson oddly failed to take into account cinema's capacity to produce the mobile sections ('movement images') set out in the first chapter of Bergson's book *Matter and Memory* (1991: 2). However, it must be noted that Bergson's attention is directed solely, in this example, at the regularity of mechanical movement and not the expressive capacities of the cinema.

6   Bergson's theory of duration is not limited to consciousness but applies to time in all contexts; an idea derived from the concrete understanding of duration, and is directed against the conceptualisation of time as a collection of points on a line.

7   This term is used by Umberto Eco in 'The Myth of Superman' to compare plot elements in serialised narratives that cannot be undone, such as death and marriage, with those elements that can be endlessly recycled and repeated, such as the battles with various supervillains.

8   An astrophysicist, by contrast, might recognise the particularity of the movement of a galaxy such that differences in direction are tangible.

9   Dunne explains how each individual follows a particular path through the world and that this path can be known in advance (1958: 121–2). This is adapted from the notion of world lines, which are also explored in *Donnie Darko* (2001).

WORKS CITED

Bergson, H. (1944) *Creative Evolution*, trans. A. Mitchell. New York: Random House.

_____ (1965) *Duration and Simultaneity: With Reference to Einstein's Theory*, trans. L. Jacobson. Indianapolis: Bobbs-Merrill.

_____ (1991) *Matter and Memory*, trans. W. S. Palmer and N. M. Paul. New York: Zone Books.

Chatman, S. (1980) 'What Novels Can Do That Films Can't (and Vice Versa)', *Critical Inquiry*, 7, 1, 121–40.

Deleuze, G. (1986) *Cinema 1: The Movement-Image*, trans. H. Tomlinson and B. Habberjam. Minneapolis: University of Minnesota Press.

Dunne, J. W. (1958) *An Experiment with Time*. London: Faber and Faber.

Eco, U. (1979) 'The Myth of Superman', in *The Role of the Reader: Explorations in the Semiotics of Texts*. Bloomington: Indiana University Press, 107–24.

Frampton, H. (1983) 'For a Metahistory of Film: Commonplace Notes and Hypotheses', *Circles of Confusion: Film Photography Video: Texts 1968–1980*. Rochester, NY: Visual

Studies Workshop Press, 107–16.

Husserl, E. (1991) *On the Phenomenology of the Consciousness of Internal Time (1893–1917)*, trans. J. B. Brough. Dordrecht: Kluwer Academic Publishers.

Merleau-Ponty, M. (1964) 'Eye and Mind', in *The Primacy of Perception*, trans. C. Dallery. Evanston: Northwestern University Press, 159-192.

Schlegel, R. (1968) *Time and the Physical World*. New York: Dover.

Szumilewicz, I. (1971) 'The Direction of Time and Entropy', in J. Zeman (ed.) *Time in Science and Philosophy: An International Study of Some Current Problems*. Amsterdam: Elsevier, 181–92.

2. RECONSTRUCTING THE PAST: VISUAL VIRTUALITY IN *ETERNAL SUNSHINE OF THE SPOTLESS MIND*

STEVEN RAWLE

Pipi: Are we in 2002?

Me: Yes.

Pipi: Fuck. Eet's late.

Me: I know.

Pipi: Time keeps going. Eet's draping through our fingers. Nothing can stop eet. [sic][1]

Michel Gondry's *Eternal Sunshine of the Spotless Mind* (2004) follows Joel Barrish's (Jim Carrey) ultimately futile attempts to both delete and retain his memories in order to cope with and control the traumatic events of his recent past.[2] In the process, the film explores the cinematic representation of memory. During the opening pre-credit sequence, Joel is impulsively compelled to skip work in order to take a train to Montauk, Long Island. While strolling down the beach there, he encounters Clementine Kruczynski (Kate Winslet), a blue-haired exhibitionist. He later sees her again in a diner, sneaking gin into her drink at breakfast. She smiles at him, but he does not reciprocate, trapped in the throes of shyness. On the train back to the city, she speaks to him; he seems withdrawn and agitated, while she is emotional and open. Eventually, they agree to see each other again, a brief relationship which culminates in an evening spent together watching the stars on the frozen River Charles. Cut to the opening credits: we see a distraught Joel, in tears, driving his car, to the soundtrack of Beck singing 'Change a Heart'. Eventually, like Joel, we discover that, in order to avoid the pain of a broken heart, Clementine has had her memories of him and their relationship erased by a company called Lacuna, Inc., something she undertook as 'a lark'. Joel decides to have the same procedure carried out.

The rest of the narrative follows the disjointed structure of Joel's relationship with Clementine as he re-experiences the events of their romance whilst it is being erased. At the end of the erasure process, which takes place overnight, Joel awakens to find himself in unfamiliar pyjamas.

We see him get ready to leave for work. He discovers that his car has been scraped by a neighbour; he leaves a note on the other car, which simply says 'Thank You!' The audience however has already seen that the car was damaged by a drunken Clementine before leaving Joel, one of the first of his memories to be confronted and deleted; it soon becomes clear that the sequence discussed above is not simply the beginning of a conventional romantic comedy, but also the ending, a structural and visual repetition that echoes the confused temporality of the film as a whole. This repetition is also reflected in the subplot intercut with the scenes depicting Joel's memory. As Joel's memories are being erased by the ramshackle team of technicians from Lacuna, a secondary narrative of memory deletion and repetition emerges. When Joel attempts to resist the procedure, Stan (Mark Ruffalo), one the Lacuna technicians, then calls on Dr Mierzwiak (Tom Wilkinson), the technique's inventor, for assistance. When he arrives, he is briefly left alone with the smitten Mary (Kirsten Dunst), Lacuna's secretary; mesmerised by the doctor, she playfully quotes out of context aphorisms to him. She kisses him, but they are caught by Mierzwiak's wife. It transpires that this is not the first time Mary and Dr Mierzwiak have had an affair, but she has had her memory erased. As revenge for Mierzwiak's lack of ethics, Mary returns his patients' files to them, complete with re-cords of their deleted memories. Meanwhile, another Lacuna employee, Patrick (Elijah Wood), has been dating Clementine, using the mementoes of her relationship with Joel to seduce her. However, she experiences some unease at the uncanny nature of the relationship, especially when they visit the frozen River Charles at night. Finally, when Joel and Clementine re-ceive their files the morning after their own night on the frozen river, they are shocked to find evidence of their prior relationship. Nevertheless, at the end of the film they decide to proceed with another relationship. This decision seems a clear attempt on the part of both characters to reclaim and manage a lost past through the repetition of prior experience, something they both intentionally erased. In the final shots of the film, we see Joel and Clementine fooling around on the beach where they first met; the shot gets stuck in a loop before fading to white. Is this a painful future repeated again and again, or a repetition of the past? As with the repetition of the pre-credit sequence, the temporality of this ending is unclear.

In what has quickly become a modern cult classic, Gondry and script-writer Charlie Kaufman have created a film that functions to present a picture of memory that works on two different levels of visual virtuality.

For the purposes of this essay, 'visual virtuality' refers specifically to the performance of memory in the text – both in terms of the narrative structure and its effect upon the audience, and the stylistic and visual function of the film. *Eternal Sunshine* in particular invokes specific relationships between images and events in the text that explore the linkages between the actual moments of character experience and perception and the virtual moments of a recollected or forgotten past. As the film features the use of both structural and stylistic repetition, Gondry and Kaufman make the relationship between actual, experienced images and events (images in particular) and virtual traces of the past of the narrative; the viewer cannot help but be sucked into the actual/virtual linkages that determine the actions and emotional reactions of the characters in the film.

The visual virtuality of *Eternal Sunshine* works on two separate levels of actual and virtual, where one refers to the function of the text while the second, deeper level relates to the activation of memory in the viewer whilst watching the film. The first and most superficial level deals specifically with the representation of Joel's memory, and the ways in which he experiences memory during the film. During his fruitless attempt to resist the memory eradication process, Joel's memory is presented as faulty, or at least prone to nostalgia. Joel's memory contradicts the unhappy relationship we know him to have had with Clementine – a relationship he is compelled to repeat at the end of the film. The representation of Joel's memory is visually manifested in a discontinuous, fragmentary fashion, depicting the separate layers of Joel's recollected past. When Joel initially discovers from some friends that

Fig. 6 Repetition compulsion in action: Joel and Clementine meet for, temporally at least, the first time in the film. Is this a reenactment of their actual first meeting?

Clementine has had him erased, we see a card from Lacuna in a close up point-of-view shot. Suddenly, the words 'Clementine Kruczynski' disappear from the card. The shot then fades out of focus before cutting abruptly to Joel in the street. The background around him is out of focus. With no warning, the film has shifted into a memory register, and it is through the memory-deletion process, signified by the lack of focus, that we learn about the process itself. Although we assume this to be conventional narrative exposition, the visual performance of the text signals its already memory-located nature.[3] Only once the erasure procedure begins does the narrative start to move backward in time. The sequences in the Lacuna offices are replayed, although in fragmented fashion, with sudden shifts into fast motion, jump cuts, shifts in location (at one point Joel is seen strapped into the brain-mapping chair, although suddenly outside on the snowy street), and fragmentary, echoey patches of unidentifiable dialogue are heard. These collapsing scenes and those that follow, including the memory of the final break-up, signal the distorting memory, the gaps in recollection and approaching amnesia, sometimes signaled by overexposed light or by white in the *mise-en-scène* (as when the titles on the books in the bookstore disappear); as Joel tells Clementine, 'It's all falling apart.'

The second level of virtuality involves the activity of the viewer. When the film returns, shot for shot, to the initial opening sequence described above, the viewer is confronted with their own past, the past of watching the film. When Joel re-awakens into the bright, overexposed sunlight, the viewer is immediately confronted with the uncanny sense of déjà vu at re-viewing the opening of the film. The recognition of a potential (and unresolved) circular temporality for the viewer implies a second level of signification to the images. The initial enigma surrounding Joel's actions – the damaged car, the uncharacteristic impulsiveness – is now resolved, as the viewer has experienced Joel's past with him, although he has no recollection of that past. The images have the past inscribed into them for the audience – the repetition is recognised as a visual narrative past, one shared by all of the audience. This secondary visual virtuality invites the audience to connect a virtual recollection to the repeated imagery, a map of the past for the audience, but not the characters in the film.[4] However, the intricacies of *Eternal Sunshine* finds the audience member directly involved in the virtuality of repeated and twice-experienced images, as the characters are, although the audience are privileged in that they are aware that the images they are re-viewing include virtual traces of the past.

Eternal Sunshine plays out as actual (at all times), as virtual (as represented recollection and as repetition) and, at times, both at once, diegetically and extra-diegetically. Thus, by drawing on the work of Gilles Deleuze, who draws liberally from Henri Bergson's work on duration and memory, this essay will discuss the manners in which *Eternal Sunshine* can be treated as a reflection of Deleuzian memory-images, and how these extend into the presentation of crystalline-images when the viewer's memory is stimulated by the function of the visual text; this is outlined in greater depth below. 'Visual virtuality' thus refers to both levels of memory in the film: the superficial represented memory and the deeper layers of viewer memory brought to the 'peaks of the present' (Deleuze 1989: 98) by Gondry's stylistic use of repetition. Gondry's stylistic and structural virtuality invokes the performance of the viewer's virtual experience at the very moment at which Joel's virtual memory of Clementine has been eradicated. Gondry returns us to the beginning of the film in a shot-by-shot repetition to raise the viewers' virtual recollection of the repeated images – although the main character's own recollection of the images has been deleted. Even though the film implies that this is Joel's first and only perception of these images, the audience infers the repetition in the film's own repetition of these images – *has* Joel experienced this before? We have, and we detect the virtual behind these actual images. Of course, Joel only senses the actual, automatic perception and understanding of these images – he cannot remember how he got here, and he does not understand what has happened to him. His own virtual recollection of going to bed has been eliminated (he has even 'forgotten' putting on the pyjamas given to him by the technicians of Lacuna). The audience, however, retains the virtual image as memory via their experience of prior perception of the narrative events. Gondry's direct invocation of visual repetition stimulates the recollection in the viewer, who experiences the déjà vu of the virtual memory-image becoming actual in the performance of the narrative when the film leaves Joel's memory.

The extension of virtual images into actual motor-extension in action is a key theme throughout the film. Although the memory of the past has been eradicated, the characters that undergo the memory-deletion process are still prone to repeat past behaviour: Joel is still drawn to Clementine, and vice versa; Mary is still inclined to repeat her affair with Dr Mierzwiak. In addition, Clementine is attracted to Patrick, who is exploiting the experiences and mementoes of her relationship with Joel. However, when Patrick 'performs' her meeting with Joel on the ice, Clementine is disturbed by the uncanny nature of the experience. The actual perception of the moment reactivates her virtual memory, despite its effective disavowal during the memory eradication process. Thus, she senses the uncanny resemblance between the actual experience and the virtual trace left by the procedure. Nevertheless, she remains compelled to repeat, in its full Freudian sense. Freud refers to repetition compulsion 'not as a matter belonging to the past, but as a force operating in the present' (2003: 36). In the Deleuzian-Bergsonian terminology adopted here, we might also see this as the virtual masquerading as the actual, where the two coalesce, the actual extension into action hiding the limited virtual trace behind the motor-extension. In *Eternal Sunshine*, then, the eradicated virtuality is experienced as a lacuna, a scar left behind on the brain (normally by a stroke or seizure), something present but intangible. The actions of Joel, Clementine and Mary are manifestations of the intangible lacuna – extensions of memory into action which act, as Freud again notes, 'to forestall the unpleasure that would be caused if the repressed part of the psyche were to break free' (*Ibid.*: 58). As David Martin-Jones notes, the idealisation and falsification of memory by Joel is a gateway to the repetition of a traumatic past; he notes that *Eternal Sunshine* 'suggests that the amnesia propagated by American cinema after 9/11 is constructing an infantilised generation who, disconnected from their nation's own complicity in events of the recent past, are doomed to repeat the same mistakes' (2006: 179). The eradication of memory is a failure in this sense, a repression (something left behind after a traumatic experience) rather than a deletion, hence Clementine's uncanny sense of déjà vu, and the shared compulsion to repeat on the parts of Joel, Clementine and Mary.

Whereas the film eventually functions as a virtuality for the viewer, it also represents virtuality in its main, memory-located sequences. For this, Gondry imagines the film in the register of something equivalent to Deleuze's recollection-images. Deleuze, following Bergson, contends that 'the recollection-image is not virtual', but that it does actualise 'a virtuality' (1989: 54). The recollection-image is a time-image only through its representation of memory – it is not really virtual, but actual. Like a flashback, it is a 'closed circuit which goes from the present to the past, then leads us back to the present' (*Ibid.*: 48). Thus, the recollection-image only *represents* the virtual, it is not virtual in and of itself. Bergson's inverted cone, to which Deleuze repeatedly refers, offers the primary model for the recollection-image. In *Matter and Memory*, Bergson constructs the example of the inverted cone to demonstrate the process and virtual location of memory and the various layers of recollection-images between the perceived actuality and the upside-down bottom of the cone, the 'motionless' past (1991: 152). The inverted cone represents the totality of the memory's accumulated virtual imagery, developed through habit and repetition. The point of contact between the sheet of the present perception and the point of the cone is the moment of synthesis, at which point the actual and virtual form a circuit into indiscernability (the moment at which Deleuze's recollection-images give way to crystal-images). For Bergson though, this is a crucial moment of fusion between past and present that steers the body: 'the memory of the past offers to the sensory-motor mechanisms all the recollections capable of guiding them in their task and of giving to the motor reaction the direction suggested by the lessons of experience' (*Ibid.*: 152–3). The synthesis is largely automatic, an immediate location of the recollection needed to process the impulse. In many senses, this is closer to Deleuze's movement-image, in which the impulse and sensory-motor movements of narrative are closely linked, although the linkages between virtual recollection and actual images become more pronounced for Deleuze when the sensory-motor schema is at its weakest. Of course, for Joel in *Eternal Sunshine*, the procedure takes places during his most motor incapable state, when he is asleep, where the link between impulse and movement has been disabled so that the memory is freed of bodily movement in the actual world. Thus, the memory-located passages of the film's narrative are locked into the inverted cone, detached from the perception of the actual world taking place outside Joel's mind. But, as the cone is detached, the base of the cone – Joel's motionless past – has also become detached. The 'totality of the recollections accumulated' (*Ibid.*: 152) in Joel's mind threatens to become disconnected from its coordinates in virtual space, as those recollections blur together and become subjectivised.

Deleuze's conception of cinematic recollection-images, which he designates *mnemosigns*, builds upon Bergson's notion of the motor-extended recollection-image: as Deleuze notes, recollection-images 'insert themselves between stimulation and response, and contribute to the better adjustment to the motor mechanism by reinforcing it with a psychological causality' (1989: 47). As noted above, the role of recollection-images is crucial in *Eternal Sunshine* in this sense. Without the 'knowledge' of the performers, the recollection-image remains in the mind as lacunae – Joel, Clementine and Mary all fall into the trap of repetition compulsion, the 'eternal recurrence of the same', to adopt Freud's phraseology (2003: 58). As Freud argues, the repressed memory returns as active behaviour in the patient, an unconscious attempt to deny the unpleasure of the recollection by suppressing the virtual memory. In Deleuzian-Bergsonian terms, this is the actualisation of a virtual memory, where the recollection-image is repressed by the subject, unknowingly manifesting the recollection as motor-extended action. Thus, the recollection unconsciously intervenes between the stimulus and the reaction. The lack of recollection in the film's main characters is akin to a repression, especially in Joel where there is such a conscious attempt to link the adult recollection to repressed and traumatic memories, which stimulates the behaviour of the (non-) rememberer. However, whilst this explains the post-procedure behaviour of the character, it does not illuminate the performance of the film's representation of memory and the recollection-images manifested by Gondry in the memory-located sequences.

Deleuze's main cinematic model for the recollection-image is flashback. This provides a key analogy for the understanding of the role played by recollection-images in *Eternal Sunshine*, where we understand the imagery of the narrative explicitly as a flashback, something located in the past, but intrinsic to our understanding of the present. The relationship of recollection to actual in the flashback is as follows:

> a closed circuit which goes from the present to the past, then leads us back to the present ... a multiplicity of circuits each of which goes through a zone of recollections and returns to an even deeper, even more inexorable, state of the present situation. ... It can, therefore, indicate, by convention [a dissolve-link], a causality which is psychological, but still analogous to a sensory-motor determinism, and, despite its circuits, only confirms the progression of a linear narration. (Deleuze 1989: 48)

The circuit between the actual and the reflection of the virtual is one of a 'sensory-motor determinism', where the recollection-images are wholly motivated by the needs of the narration, which seeks to validate, or explain, the events of the present through the recollection of the past. In many ways, this not only acts as a reminder of the repetition compulsion of the three main characters (and in some senses also of Gondry, whose work in film and music video is rife with repetition), but also a sign of the representation of memory in the film. The narrative structure of *Eternal Sunshine* feeds off a key actual/virtual circuit between the pre-credit opening sequence, Joel's realisation of Clementine's actions and her public dismissal of him, Clementine's uncanny experience of déjà vu with Patrick (something the audience has experienced as an actual narrative present and past in the pre-credit sequence and in Joel's mind) and the information relayed to us through Joel's exploits inside his own mind. By Deleuze's terminology, the circuit between the present of the narrative and Joel's recollected images is most like a flashback, although it always resembles a present of the narrative as it involves a present agency above that of simple actual motor-extension. Joel retains an image of motor-extension, although it is only an image within his own ever more distorted past, where the circuit between past and present is particularly active, although only in the sense that the present is operational in the past as a reflection of Joel's subjectivity. However, the past and present form a more marginal, reducing circuit through the film as Joel's memory is eradicated, despite his attempts at an active agency, which prove illusory – it was only ever an image in his own mind.

The sequences of *Eternal Sunshine* that are located entirely within Joel's mind only represent the virtual sampling of his memory – although they are entirely replayed through his subjectivity. There is a tendency to accept the images in the memory sequence as objective, an effect of the cinematic apparatus, which suggests to us that all images captured by the camera represent a 'truthful' reality. In *Eternal Sunshine*, Joel's virtual memory is distorted by his subjectivity, his nostalgia for his relationship with Clementine (she appears in his memory as idealised, perfect at times); as such, the actual, represented virtuality of Joel's memory portrays less of the past Joel, than it does of the present Joel. This is made explicit in the sequences where Joel appears in his memory as a child, although still Carrey – he is an actual,

present Joel (an adult without motor-extension wandering his own mind), rather than the virtual Joel, who would surely appear as a child. Under these circumstances, due to the subject's interference, memory becomes the simulacra of the past.

Fig. 7 Memory becomes the simulacra of the past as Joel inserts his adult image into disintegrating memory of his childhood, signified by Jim Carrey's performance as the child Joel.

Joel's memory is based only tenuously on an unseen original (a fiction within the fiction). The represented memory – Gondry's first layer of visual virtuality – is a mass of nostalgised and distorted fragments blended into a single image of 'memory'. The narrative images that take place within Joel's mind do not stimulate the viewer's own memory of these events, and as such our knowledge of Joel and Clementine's relationship is filtered through Joel's personal memory of those events: the arguments, the final confrontation and break up; their first encounter; the sexual games they played together; and fun times narrating drive-in movies are all relayed to us through Joel's memory of those events. The 'recollection-image', Deleuze argues:

> does not deliver the past to us, but only represents the former present that the past 'was'. The recollection-image is an image which is actualised or in the process of being made actual, which does not form with the actual, present image a circuit of indiscernability. (1989: 54)

The recollection-images in the narrative of *Eternal Sunshine* represent Joel's accumulated virtual recollections, but as they are actualised for the viewer, there is a tendency to forget the subjectivity that is relaying them to us. The subject warps the recollection-images before us, making them less than virtual, but suggestive of more than simply an actual narrative image of past events (as the cinema almost always is); it is not our recollection, but the recollection of an Other subjectivity which we may confuse as the performance of a history, however personal.

The idealised, fragmented memory sequences of *Eternal Sunshine* are engaged in the process of *being-made-actual*. They represent not only a former present, but also the actualisation of an image that does not form a circuit with its virtual counterpart to the point of indiscernability – that is reserved for the crystalline-image in which the virtual and actual faces of the crystal are merged into an indiscernible, fluctuating and interchangeable indiscernability. (Gondry creates the potential for this in his later use of repetition, something not signalled by the creation of recollection-images.) Jason Sperb (2005) examines the role of light played in the film and its meditation on 'the artificiality of mental recollection' and 'the notion of characters living in and perceiving the immediate moment, as opposed to putting themselves into the past'. He implicates the role of the recollection-image in his thesis, suggesting that the recollection-image engages the rememberer not with a virtual past, but with a limited, blinkered view of the past engaging more with the present than a remembered past. However, the role of virtual images, as previously noted, in the process of *being-mage-actual*, rather than limiting the perception of the past creates actualised images of the past that, as Laura Marks contends regarding the recollection-image, have 'no match in the recent image repertoire'

(1994: 251). The recollected imagery of Joel's immediate remembered past, his relationship with Clementine, have no equivalent in the shared consciousness of the actual motor-extended events of the relationship. Rather, Joel's nostalgic, idealised remembering tends to combine virtual traces of other events, childhood trauma, adolescent humiliation, where recollection-images represent not the practice of remembering itself, but the practice of forgetting. The recovery of long-repressed fragments of memory restores the virtual traces to an actualised state, especially in the sequence with the dead bird, where Joel and Clementine switch between their adult selves and their childhood equivalents (using a photographic image of what is presumably the young Clementine seen earlier in the film). The recollection-image then is part past, part present and part other past, idealised and filtered through Joel's sub- and unconscious memory – the reflection and remembrance of not one, but multiple pasts, both personal and impersonal ('unofficial' and 'official' histories in Marks' terminology).

Gondry's visual virtuality combines multiple virtualities in its creation of recollection-images, in which the 'real' past is unrepresentable, not through its limitations, but through its lack of limitations. Joel's memory is incapable of both remembering *and* forgetting – signified by his return to a deleted memory, and his reclamation of forgotten and repressed memories to help him remember Clementine. The paradox of Joel's memory lies in its indiscernible convergence of virtual fragments into fragmentary, actualised imagery with no virtual equivalent in his or our image repertoire. As such, the virtual is often processed in an actual fashion – as when Joel narrates his thought to Clementine in his memory of their first meeting. He notes details, like the 'intimate' way she snatches chicken from his plate. This is also the case during his memory of the drive home with his friends following the first meeting with Clementine – multiple virtual images collide as fragments (as they do in the repeated scenes in Lacuna's offices), motivated by Joel's nostalgic reflection on his relationship with Clementine; he takes one final tour of the memories, before they are supposedly gone forever. Perhaps these are the fragments he retains, not forgotten, but repressed (lacunae), the source of his compulsion to repeat.

Although the narration is in the process of *being-made-actual*, Joel's recollected image, the virtual actualised, does not bear any resemblance to the 'real' past, as the performance of Joel's memory relocates the events within his perception of image, time and thought (rather, events have the curious sensation of resembling the future, which is the narrative's past). Despite this, the images within the film continue to merely *represent* virtuality. There is no actual equivalent in the film for the recollection-images; 'Memory is not in us', as Deleuze contends (1989: 98). The images are not virtual for the viewer, because they do not correspond to any previously experienced memory, only the traces of Joel's memory which are actualised as recollection-images, unremembered, fragmented and distorted. Importantly, they are *only* actual for the audience; this is purely a simulacrum of memory. When they can be remembered by the audience, as with Joel's meeting with his neighbour at the beginning of the film, lines are fragmentary, events are changed and, through Gondry's use of extreme shallow focus, eroded. The viewer finds Joel in 'the process of replacing actual images with virtual images' (Marks 1994: 254).[5] But, crucially, the viewer does not share in the process of actual-virtual substitution; they are only aware of the 'volatile' recollection-image.

'There is no doubt', Deleuze contends, 'that attentive recognition, when it succeeds, comes about *through* recollection-images: it is the man I met last week at such and such a place...' (1989: 54). Attentive recognition is Bergson's concept of the activation of virtual memory by the actual image in front of the individual:

> At each moment of an attentive perception, for example, new elements sent up from a deeper stratum of the mind might join the earlier elements, without thereby creating a general disturbance and without bringing about a transformation of the whole system. (1991: 104)

Attentive recognition is a further moment of synthesis, although ultimately one more complex and fruitful than the automatic recognition. Here, the actual image calls to mind a host of potential virtual linkages for the viewer. Marks describes the process as 'a *participatory* notion of spectatorship' (1994: 256; emphasis in original). Whereas forgetting is linked to the motor extension of stimuli into action – the compulsions to repeat for several of the main characters – attentive recognition detaches the image from its extension into action. Thus, it stimulates the *active* connection of actual to virtual by the rememberer, or the viewer. Crucially, for Joel, his period of memory eradication comes at the point where he is most motor inactive, while he is asleep; this stimulates his descent into the virtual realm of his mind. However, his emergence into motor sensation is not necessarily the emergence into the eternal sunshine of the spotless mind, if his mind is even ever spotless.

Gondry eventually returns the viewer to the beginning of the film as Joel wakes up from his night of memory eradication. He stares up at the blinding light pouring into his window, unable to see clearly. The viewer however is able to see clearly that the sequence is tainted by repetition. Joel emerges into the sunshine as a kind of cypher, rooted purely in the perception of the present actual moment; he darts around, suddenly noticing the unfamiliar pyjamas given to him by the Lacuna technicians. However, Gondry's use of shot-for-shot repetition brings the issue to the fore for the viewer. Although Joel does not sense the uncanny feeling of déjà vu felt by Clementine when she spends her night on the ice with Patrick, the viewer *is* struck by the sense that he or she has seen this all before; from the point-of-view shot of Joel's perspective looking at the window, over-exposed and slightly out of focus like the film's first shot, to the exact repetition of Joel's impulsive decision to take the train to Montauk. The viewer is suddenly confronted with the performance of the past in the present – what are we actually seeing now? Is this a repetition of the past, and was the pre-credit sequence a foreshadowing of future events? Or is this the repetition of the past in the present? Has Joel done all this before, as Gondry's stylistic repetition implies? As Joel repeatedly asks himself, 'why do I always…?'

Joel's uncharacteristic, impulsive behaviour continues his extension into the actual moment – a reflection of Deleuze's Action-Situation-Action (ASA) small form of the action-image,[6] not to mention his forgotten memory that compels him to repeat the past. For the viewer though, this is explicitly the past, as Gondry's visual virtuality, his use of shot-for-shot repetition, goes beyond the recollection-image into the crystals of time to the point where actual and virtual are indiscernible. At the moment where the circuit between virtual and actual becomes multiple to the point of imperceptibility, the image, Deleuze asserts, become crystalline, becoming an image of time itself, divorced from movement. The crystal-image, Deleuze contends, has multiple sides of virtuality and actuality: 'the actual image itself has a virtual image which corresponds to it like a double or a reflection. In Bergsonian terms, the real object is reflected in a mirror-image as in the virtual object which, from its side and simultaneously, envelops or reflects the real: there is "coalescence" between the two' (1989: 68).

The circuit between the two sides of the crystal forces images of virtuality and actuality – the pure recollection and present perception (past and present) – to merge in an irreducible unity to the point of indiscernibility ('coalescence'). This 'smallest internal circuit' is in a continual state of flux:

> the virtual image becomes actual, it is then visible and limpid, as in the mirror or the solidity of finished crystal. But the actual image becomes virtual in its turn, referred elsewhere, invisible, opaque and shadowy, like a crystal barely dislodged from the earth. The actual-virtual couple thus immediately extends into the opaque-limpid, the expression of their exchange. (*Ibid.*: 70)

Gondry's repetition creates a crystal circuit between the original moment – once actual, now virtual – and the repeated moment, which is actual and virtual at once. The virtual image, the past, becomes 'invisible, opaque and shadowy', reflected in the mind of the spectator. In this moment, the image goes beyond recollection into attentive recognition, wherein the viewer shares in Joel's déjà vu, his barely cognizant sensation of the past operating in the present. However, without the shared virtual image of the past held by the viewer, Joel extends virtuality into motor extension (of impulse into action). On the other hand, the viewer who enters the diegesis with a relatively spotless (narrative) mind experiences the participatory efficacy of attentive recognition, delving into the recesses of the virtual mind to find the 'double or reflection' that corresponds to this actual image. In stimulating the viewer's own memory in this fashion, the film hints at a continuing virtuality into a state of perpetual eternal return – does the film return the viewer to the past, or this is a new present? If it is a new present, then the situation has the capacity to repeat into eternity, memory erased, repressed and then repeated again and again. In fact, in an earlier draft of Kaufman's screenplay, the film was to end with Clementine returning to Dr Merzwiak's office to have the procedure performed again – a glimpse at the computer's monitor would reveal to us that she had had multiple procedures carried out to erase Joel again and again.[7] Gondry's use of stylistic and structural repetition hints at this outcome by stimulating the viewer's own virtual recollection of the narrative past, while hinting at a continual actualisation of the virtual lacunae of memory. There can be no eternal sunshine for a 'spotless' mind, as Mary's part remembered, part forgotten aphorisms prove, painful fragments remain and the unremembered virtual will extend into action again and again.

The role of repetition in this recovery of the past in the present moment is crucial.[8] Repetition signifies the collapse of past memory and present perception into a homogeneous circle of eternal return.[9] Gondry even ends the film with a crystal-image that presents the erosion of both the virtual *and* actual, whilst simultaneously signifying the potential perpetuation of repetitious cycles of behaviour for Joel and Clementine. The final shot of the film becomes stuck in a loop (a metaphorical reflection of the plight of the main characters), which slowly degrades to white. As the sequence progresses, the difference between what is actual in the present and what is virtual in the past becomes totally indiscernible. As a consequence, the ending is open, stimulating a series of interpretations that read the ending as either happy or sad.[10] Joel and Clementine will either get it right through practice or experience a frustrating, absurd recurrence of unhappiness; this seems to reflect more on the virtual linkages that the audiences have brought to the film themselves, their own personal histories projected onto the film in a particularly participatory way – the crystalline imagery stimulates the activity of attentive recognition, as the viewer brings virtual images to the actuality of the narrative's own imagery. Gondry's visual virtuality motivates other virtualities by directly stimulating the processes of memory in the viewer.

Eternal Sunshine of the Spotless Mind indulges in multiple plays with the representation and invocation of memory. Gondry's use of visual virtuality creates memory-images in two different fashions. Primarily, during the sequences of Joel's memory eradication procedure, Gondry's imagery explores the creation of recollection-images in the use of specific fragmented *mise en scène* and the distortion of boundaries between memories that collapse or are

Fig. 8 A brief moment of domestic harmony in the tumultuous relationship between Joel and Clementine.

redrawn. Where the recollection-images are signified only as the representation of memory is in the lack of corresponding memory in the viewer; 'the memory is not in us,' as Deleuze noted. Here, there is no implication of repetition in the imagery, only in the desire of the characters to compulsively repeat unfulfilling behaviour. The second level of visual virtuality occurs specifically where repetition is invoked by Gondry, where crystals form in the coalescing of the viewer's virtual memory of the text and the actual, present performance of the text (expressly, the shot-for-shot repetition of the opening sequence and the degrading final loop and fade to white). At these moments, past and present are indiscernible, stimulating a sense of déjà vu in the viewer. Finally, the memory *is* in us, although paradoxically it is not in the characters. The invocation of repetition, fragmentation, distortion and the representation of the virtual through recollection-images draw the viewer into the virtual/actual play of the film, motivating the participation of memory in the process. This is something that Gondry carries into later work in *The Science of Sleep* (2006).[11] In the opening sequence, Stéphane presents the recipe for a dream, adding a handful of spaghetti to represent 'memories of the past' – when he senses rejection later in the film, he repeatedly screams, 'I don't want to be spaghetti!' What Stéphane really fears is becoming lost in the virtual vaults of memory, forgotten in the present world, and recovered only in processes of thought and dreams; he tends to live in the actual register of present experience, even in his dreams. *Eternal Sunshine of the Spotless Mind* on the other hand is a veritable feast of spaghetti for its characters *and* its audience.

NOTES

1   Michel Gondry (2003) *I've Been Twelve Forever: The Work of Director Michel Gondry*, DVD notes from *The Work of Director Michel Gondry*. Palm Pictures, n.p.

2   In *Deleuze, Cinema and National Identity*, David Martin-Jones likewise contends that *Eternal Sunshine* maps onto Deleuzian territory in its evocation of American self-identity dealing with recent trauma, specifically the spectre of 9/11 in recent cultural and political memory. He contends: '*Eternal Sunshine* depicts characters coming to terms with a recent trauma in their personal lives ... [It] suggests that Joel and Clementine will retrace the two years leading up to their break up, despite the pain this entails, in order to attempt to change it. They consciously acknowledge their own complicity in creating the trauma and endeavour to stop it from happening again' (2006: 176–7).

3   Later, when Joel returns to Lacuna for his procedure, he steps in front of a car in the street; the driver tells him to 'wake up'. This is another example of the subtle ways in which Joel's degrading memory is signified by the text.

4   As a consequence, the film also maps onto speculative territory involving the viewer's own experience of unhappy memories; would they have them eradicated, if the technology was possible (another technology of personal mutilation for supposed personal 'improvement')? Would they not? In this manner, the viewer is placed in a position of identification with the protagonist, a further layer of visual virtuality, although of a different order. Christopher Grau (2006) reflects on the philosophical and moral ramifications of the process.

5   Marks is here discussing Atom Egoyan's *Calendar* (1993).

6   The small form of the action image is 'a reversed sensory-motor schema' where the milieu is stimulated by the action, rather than the opposite in the large form, in which the determined milieu stimulates action from the impulse-image – a moment

in which the sensory-motor extension is activated by surrounding stimulus, as in the recollection-image; in the action-image, external factors stimulates motor-extension, rather than the internal vicissitudes of memory (see Deleuze 1986: 141–51, 160–4).

7   *Internet Movie Database* 2007.

8   David L. Smith (2005) has also noted the importance of repetition for the narrative function of *Eternal Sunshine*. He discusses the role of quotation as 'metaphor for repetition'. He cites Mary's use of Bartlett's to quote, among others, Nietzsche and Pope (including the film's title) as a wide-ranging symbol for the various means of quotation and repetition that bring meaning and structure to our lives in the form of psychology, linguistics, reproduction and popular culture. These, he argues, are 'ways we both use the past and are constrained by it'. Smith might also include the narrative structure and visual performance of the film as ways in which its characters are 'constrained' by the past.

9   A crucial concept for both structural and behavioural models of repetition (in Deleuze and Freud), eternal return is an important component of Nietzschean philosophy. In *Thus Spoke Zarathustra*, Nietzsche expounds his nihilistic view of experience with the proclamation that 'God is dead' (2003: 41). The repetition of eternal return is essentially nihilistic in itself, destructive, negating meaning. Present moments are emptied of the uniqueness of experience as all that can be has been before in the past and all that will be has already been. For Joel and Clementine, the eternal recurrence is only hinted at, as the repetition merely hints at the eternal, yet the crystalline confluence of virtual and actual brings the repetition to the fore in the minds of the audience, who see beyond the singular repetition at the film's conclusion.

Nietzsche's theories of eternal return and the negating, destructive power of repetition are a significant influence on Deleuze in *Difference and Repetition*, in which he discusses the signifying potentials of repetition, and the consequential difference revealed in eternal return. Deleuze argues that the 'natural' systematisation of repetition can sustain three repetitions before the mechanism comes to signify itself, turning all subsequent recurrences into pure repetition. Deleuze's 'triadic structure' sees the third moment that implies a systematisation of repetition as 'the revelation and affirmation of eternal return' (1994: 92). The eternal return can at times be hinted at in cyclical repetitions that do not reach a third level, 'which alone merits the name of eternal return' (*Ibid.*: 93). *Eternal Sunshine* on the other hand does not get this far; it really has only one repetition. This single repetition merely hints at the eternal return, and the cycle of repetition in which the two protagonists are trapped. When we reach the final shots of the film, however, we get a fuller sense of the eternal return as Gondry repeats the final shot of the film in a loop, eventually fading to white; more than anything, this signifies the eternal recurrence of *Eternal Sunshine*.

10 My own work with students on the film has thrown up a host of interpretations of the future of these two characters, some positive and some negative – in many ways this may be a clean slate onto which viewers can project their own virtual experience of romance onto the possibility of success or failure for our two protagonists' second chance future together.

11 *The Science of Sleep* appears to continue *Eternal Sunshine*'s concerns with memory and recollection, although in a different Deleuzian register of *onirosigns* (dream-images, 'where a movement of world replaces action' (1986: 335) as opposed to *Eternal Sunshine*'s *mnemosigns*. Drawing particularly on Gondry's earlier music video work, the film includes references to the homemade theatrical cityscape *mise en scène* of Björk's *Bachelorette* (1997), the collage animation of *Human Behavior* (1993) or *Hyperballad* (1996), both also for Björk, and the giant hands from The Foo Fighters' *Everlong*

(1997). The *mise-en-scène* of *The Science of Sleep* echoes Gondry's earlier work, in addition to the once again memory-located portions of a narrative that deals explicitly with past experience, in particularly Stéphane's difficultly in dealing with his father's death, something which has autobiographical roots in the death of Gondry's father.

WORKS CITED

Bergson, H. (1991) *Matter and Memory*, trans. N. M. Paul and W. S. Palmer. New York: Zone.

Deleuze, G. (1986) *Cinema 1: The Movement Image*, trans. H. Tomlinson and B. Habberjam. London: Athlone.

_____ (1989) *Cinema 2: The Time-Image*, trans. H. Tomlinson and R. Galeta. London: Athlone.

_____ (1994) *Difference and Repetition*, trans. P. Patton. New York: Columbia University Press.

Freud, S. (2003) *Beyond the Pleasure Principle and Other Writings*, trans. J. Reddick. London: Penguin.

Gondry, M. (2003) *I've Been Twelve Forever: The Work of Director Michel Gondry*. New York and London: Palm Pictures.

Grau, C. (2006) '*Eternal Sunshine of the Spotless Mind* and the Morality of Memory', *Journal of Aesthetics and Art Criticism*, 64, 1, 119–33.

Internet Movie Database (2007) 'Trivia for HYPERLINK "*http://www.imdb.com/title/tt0338013/*" \t "_popup7635" *Eternal Sunshine of the Spotless Mind* (2004)'. On-line. Available at: http://www.imdb.com/title/tt0338013/trivia (accessed 18 May 2007).

Marks, L. U. (1994) 'A Deleuzian politics of hybrid cinema,' *Screen*, 35, 3, 244–64.

Martin-Jones, D. (2006) *Deleuze, Cinema and National Identity*. Edinburgh: Edinburgh University Press.

Nietzsche, F. (2003) *Thus Spoke Zarathustra*, trans. R. J. Hollingdale. London: Penguin.

Smith, D. L. (2005) '*Eternal Sunshine of the Spotless Mind* and the Question of Transcendence', *The Journal of Religion and Film*, 9, 1. On-line. Available at: http://www.unomaha.edu/jrf/Vol9No1/SmithSunshine.htm (accessed 10 April 2006).

Sperb, J. (2005) 'Internal Sunshine: Illuminating Being-Memory in *Eternal Sunshine of the Spotless Mind*', *Kritikos*, 2. On-line. Available at: http://garnet.acns.fsu.edu/%7Enr03/Internal%20Sunshine.htm (accessed 10 April 2006).

3. DEATH EVERY SUNDAY AFTERNOON: THE VIRTUAL REALITIES OF HIROKAZU KORE-EDA'S *AFTERLIFE*

ALANNA THAIN

A group of people take their seats in a cinema. The lights dim, the projector comes to life, its beam of light washing over the faces in the crowd. Some are about to watch the finished fruits of their labours as filmmakers projected for the first time. Others will see one moment of their life, plucked from the stream of their experiences, worked through by filmmakers, cameras, sets and shooting and finally spilling from the projector onto the screen. This one moment they have chosen to be their eternity, a singular expression of an entire life. When the projector begins, the lights go down. When they come up again, those who have just seen their memories played out are gone. Where did they go?

This is a scene from Hirokazu Kore-Eda's second feature film, *Afterlife* (*Wandafuru Raifu*, 1998).

There is little that is other-worldly about this film, except in the heightened uncanniness of everyday moments where what is most familiar becomes strange, the vertiginous experience of standing aside from yourself and looking in on your own life. In *Afterlife*, characters are asked to experience paramnesia, or déjà vu, when, as Henri Bergson writes, 'whoever becomes conscious of the continual duplicating of his present into perception and recollection will compare himself to an actor playing his part automatically, listening to himself and beholding himself playing' (in Deleuze 1989: 79). Here, it is not accurate to say that film functions as a metaphor for death and memory. Instead, the film makes literal the idea that cinema is a memory machine; as much a meditation on cinema as it is on death, *Afterlife* investigates a cinematic state that I have termed 'immediation', a state of suspense between the virtual and the actual, what Gilles Deleuze calls the cinema of the time-image. While ostensibly about the 'actual deaths' of the characters, the film actively explores the intensities of the 'little deaths' that occur in the realm of the virtual. Memory is not then that most personal possession of an individual, a subjective interiority; it becomes that which takes us outside of the self.

In *Cinema 2: The Time-Image* (1989), Deleuze traces a cinematic virtual in which the distinction between real and imaginary is supplanted by an (in)distinction between virtual and actual, where the virtual is not opposed to the real. As Gregory Flaxman describes this, 'the virtual is the reservoir on which thought draws in order to bring about the actual' (2000: 31); note that in French, 'actuel' has the sense not only of the actual as the real, but also of 'at the present time'. Thus in Deleuze, the virtual is frequently aligned with the past, with memory, but not merely as a collection of past actualities. Rather, it is a domain of 'pressing potential', and in the cinema of the time-image, the virtual and actual enter into an oscillating exchange: 'the actual image beside a kind of immediate, symmetrical, consecutive or even simultaneous double' (1989: 68). The virtual doubles the actual, but this doubling itself is perfectly real; 'it is at the point when images become ambiguous – when we cannot tell what is real and what is imagined, what has happened in the past and what is happening in the present – that we begin to see the outlines of how Deleuze understands the virtual aspect of the cinema' (Flaxman 2000: 31–2). It is in this sense of the ambiguous image, embodying the doubling of the actual/virtual in the real, that I understand the intimate relation between cinema and memory in *Afterlife*. The force of memory in this film functions as a pausing or suspension of the actual, a warping of the normal, habitual or everyday, an impingement of the virtual on the actual that renders it ambiguous, and thus, generative.

After viewing their recreated past, characters disappear into the ether between bodies and screen, living only in the repeated loop of their memory films, seemingly lost to past and future, condemned to an eternal present. It appears a horrifying fate; although the memory films do not record the moment of death (how characters have died is never directly addressed) they do ostensibly suspend life in an eternally unchanging manner. Recall André Bazin's contention in 'Death Every Afternoon' (on a film of a fatal bullfight) that the greatest obscenity of cinema is its ability to repeat what is most singular — death:

> Death is surely one of those rare events that justifies the term ... cinematic specificity ... I cannot repeat a single moment of my life, but cinema can repeat any one of those moments indefinitely before my eyes. If it is true that for consciousness no moment is equal to any other, there is one on which this fundamental difference converges, and that is the moment of death. For every creature, death is the unique moment *par excellence*. The qualitative

time of life is retroactively defined in relation to it ... *Doubtless no moment is like any other, but they can nevertheless be as similar as leaves on a tree, which is why cinematic repetition is more paradoxical in theory than in practice.* Despite the ontological contradiction it represents, we quite readily accept it as a sort of objective counterpart to memory. However, two moments in life radically rebel against this concession made by consciousness: the sexual act and death. Each is in its own way the absolute negative of objective time, the qualitative instant in its purest form. Like death, love must be experienced and cannot be represented (it is not called the little death for nothing) without violating its nature. This violation is called obscenity. The representation of a real death is also an obscenity ... We do not die twice. (2003: 30; emphasis added)

Bazin claims that in life, we frequently minimise our awareness of both difference and repetition: 'Doubtless no moment is like any other, but they can nevertheless be as similar as leaves on a tree, which is why cinematic repetition is more paradoxical in theory than in practice'. Difference is presumed, repetition reduced to the similar, time indirectly represented as number ('leaves on a tree') and cinematic repetition is strange and paradoxical not in experience but only when abstracted from lived conditions. This minimisation of the vertiginous gap between difference and repetition is what Bazin compares to the workings of memory – here, I would argue, habitual or functional memory, what Bergson calls an actualisation of a memory image. Cinematic repetition is likewise usually experienced in the same fashion, as a lived experience, what Bazin calls an 'objective counterpart' to memory in the sense I have just described. A violation of love or death is to render the immemorial repeatable by turning it into a representation – representing (seen as the only alternative) what should only be experienced.

Yet there is an ambivalence in Bazin's essay precisely over the nature of cinematic specificity, which can paradoxically release us from lived experience, and it is the effects of this release, better characterised as a 'suspension of lived experience', that Bazin wrestles with here. Essentially, Bazin asks how we can reconcile this obscenity of cinematic specificity, its 'metaphysical violation', with reality itself – 'we do not die twice'. Here we may remember Deleuze's discussion at the end of *Difference and Repetition* (1994), where he claims that every death is double, that while we experience an actual death, life is also composed of a multitude of virtual deaths.

As Deleuze and Guattari put it in *Anti-Oedipus*, 'The experience of death is the most common of occurrences in the unconscious, precisely because it occurs in life and for life, in every passage or becoming. *It is the very nature of every intensity*' (1983: 330; emphasis added).

If *Afterlife* is a version of virtual reality, it is in the way that it explores memory as the affective link between difference and repetition, where memory and death are not opposed, but both a form of afterlife that is perfectly real, yet outside of everyday lived experience.

The problem for Bazin is in trying to understand the virtual/actual relation through the lens of the real and opposing virtuality to reality. He acknowledges the paradox of his position, claiming that while the bullfight on film is not the same as seeing it in person, it does give him its 'metaphysical kernel' – death. Yet at the same time, the obscene for Bazin lies in its repeatability. Or is it less the repeatability than that it is different every time, that cinema can heighten our sense of the difference in repetition, that what is repeated is difference even under the bare repetition of the same image repeated as a loop, as in the memory films? In this sense, the lived experience of cinema, like the habitual or functional form of memory, is displaced by the relived, or the unlived as yet, the other face of death as afterlife, memory in its generative form. Only cinema can 'draw the passage' between one state and another – film is characterised by this movement between, this solicitation of affect that reshapes the self. This reshaping is an anamorphosis of the self, not as the loss of an original essence, but as a kind of virtual death. Bazin indicates the crucial importance of affect in the experience of this death with a little pun: 'Thanks to film, nowadays we can desecrate and show at will the only one of our possessions that is temporally inalienable: dead without a requiem, the eternal deadagain of the cinema' (2003: 1).

In the French, 'dead-again' is written *re-morts*, a homonym for *remords*, or remorse. Dead-again is figured, through a gap in perception between eye and ear opened up by the homonym, in terms of affect as remorse. This double audition of Bazin is the marker of his ambivalence, opening a gap that solicits the virtual. He attempts to recuperate this in terms of the original reality of the moment of death, but once again, his analysis is defigured by cinematic excess when he claims that death on screen is as moving as the 'real instance that it reproduces': 'In a certain sense, it is even more moving because it magnifies the quality of the original moment through the contrast of its repetition' (*Ibid.*: 32), a repetition which, though lacking originality, still has a stronger affective intensity. In *Afterlife*, it is not through spectacular or explicit imagery that death is evoked. It is in the very banality of the memory films (one moment like any other, both in the type of moments typically chosen and in the looping of the films themselves) that the genuine strangeness of repetition and memory as a kind of virtual death comes through. In fact, what the memory films and *Afterlife* reveal is the generative force of this repetition, the difference at the heart of the repetition of memory and cinema alike.

Afterlife, blending documentary and fiction, memory and its simulation, is located between the subjective and the objective, displacing this polar opposition. This is the virtual reality of affect, akin to what Nicole Brenez describes as 'a type of Bazinian exigency maintained in the heart of a type of non-Bazinian analysis that no longer takes the real as second nature or as the second nature of film' (1997). The cinematic double of the memory films produced over the course of a week is not a mediation of memory or experience; in this case, attention to the formal qualities of the medium highlights temporality as becoming. I use the affects of love and memory in *Afterlife* to explore the relation between cinema, death and the relived body: cinema as suspended animation, or immediation.

There is an intimate connection between cinema, love and memory; but the intuitive nature of this connection is difficult to explain. All three involve a virtual reality of affect that exists between the objective and sub-jective, and a tension between experience and knowledge.

In *Afterlife*, this in-between space is explored via an infidelity at the heart of love and memory that requires both a connecting and a forgetting. A blend of documentary and fiction techniques, the story is set in a way station to the afterlife, where the recently dead must select, from an entire lifetime, one memory to be their eternity. Through the course of the film, layers of memories are carefully peeled back, beginning with a first, hesi-tant recitation by the bewildered newly deceased, moving towards the goal of a restaging of that memory, to be filmed on a sound stage and recreated with actors and props, all in the space of a week.

The curious disjunction between living and reliving an experience, between possessing and being possessed by our memories is explored through this deliberate recreation, ultimately leading to a final screen-ing where, once the participants see their final cut, they vanish into the afterlife. The film crew (the memory workers themselves) is made up of the dead who have been unable or unwilling to make a choice and move on.

Here, memory is explicitly linked to the cinematic experience, in which the artificiality of describing and objectifying the past is merged with the vitality and absorption of cinema in a kind of suspended animation. In many instances, love acts as the hinge between cinema and memory, as it also pulls between the objective and subjective poles of the self.

Kore-Eda's early career was largely based in documentary filmmaking, a body of work marked by a repeated concern for the reanimation of memory enabled by cinema. As James Ellis describes: 'In all his documentaries, Kore-Eda looks at the role of memory in shaping a person's life and the extent to which afterlife can be achieved through other people's reminiscences' (2003: 32–3). His first fiction film, 1995's *Maborosi no Hikari*, based on a short story by Teru Miyamoto, explores the same zone of memory inhabited by the absent presence of love and loss. In this story, Yumiko, a young woman loses her husband to an apparently unmotivated and unanticipated suicide. Years later, after remarrying a widower who, like her, is unable to let go of her past, Yumiko struggles to comes to terms with the thought of living with the unanswered question of her first husband's motives.

As with *Afterlife*, Kore-Eda draws on a formal naturalism is the film's style, with shots, lighting and setting becoming imbued with emotion and memory, conveying in a subtle palette the ungrounding force of a Proustian memory, in which the past irradiates the present in its fullness. As Kore-Eda describes: 'I constructed every scene in this film not for the purpose of telling her story, but to invite the audience to feel the light, the sound and the darkness that Yumiko was feeling at that moment' (in Feinsod 1996).

In his films following *Afterlife*, Kore-Eda has continued to explore the liminal terrain between documentary and fiction, with feature films that draw on real events ingrained in the collective consciousness of the Japanese people, such as *Distance* (2001), about the aftermath lived by the surviving relatives of people involved in a terrorist suicide attack, and the highly acclaimed and emotionally wrenching *Nobody Knows* (2004), about young children abandoned in an apartment by their mother who struggle to make an existence for themselves, a film frequently compared to Truffaut's *The 400 Blows* (1959) for its astonishing child actors and the unsentimental fidelity of Kore-Eda's depiction of their tragic lives.

Kore-Eda is at the forefront of a new interest amongst contemporary Japanese filmmakers in films that push the generic boundaries of documentary and narrative fiction. He drew heavily on his documentary background when preparing *Afterlife*, interviewing over five hundred people, asking each the same question 'Which one memory would you choose to take with you into the afterlife?' (*Afterlife* press kit). To see this film is to realise that any answer is less interesting than the act of enquiry itself. Kore-Eda incorporated the results of these interviews in several ways. The beginning of the film is largely taken up with the early stages of the collection of memories from the newly dead; for these interview scenes, Kore-Eda mixed social actors narrating real memories, professional actors drawing on their own real memories and professional actors working from a script.

The memories range from simple sensations – a man recalls a moment from babyhood, lying bathed in autumnal sunlight – to moments where the personal and historical merge – several of the older dead recite wartime memories, including an elderly man who describes his experience as a starving POW captured by Americans, who charms them into feeding him chicken and rice. In his original interviews, Kore-Eda was struck by the way in which the narration of memories involves a certain amount of fabulation, but noted that it is the difficulty of memory, its imperfection and insistence on repetition that creates an emotional experience. He says: 'Human emotions are the sparks that fly when truth and fiction collide. I wanted to explore the consequences of such collisions by investigating the uncertain area between objective record and recollection' (*Ibid.*). In doing so, he gets at a key element of the cinematic experience – the record that is always a memory, the repeatable that solicits change.

In his essay 'The Image of Proust', Walter Benjamin writes: 'An experienced event is finite – at any rate, confined to one sphere of existence; a remembered event is infinite, because it is only a key to everything that happened before and after it' (1969: 202). *Afterlife* describes such an experience of memory. Deleuze's cinema books explore the Bergsonian splitting of time – into the present that passes and the past that is preserved – as a means of reanimating images of past events. In *Cinema 2: The Time-Image*, Deleuze makes a distinction between images that are actualisations of memory, and thus which remain in the realm of the action image, and virtual images, which include images of the past that resist actualisations in their indeterminacy; it is in the indeterminacy that a genuine time image appears. The time image is associated with a suspension of action, an uncertainty about how to react. This view of time resists a linear understanding in favour of a layered and convoluted time. What it suggests for memory is that the past is never strictly in the past as completed, but that each experience of memory has the potential for re-animation. Each time-image vibrates in this suspended relation between the virtual and actual; while workers and deceased alike in *Afterlife* strive to achieve fidelity to the memories, there is never a strict sense that they are uncovering a truth. Each instantiation of the memory image is instead caught up in its own production. As Laura Marks puts it:

> The time-image ... questions everything about how this particular image got to be constructed from a given perspective. It thus compels the viewer to start the act of perceiving all over again, choosing which part of the available image is relevant. In fact, Deleuze argues, cinema necessarily pulls the viewer between objective and subjective poles, between accepting and reflecting upon a given image. (2000: 42)

Marks goes on to say that 'the image is barely a beginning' (*Ibid.*). This key-like quality to memory is explored in several ways; one concerns the question of sensation or affect that the film produces in the audience, and which is also a key component of memory. In *Afterlife*, the image has a certain thinness, the result of a number of qualities: the use throughout of natural light, minimalist sets and costumes, a subdued palate, the avoidance of non-diegetic music, a restriction of most scenes to two or three characters, and a spartan and reserved sense of framing. Despite this, the film is enormously moving and has a vividly synaesthetic sensibility. Through this very restraint, the film solicits the 'sensation' of memory as a kind of affect; the key-like quality of remembered experience. A flood of memory can be unleashed by a simple trigger; a scent or a colour, a brush of texture reveals the thinness of the gap between present and past, or rather, when memory surges in to occupy the gap generated by the Bergsonian splitting of time between the present and the past. The film remains resolutely in the grip of this immediation, and asks questions about the trigger rather than the memories themselves. We can see this in particular in two related scenes, where the film explicitly solicits a visceral sensation on the part of the spectator, but in order to comment on the involuntary nature of memory.

Shiori Satonaka (Erika Oda) is a junior memory worker, clearly dissatisfied with her life, in particular when it comes to her sense of being loved. It is suggested that she suffers from an unsatisfying relation to her mother. At

a strategy session, the memory workers discuss one client whose memory
is of being four months old. A senior
worker notes that some people claim
to recall being in the womb, noting
in passing that being submerged in
a bathtub is said to be the closest experience to this. Shortly afterwards,
we see a large industrial tub, filled to
the brim with water and Shiori, com-

Fig. 9 Shiori trying to stimulate a genuine memory
of her own in a bathtub.

pletely submerged. She comes up, gasping for air. Clearly, she has been
trying to stimulate a genuine memory of her own, hoping the analogous
experience will lead her to a kind of truth. Just as clearly, it hasn't worked.
Shiori, like many of the characters in the film, struggles with the idea both
of the loss of self but also the terrible uncertainty of not being sufficiently
lost in another person or relation.

In a later scene, Shiori again reacts to loss through an intensification of
physical, tactile experience. Having learned that her co-worker Mochizuki
(Arata), whom she clearly loves, has decided to choose a memory and move
on, she flees to the snow-covered roof of the institution. For long moments,
we see her violently sloshing around in the snow, her damp breathy sobs

and the icy slush of the spring snow
against her boots the only sound. In
a film where sound effects are mini-
mised, where dialogue has been the
primary sound, the effect is striking.
The viewer sees and hears the snow,
but also feels the damp chill and cold
air. It is an astonishingly synaesthetic
moment; what is fascinating, though,
is that this 'reality', this material
sensation is not contrasted to the im-

Fig. 10 Shiori vents her frustration and grief when
she learns of Mochizuki's decision to move on.

material recreation and thus artificiality of the film; its part and parcel of
it. Shiori, who has sworn that she will refuse to forget Mochizuki, that she
will keep him inside of her, is in effect trying to freeze time as a memory
on that frozen roof, the snow a trigger to help her recall the moment and
how she feels. In this highly synaesthetic moment of experience, Shiori's
intensification of the now, we also get a genuine time image, in her helpless

consciousness of the splitting of time; in this scene, we see enacted Nadia Seremetakis's claim that 'the senses defer the material world by changing substance into memory' (1994: 29). But in turn, and as the memory films show, Shiori's promise of a memory owned and preserved in unchanging form is impossible to keep, an infidelity to the self that is the only fidelity to time. A genuine memory, and not simply a memory-image, will always retain its power to re-emerge into the present and thus displace the self. Memory itself, in occupying the gap between the present that passes and the past that is preserved, surges in this space of deferral, intertwining with the senses in an affective indeterminacy. Mochizuki's choice of memory for his own film will complement this scene.

Afterlife draws a connection between the transformative and synaesthetic quality of film, in which feeling or affect is real even when the source is non-objective, and emotion, which likewise can be felt but not quantified. Many of the memories evoked rely strongly on the embodied senses: touch, smell and taste; the continual challenge addressed by the memory workers is how to convey these sensations through sound and picture alone. If the newly dead must in some way do away with their bodies, cinema offers an alternative type of experience; while not able to keep for the dead their corporeal existence, *Afterlife* strives to tap into the incorporeal dimension of the body. It is not a question of adequacy of representation; although much of the film's charm lies in its careful presentation of the process of reconstructing the memories – refitting the wings on an airplane to more closely resemble a Cessna, stringing wads of cotton along wires to simulate clouds, the production team shaking a school bus to induce movement – there is no attempt to argue for a seamless simulation. In fact, the gap between the memories and the recreation is highlighted during the sequences in the studio. One man, who has chosen the memory of a cool breeze washing over him as he rode the school bus on a sweltering day, remarks, when the director of his memory plays back a tape of street noises while they are on the set of the bus, 'that brings back memories'. He is immediately aware of the redundancy of such a statement; looking on at the little boy being carefully spritzed to resemble his young, sweating self, his reaction conveys bemusement and a sense of being out of place. Again and again we see this reaction as the newly dead turn over their memories to directors, actors and crew; they are set apart from themselves, but only in order to see that this is the nature of memory, in the strong sense of the time-image.

Stylistically, *Afterlife* draws on many of the conventions of *cinema verité*. This has the effect both of 'shoring up' a sense of realism, but also of simultaneously pointing to memory as a kind of style and to a tension between event and recording. Particularly in scenes directly connected to the process of creating the memories – the interviews with the newly dead, the meetings of the memory workers – these conventions give the film an improvisational sense. Handheld and jerky camerawork, use of available lighting, imperfect framing and interviews in which the off-camera interviewers are deliberately kept out of sight keep the audience focused on the facts at hand. However, from the beginning these devices are intercut with more conventional 'fictional' camerawork, and as the memory workers become increasingly and personally involved in their work, there are a number of scenes which illustrate this breakdown.

The generative perspectival nature of memory is continually emphasised throughout the film, and is set off by the play between documentary and fiction. For example, consider a scene between Shiori and one of her clients, a young girl of around twelve. The girl describes her happiest memory with cheerful enthusiasm. 'I believe it is called "Splash Mountain"', she says, describing her wonderful day at Disneyland that culminates in delicious pancakes. Shiori looks on with annoyance and boredom. Shortly afterwards, she meets with the girl and asks her to reflect on her choice. At first we suspect Shiori does so because the choice lacks a personal edge, or she might regret spending all eternity in Disneyland. However, it soon becomes evident that Shiori is simply sick of girls choosing Disneyland. 'You see, you're the thirtieth one to choose Disneyland since I've been here', she says kindly. The girl, chastened, agrees and shortly afterwards we see her solemnly reciting a new memory of being held by her mother to her lead memory worker, without giving him an indication that her change of heart was motivated by anyone but herself. In an almost shocking cut away, we see Shiori seated behind him with a small smile on her face. It's shocking because the film, in using the conventions of *verité*, has been creating the sensation of non-intervention; the workers are simply there to recreate, as accurately as possible, the memories of the clients. Shiori's actions, manipulative and motivated by personal reasons, are not only suspect in the context of her job, but in the stylistic context of the film itself. Shiori violates the non-interventionist rules of documentary, and it calls the entire process of the memory work into question. Can this girl in effect trust her own choice? Later, however, she thanks Shiori for making her change her mind. Shiori's intervention pays off; it suggests that all our memories are in part a result of this type of manipulation and collective experience. The film as a whole also rejects the distinction between 'truth' and representation, and instead, curiously for a film about the dead, insists on embodied and collective experiences.

Afterlife plays throughout on a tension between reactions and familiarity. Characters in the film are encouraged to explore their memories in interviews, and they bring out moments from their past like well handled objects. In their recitations there is a certain distance from the present moment, rendered through a slight glaze in the eyes, a loss on focus on the listener; the otherness of their memories manifests in the way they become a little bit removed from themselves. It is in choosing a moment of their own experience, looking inside themselves, that we see the separation from self, a hollowing out of interiority. It is in this sense that we are 'in time'; there is an acknowledgement of the overlapping nature of multiple times that go beyond individual experience. Likewise, in reconstructing their memories characters are asked to alienate themselves, to spell out in as much material detail possible all the elements: to try to reproduce the ineffable by means of the material. The entire film is about the mysterious nature of this alchemical transformation.

Afterlife explores the generative quality of memories in particular through the entwined tales of memory worker Mochizuki and his troublesome client, the elderly Ichiro Watanabe (Taketoshi Naito), who, faced with a life of mediocrity, cannot choose a memory. Instead, he insists on his desire to find some (external) 'evidence of his life'. Mochizuki patiently retrieves from the archives a collection of videotapes – the record of Watanabe's entire life – for his review. When Shiori and Mochizuki check on his progress, they find him watching footage of himself at home with his wife Kyoko (Kyoko Kagawa). Watanabe describes his arranged marriage as ordinary, not based on a great passion. 'Her fiancé was killed in the war', he notes. Mochizuki is struck by something in the tapes; questioned later by Shiori, he reveals that he was Kyoko's fiancé. Mochizuki, although in appearance a young man in his early twenties is, in fact, Watanabe's contemporary. Eventually, Watanabe chooses as his memory a late-life conversation with his wife on a park bench; ironically, they discuss a plan to start going to the movies more often. Watching footage of his younger self, Watanabe sees himself proclaiming his desire to make his mark on the world. At an awkward first meeting with his wife-to-be, Watanabe berates his younger self: 'do something! Say something!' Yet in the end, he chooses a moment of being rather than doing; or rather he comes to realise that it is in the being that we are. Sharing a moment with another person, rather than accomplishing a singular act, becomes Watanabe's evidence that he was.

When Mochizuki later goes to collect the videos after the weekly screening has sent Watanabe on his way, he finds a note thanking him for his kindness in not revealing what Watanabe nonetheless understood, that he was Kyoko's fiancé. Mochizuki tells Shiori that he was motivated not by kindness, but by envy, but Shiori, retrieving Kyoko's memory from the vaults, discovers that Kyoko has cho-

Fig. 11 Shiori searches the archives for Kyoko Watanabe's memory film.

sen a moment where she and Mochizuki sat on a park bench, the same as in Watanabe's film, saying nothing. The sweetness of that silent moment was repeated with a difference in Watanabe's film, and Mochizuki repeats it yet again when he finally decides on his memory.

Mochizuki's film challenges the understanding that the film is only concerned with the 'actualisation' of memory images. It takes place on the well-used park bench, and during shooting appears to be merely a film of him sitting, lost in thought. During the filming, all of his colleagues, save Shiori, appear happy and congratulate him on choosing. They gather for an intimate screening, as this week's dead have already gone through. The lights dim, and unlike before, we see the film; first, Mochizuki alone on the park bench, lost in thought, and then the reverse shot – the crew filming him. His memory of love and connection has been formed in limbo.

In Mochizuki's film, the only film we see projected, the complex time of memory is manifested. Although it is in choosing a memory that Mochizuki is freed from limbo, from his state of suspended animation, there is no actualisation of the time-image to be found. Instead, his film enacts the multidirectional, layered flow of time: it connects his past with Kyoko's

Fig. 12 The reverse shot of Mochizuki's memory film, showing his colleagues at the institution.

and Watanabe's. He retains his past, albeit a 'suggested' past inspired by Kyoko's film. In her choice, the park bench is 'dynamised' by her memory; later, with Watanabe's choice, it is not a question of a poor repetition, a failed analogy, but of the incompossible worlds, all of which are present. Mochizuki also retains his present; in reusing Watanabe's bench he keeps alive the events that have led to his decision. In including his fellow caseworkers and the act of filming, he chooses to not only take a memory, but the act of remembering, as his experience. When he tells Shiori that he has chosen, Mochizuki says 'I was a part of someone else's happiness. What a wonderful discovery.' At the time, Shiori cannot accept this; she tells Mochizuki: 'I won't choose. I will keep you inside me forever.' *Afterlife* turns on the impossibility of this promise, suggesting the impersonal nature of the most personal memories, the connections and expansion of the self it demands, and the infidelity to the self that the ungrounding force of memory produces. It is in this sense, then, that we return to Benjamin's words: remembered events are only keys to all that have gone before and after.

Shiori, caught up in the experienced event, is not ready to choose. One other scene illustrates her dilemma. Sent into town to scout locations for the memory shoots, Shiori wanders aimlessly. As always in *Afterlife*, we are continually shown the mechanism of things. Earlier in the hallway of the way station, Shiori looks up at the moon through a skylight, only to find it is just a painted image; she tries for an artificial semblance of the womb to replace her lost time of oneness with her mother. In town, Shiori pauses by a giant sculpture only to have it come to life as a clock; Shiori, a ghost, encounters the durational time of the clock sculpture, in which the relentless, measured ticking of linear time is momentarily displaced by the mechanical song the clock releases to mark the hour. Although the song plays automatically as it has done hundreds of times before, Shiori's delight and engagement in this scene is an affective experience of surprise and possibility; this regularity of the clock's song does not undo the evocative durational time of the music. It is by recognising the releasing of the past through repetition, of knowing that memory, like time, is not internal to us, but that we are internal to it, that the connection between the clock and Shiori as a memory worker is suggested. While this music in some ways holds to the documentary convention from *cinema verité* not to use non-diegetic music, it at the same time asks us to consider its effects, even when we can see the mechanism. Like the experience of music, it is eternally repeatable, but the presence of the audience prevents it from ever being the same. To understand the source or the origin is not to understand the mystery or the experience. In some ways it is a rejection of a singular originality, and this is what makes it an allegory for film as well.

In the end, the realised memories of the dead are a moment of pure virtuality; they collapse the distance between the dead and their memories as they disappear in a flash. Even so, the memories persist in the vaults of the way station, in the minds of those left behind, and resist pure virtuali-sation, keeping *Afterlife* well situated within the time image by preserving that uncertainty.

Afterlife offers a cinematic version of the virtuality of memory as an expe-rience of qualitative transformation, when we become strange to ourselves in order to become something else. The real material ghosts of *Afterlife* are not only the characters, but the films themselves, the experience of a 'film body' as relived in the telling or witnessing of memory, and in the solicita-tion of the unlived-as-yet as the infidelity at the heart of the self. *Afterlife* explores the way that cinematic memory can give rise to new experiences of corporeality, but also how cinema solicits the experience of what Brian Massumi calls the 'incorporeal yet perfectly real' dimension of the body, the dimension of the virtual. The virtual in *Afterlife* is to be understood not as an alternative to reality itself, but instead, in Deleuze's terms of 'hav-ing the power to produce effects'. Better yet, the power to produce affects; in *Afterlife*, the memory films themselves become a kind of special *effect* turned special *affect*, producing the suspended body of cinema out of the dead.

WORKS CITED

Afterlife press kit. Artistic License Films. Online. Available at http://www.artlic.com/press/kits/afterlif.html (accessed 27 March 2010).

Bazin, A. (2003) 'Death Every Afternoon', in Ivone Margulies (ed.) *Rites of Realism: Essays on Corporeal Cinema*, trans. Mark Cohen. Durham: Duke University Press. 27-31.

Benjamin, W. (1969) 'The Image of Proust', in *Illuminations: Essays and Relections*, trans. H. Zohn. New York: Schocken, 201–15.

Brenez, N. (1997) 'The Ultimate Journey: Remarks on Contemporary Theory,' trans. W. Routt, *Screening the Past*. Online. Available at http://www.latrobe.edu.au/screeningthepast/reruns/brenez.html (accessed 27 March 2010).

Deleuze, G. and F. Guattari (1983) *Anti Oedipus: Capitalism and Schizophrenia*, trans. R. Hurley, M. Seem, and H. Lane. Minneapolis: University of Minnesota Press.

Deleuze, G. (1989) *Cinema 2: The Time Image*, trans. H. Tomlinson and R. Galeta. Minneapolis: University of Minnesota Press.

_____ (1994) *Difference and Repetition*, trans. P. Patton. New York: Columbia University Press.

Ellis, J. (2003) 'Afterlife', *Film Quarterly*, 57, 1, 32–7.

Feinsod, M. (1996) 'A Conversation With *Maborosi* Director, Hirokazu Kore-Eda', *indiewire*, 5 September, 1996. Online. Available at http://www.indiewire.com/people/int_kore-eda_hiro_1_960905.html (accessed 27 March 2010).

Flaxman, G. (2000), 'Introduction', in G. Flaxman (ed.) *The Brain is the Screen: Deleuze and the Philosophy of Cinema*. Minneapolis: University of Minnesota Press, 1–57.

Marks, L. (2000) *The Skin of the Film: Intercultural Cinema, Embodiment and the Senses*. Durham: Duke University Press.

Seremetakis, C. N. (1994) 'The Memory of the Senses, Part II: Still Acts', in C. N. Seremetakis (ed.) *The Senses Still*. Oxford: Westview Press, 23–44.

4. 'PROSTHETIC MEMORY' AND TRANSNATIONAL CINEMA: GLOBALISED IDENTITY AND NARRATIVE RECURSIVITY IN *CITY OF GOD*

RUSSELL J. A. KILBOURN

'Why remain in the City of God where God has forgotten you'?

— City of God

FILM, LANGUAGE, MEMORY

In a fundamental sense every narrative fiction film is invested in memory, including those films that neither thematise nor represent memory – in a flashback, for example. I begin from the precept that 'memory' today derives its primary meaning and, in a sense, its existence as such, from visually-based technologies like cinema, which is not merely one of the most effective metaphors for memory but, alongside photography, television and new media, is *constitutive* of memory in its most meaningful sense. This is the direct result of cinema's status as pre-eminent narrative mode in the twentieth century; the primary purveyor of an iconic realism characterised by the representation of three-dimensional space as well as 'objective' and 'subjective' temporalities.

This essay explores, through the Brazilian film *City of God* (Fernando Meirelles and Katia Lund, 2002), what Nestor Garcia Canclini calls the tendency of filmmakers in a transnational cultural landscape 'to conform to generic cinematic codes (*cine-mundo*) in order to lure international audiences' (cited in Alvaray 2008: 62). Canclini's implicit critique glosses over the very significance of such generic codes, which, in producing an international style consequently form the basis for an artificial collective memory-system – in its broadest sense the matrix within which transnational identities are generated, appropriated, recontextualised and resignified, as a function of the modes of cultural consumption characteristic of late modernity. Behind this is the problem of defining 'Brazilian' over-against properly transnational (not to speak of 'global') cultural production – a problem arising in part from the gap between critical-theoretical discussions (such as this one) and the 'reality' of self-expression and self-representation on the cultural level.

What does it really mean to think of cinema as a kind of *global* memory system; as both source and archive of our collectively most cherished memories? To consider cinema as a principal mode of *collective* cultural memory it is necessary to begin with Hollywood, as one of the first film industries to achieve truly 'global' appeal. The precise identity of this 'we' aside, this line of enquiry leads to the more general question of cinema's legibility across borders, its status as global vernacular or *lingua franca*.[1] To think of film in these terms is obviously problematic. Historically, film is a medium with very few 'speakers' in relation to viewers. Today many people around the globe have access to the means of production, but for much of cinema's history the vast majority have been neither 'speakers' nor 'writers' but 'readers,' or rather, viewers. Concomitantly, worldwide levels of what Elizabeth Ezra and Terry Rowden call 'cineliteracy' are higher than ever before: a 'global cineliteracy ... created and made necessary by the degree to which capitalism as the catalytic agent in the expansion of popular culture has undermined the viability of cultural or national insularity' (2006: 3). Further, there is the post-1970s film theory reaction to the idea of cinema as a language – presupposed all over again by this notion of 'literacy'.[2] But debates about language do not negate the question of the 'we' that claims to own or determine the meaning of such a thing as memory, recognised – like 'History' – to be inextricable from the discourses and media in which it is constituted.[3]

In order to clarify my argument, I will isolate two distinct (but interconnected) ways in which film as artificial memory manifests in *City of God*. First, there is memory represented via specific formal-stylistic features, a specific cinematic vocabulary or set of codes, typified by such temporally disjunctive strategies as the flashback.[4] Initial reviews tended to focus on *City of God*'s obvious flashback structure, represented microcosmically in the opening 360-degree 'matrix-style' shot,[5] motivated by the drive to dynamically represent the recursive non-linearity of narrative time.

Second, there is memory as (cinematic) intertextuality, in which cinema's own past (and ever-present present) constitutes an archive potentially accessible within or through *any* film, but which tends to operate in specific, motivated instances of intertextual appropriation and recontextualisation (e.g. Jameson's 'nostalgia film' [see below]). *City of God* is typically intertextual and transcultural in its generation of meaning – belonging as it does to a category of film whose visual style derives largely in response to contemporary Hollywood and North American pop culture generally.

CITY OF GOD AS BRAZILIAN 'NOSTALGIA FILM'

From its appearance in 2002 *City of God* marked a milestone in the histories of both Brazilian and 'world' cinema. The film's powerful visual style seemed ideally suited to the expression of its distinctively Brazilian subject. Meirelles (along with fellow Brazilian director Walter Salles) have come to represent 'a trend concerned with reshaping Brazilian film language in line with both national and international audiences' tastes, while at the same time striving to respect the dramatic reality of the country' (Neto 2002: 10-11) – a 'dramatic reality', in whose peculiar history cinema plays a significant role.[6] More than one critic has pointed out a certain affinity between the current 'new wave' of Brazilian films and the 1960s Cinema Novo movement,[7] whose aesthetic was predicated on the political goal of 'social transformation' (Espiritu 2003: 290). Theorist and filmmaker Glauber Rocha's famous manifesto, 'An Esthetic of Hunger', called for 'a cinematic style appropriate to the social realities of Brazil' (Johnson & Stam 1982: 286).[8]

Karen Backstein identifies *City of God*'s inherent contradictions in this respect: 'Is the film ... an indictment of Brazil's huge economic gap between the have and have-nots? Is it ultimately an attempt to reach the global market through a presentation of energetic violence? Or is it both? ... Ironically, despite the poverty of the people depicted, the filming is far more "aesthetic of postmodernism" than what ... Rocha called the "aesthetic of hunger"' (2003: 39). For Ismail Xavier, *City of God* 'deals with social concerns, but expresses them in the language of MTV, rap and disco cultures familiar to young people of the same age as its protagonists. This style has made *City of God* the most successful Brazilian attempt since the mid-1990s to render social drama palpable to a mass audience' (2003: 28).[9] In addressing the film's 'documentary-like quality' Backstein points out that

> the quasi-location shooting, done in a *favela* (although not Cidade de Deus itself),[10] as well as the use of primarily non-professional actors, tend to blur the line between the fake and the real. Thus, the relentless violence of the narrative, and its depiction of a world ruled by guns and ruthless criminals,

combine to turn the Rio hills into something akin to the lawless 'Wild West'
of the American 1800s – except that the rapidly edited images, frequently
shot with a hand-held camera, are more MTV than John Ford. It's also far
more apocalyptic than Ford could ever have imagined, with children barely
out of diapers the coldest and most heartless of all. (2003: 39)

City of God's commercial success, as much as its content, sets it at odds with
the legacy of Cinema Novo. While filmmakers like Rocha 'realised that
the "popular" was often the subject of their films', the films themselves
never achieved a mass popularity (Espiritu 1982: 290) – a paradox faced
by all modernist avant-garde movements seeking by cultural reforma-
tion to inspire social revolution: 'while Rocha's intensely confrontational
and difficult films, wonderful as they are, were never the best vehicles for
reaching a mass audience, Meirelles' engaging imagery and fast-paced alternative can threaten to overwhelm its very real socio-political concerns'
(Backstein 2003: 39).

City of God's critical and commercial success also means that compari-
sons with Brazil's variegated cinematic past are as inevitable as they are
revealing of this film's status as a kind of contemporary Latin American
version of what Fredric Jameson in the early 1990s labeled the Hollywood
'nostalgia film' (1999: 279–96). This kind of postmodern film facilitates
the reification and consumption of the past in the form of 'glossy images',
discouraging any meaningful historical consciousness in the viewer (1999:
287). At the same time – in line with the quasi-universal film language
invoked above – *City of God* can be considered a paradigmatic instance of
what David Bordwell has labelled 'intensified continuity': 'the baseline
style for both international mass-market cinema and a sizeable fraction of
exportable "art cinema"' (2002: 21–2).[11]

Utilising Bordwell's category and building on contemporary notions of
artificial or 'prosthetic' memory, I read *City of God* in its historical context
as a quintessentially 'postmodern' film, invoking this term mindful of
the postcolonial criticism of postmodern theory's 'provincial' and arrogant disregard of the disempowered diasporic other, residing outside
the Northern hemispheric 'society of the spectacle'.[12] Therefore (going
beyond Jameson) I invoke a contextually specific, transnational usage
of 'postmodern', refering to those contemporary films characterised in
aesthetic terms by an 'intensified' continuity, as opposed to forms of dis-
continuity, disjuncture and Brechtian distanciation characteristic of the

post-war international art film.[13] In political-economic terms, this newer category of film is postmodern insofar as it is the product of the 'transnational expansion of capital' (Walsh 1996: 487).[14] Therefore the diasporic and the transnational, although intimately related, are not coterminous.[15] This modernist/postmodernist differentiation is already complicated, however, by the fact that many contemporary instantiations of the art film – defined on one level by its implicit or explicit critique of the commodification of the image – can also be categorised as 'postmodern' in their stylistic departures from this modernist tradition.[16] Ironically, unlike the plurality of modernisms that arose around the world in the first half of the twentieth century, this 'transnational' postmodern appears to be – on the visual-stylistic level at least – a far more globally consistent category.

What is of interest here is the inflection of an international or 'universal' film language with potentially global, mass-market appeal by a radically *other* cultural idiom. As a recent film that is at once transnational and regionally specific, *City of God* represents (to the non-Brazilian viewer) an ironically spectacular instance of such marked cultural hybridity. In its representation of the recontextualisation of Northern hemispheric youth-subcultural signifiers within the specific socio-economic context of Rio's *favelas* from the 1960s to the early 1980s, *City of God* exemplifies what Robert Stam describes as the 'tension between cultural homogenisation and cultural heterogenisation, in which hegemonic tendencies ... are simultaneously "indigenised" within a complex, disjunctive global cultural economy' (2000: 287). This is in keeping with a sense of 'transnational' comprising 'both globalisation – in cinematic terms, Hollywood's domination of world film markets – and the counterhegemonic responses of filmmakers from former colonial and Third World countries' (Ezra & Rowden 2006: 1).[17]

Unlike *Amores Perros* (2000), *21 Grams* (2003) or *Babel* (2006) – the films (all by Mexican 'auteur' Alejandro Gonzalez Iñárritu) alongside which Meirelles is often included as part of a so-called 'Latin American New Wave' – *City of God*'s complex narrative structure is internally justified by aspiring photo-journalist Rocket's (Alexandre Rodrigues) voiceover. This classic technique for the amplification of verisimilitude gains new life through the implicit analogy between photographer and story-teller in self-conscious difference from the gun-wielding gangster.[18] As Backstein observes, 'the verbal equivalence of "shoot" with both pistol and camera has rarely seemed as pointed' as in *City of God* (2003: 3),[19] where the symbolic phallicism of the gun 'justifies' a degree of prosaic violence whose verisimilitude is countered by the camera's metaphorical violence – a reminder that (nodding to the viewer's own cineliteracy) even in the City of God violence is not quite real until it is mediated through the image.

The representation of violence changes across the film. In the film's opening section the 'Tender Trio' never actually shoot anyone, brandishing their guns instead as obvious (and potentially parodic) phallic emblems. After the opening frame narrative with the runaway chicken, the film's alignment of camera and gun, from the intra-diegetic (Rocket's photography) to the extra-diegetic (the film camera itself), develops gradually until the advent of L'il Zé as trigger-happy lord of the *favela*. Photography is thematised from the start, incorporated into the fabric of the film in the whirr of the camera motor heard over each freeze-frame as Rocket introduces the principal characters. The implication, so easy to miss as it is subsumed within the diegesis, is that Rocket 'remembers' via a naturalised visual technology: prosthetic snapshots which are then reassembled in order to facilitate narrative meaning. The alignment of camera and gun climaxes (literally) in the scene, reprised at the end, of Rocket poised to take a photo of L'il Zé and his gang, only – instead of the click of the camera shutter – we hear the crack of a rifle and see – instead of the expected freeze-frame image – another nameless death. By the film's close Rocket has quite literally become the embodiment of 'collective memory' in the *favela*, as the controlling gaze of the camera (in both senses) temporarily supersedes the authority of the gun.

The remaining discussion divides into two parts: in the first I further elaborate the theoretical model within which *City of God* is considered in the context of collective cultural memory. In the second part I look closely at three separate shots (or shot-sequences) from the film, in order to shed light not merely on the diverse ways in which memory manifests and signifies in a contemporary, cinematically conditioned context, but also to illuminate the central contradiction of cultural heterogeneity inevitably circumscribed by memory's engagement within the spatio-temporal realism of film.[20] Historically, as a photographically-based medium, film reproduces the illusion of three-dimensional Cartesian space in relation to which and within which a rational, all-knowing, all-seeing subject – of 'Western' art history and capitalism alike – is constituted as the very ground of a 'realist' aesthetic.[21] The question posed so often today (especially in a Cultural Studies discourse) is to what degree storytellers have successfully negotiated the distance between *this* subject and a contemporary subject-agent constructed out of the fragments left over from the post-colonial deconstruction of a realist-imperialist episteme.[22]

ARTIFICIAL MEMORY

In a contemporary visually-based culture, memory as 'technology', technique or 'art' (Gk. *tekhné*) all but displaces 'natural' memory by supplementing and augmenting it, *hypomnesically*, prosthetically, in a homology with the classical 'art of memory' (*mnemotechnics*).[23] As with Rocket's eidetic snapshots, memory in the age of photography and film has acquired a second-order quality; or rather (as with identity and 'reality' itself), an artificial or simulacral double has developed alongside authentic', 'natural' memory – to the extent that, in a very meaningful sense, they are indistinguishable. Differences arise, however, in terms of the manner in which such an artificial memory functions, and how it is *valued* in contemporary global culture(s). For Jonathan Long, modern subjectivity is 'ineluctably dependent on external mnemotechnical prostheses' (2007: 163), resulting in what I call the de-ontologisation of memory; its grounding in social reality and its representations rather than an extra-cinematic, subjective interiority. This is a collective, thoroughly *artificial* memory, constituted through and by means of primarily visual media, most significantly cinema; memory as visual-auditory representation in a perpetuation of a Euro-centric privileging of vision over other faculties and senses.[24]

Moreover, cinema in this view provides the viewer with not only the *content* and *form* of memory, but also with its own 'directions for use':[25] the required codes and conventions for understanding and using this crucial prosthetic technology – an 'art of memory' for the twentieth century and beyond, but one that is merely immersive rather than functionally interactive. In short, 'cinematic memory' in this sense at best supplements and at worst destroys 'natural' memory by naturalising the technical and artificial, providing a seemingly 'universal' objective visual language for the representation of the subjective (re-)experience of the past. This process acquires a heightened significance in a film like *City of God*, in its self-reflexive fictionalisation of the 'real-life' world of *favela* drug culture, with its perpetual cycle of violence, ironically productive of a set of culturally and historically specific meanings which may only *appear* to lend themselves to transmission as publicly available 'memories' via the film's adroit exploitation of the new global film vernacular. My reading of this film therefore presupposes a larger argument about the irreducibly exteriorised, ethically charged and eminently *cinematic* nature of postmodern memory and thus of the degree and quality of agency implicit in the visually constituted subjectivities that provide the ground for identity, whether individual or collective.

Maurice Halbwachs' post-Holocaust concept of 'collective memory' informs contemporary theories of 'artificial memory', a term coined by Steven Rose in the early 1990s to oppose to a 'natural' or 'authentic' memory (see Hoskins 2004: 6–7). Halbwachs emphasises the irreducibly *social* character of modern collective memory, which differs fundamentally from a more pervasive model of memory (such as Freud's) in its insistence on the 'completion' or fulfillment of individual memory in the memories of others (see Storey 2003: 101). Marianne Hirsch's 'post-memory' and Alison Landsberg's 'prosthetic memory' each represent a less sociologically constrained theory of artificial memory in which representations in effect 'precede' reality; hence the application of the term 'postmodern' to these approaches.

Landsberg's notion of 'prosthetic' memory is predicated on the assumption that, long before television or new media (preceded of course by photography), cinema as a mass medium already constituted a form of memory as both storage place and retrieval mechanism, existing independently of the body and in complex relation to the mind. Cinema, in this view, is both a form of collective memory and a medium from which the viewer may glean information about the past – however banal or trite or inaccurate. Troublingly for some, Landsberg is concerned less with questions of historical 'accuracy' or the recuperation of an 'authentic' past and more with the ethically empowering potential for the individual of such an expanded mnemic dimension: 'The cinema and the technologised mass culture that it helped inaugurate transformed memory by making possible an unprecedented circulation of images and narratives about the past. Thanks to these new technologies of memory on the one hand and commodification on the other, the kinds of memories that one has "intimate", even experiential, access to would no longer be limited to the memories of events through which one actually lived' (2003: 146). For Landsberg, '"prosthetic memories" are indeed "personal" memories, as they derive from engaged and experientially oriented encounters with the mass media's various technologies of memory' (*Ibid.*: 148). In other words, the most immediate 'experience' referenced by prosthetic memory is this encounter with the unavoidable layers of telecommunicative mediation: the 'memory' itself is merely the audio-visual 'content' that is publicly available and utterly visible. In Paul Burgoyne's words, 'electronic or audio-visual *lieux de memoire* (sites of memory) have created a kind of second-order memory system that is fast becoming a second-order reality' (2003: 225).

Landsberg's utopian privileging of capitalist-consumerist pop culture does little or nothing, however, to get us beyond the ethico-political contradictions of a culture in which the visual image is the ultimate commodity form, whose transcultural 'consumability' may mask its complexity and its resistance to facile interpretation. For an understanding of a film like *City of God* it is necessary to cross Landsberg's notion of collective artificial memory produced through the consumption of pop cultural commodities – most notably mainstream films – with the *post*-postcolonial idea of 'diasporic identification' within the context of transnational cinema: 'As a lived condition, diasporic identification entails an imaginative leap beyond the particulars of one's own experience. It functions as the postnational version of the "imagined community" that Benedict Anderson famously theorized' (Ezra & Rowden 2006: 8). In contrast to the nation, the transnational represents a new category of 'imagined community', one defined not in terms of virtual parameters but in terms precisely of the productive *absence* of specific spatio-temporal limits. In other words, 'diasporic identity' is to space what 'postmemory' is to time: their intersection is crystallised in a film like *City of God*, producing (or presupposing) two distinct subjectivities: that of the viewer, charged with the task of decoding the film's specific meanings, and that underpinning the characters themselves. The first is a potentially transnational agent, immersed in and engaged with the film as mnemonic prosthesis mediating a globally consumable narrative; the second a representation of a specific diasporic identity, the objectified subject as narrative function. These two subjectivities are caught in a specifically inflected version of the classic relation of identificatory intimacy and voyeuristic distance – an ontological gap that can only be bridged by means of film style.

GLOBAL CULTURE AND FILM STYLE

Thanks to globalisation the introduction of more 'foreign' (i.e. non-English language)[26] material into the purview of a North American-based,

Anglophonic popular culture has occurred alongside the burgeoning of a global youth culture whose superficial homogeneity – indeed, whose very existence – is itself a product of the fertile synergy of telecommunications media and generationally specific marketing. Although it seems clear that such a youth cultural identity formation is as much media construct as lived reality, there is no doubt that a whole new class – or generation – of ever more youthful consumers has emerged since the 1960s as a significant economic force.[27] Historically, this cohort has been in the making since World War II: 'The dominant perception of youth has changed over the last half-century, largely in response to the growth of teenagers and, increasingly, children as a huge consumer market. Whether this development has contributed to the *empowerment* of young people is open to question' (O'Brien & Szeman 2004: 66). But what kind of 'power', and in what context? It is no accident that the first section of Meirelles' film is set in the late 1960s, when a youth-centred counterculture was first going global, producing new subject positions out of the contradictory relation between freedom, empowerment and self-determination, on the one hand, and consumerism on the other. In the City of God *favela*, of course, this transformation takes a darkly parodic form. In the context of contemporary Brazilian cinema one inevitably runs up against the social-cultural *difference* between the 'typical' North American teen-consumer and her/his counterpart in specific, developing-world, post-colonial subcultural formations, whose existence is paradoxically dependent upon and yet completely *outside* of the *Northern* American 'society of the spectacle'. The boys and young men in *City of God* present a powerful example of this paradoxical subaltern subjectivity; theirs is a world, and set of identities, after all, defined historically by the *lack* of the means and therefore the agency to acquire specific commodities and consumer goods.

Moreover, the *favela* depicted in the film is deliberately located far *outside* the city centre; these are not 'inner-city' gangs in any Northern hemispheric sense.[28] The various characters and their interconnected stories do not convey a self-conscious alienation from the desired mainstream North American cultural values, ideologies or myths; *City of God* is concerned with a far more fundamental form of alienation:

> The film ... gives powerful expression to the feelings of class and racial dis-
> enfranchisement that create a subjectivity under siege in a society swamped
> by images of glamour and sex appeal and a rhetoric of advertising intent

on the exploitation of mimetic desire. ... Young people's expectations are shaped in daily contact with a vision of consumption way beyond their reach. ... *City of God* adds a new piece to the mosaic of violence composed by recent Brazilian cinema. It adds up to a picture of a consumerist society of scandalous social inequality. (Xavier 2003: 30)[29]

With the film's framing sequence – a carnivalesque montage of communal feast, close-ups and frenzied chicken hunt, cut to the rhythms of samba music (see Nagib 2004) – we are very far from Rocha's revolutionary axiom: the 'aesthetic of hunger' is ironically inverted in the 'chicken's-eye-view' subjective camera. This scene has been described as 'Rabelaisian' (Xavier 2003: 29), echoing Robert Stam's discussion of the 'carnivalesque' foundations of indigenous Latin American popular culture (2005: 317–23).[30] In contrast to Cinema Novo and the legacy of avant-garde film practice, post-war Brazilian commercial cinema (epitomised by the *chanchada* genre) sought to measure up at all costs to the aesthetic standard of Hollywood (see Vieira 1982) – a desire often presented as an auto-parodic impulse within the films themselves, drawing attention to the inevitable disparity in production values between Brazilian and American popular cinema up to the 1980s. In *City of God*, by contrast, the carnivalesque parody is also directed outward, at a global culture (and audience), once again qualifying the film's status as 'transnational' Brazilian product. In fact, the production values, coupled with its internationally appealing style, suggest that what is exemplified in a film like *City of God* – not to speak of the so-called 'Latin American new wave' as a whole – is not merely the emergence (in Brazil, Mexico, or elsewhere) of a new transnational cinema, but also, perhaps in equal measure, the 'Latin Americanisation' of the dominant cinematic mode.[31]

INTENSIFIED CONTINUITY AS CINEMATIC *LINGUA FRANCA*

The social reality represented in *City of God* is the ironic inversion of the self-contradictory subcultural reality of Northern hemispheric youth found in many Cultural Studies accounts.[32] As noted above, the boys and young men of Rio's *favelas* live wholly outside of the neo-bourgeois ideal the desire for which they desperately express in their self-construction as gangsters whose moral code is determined by the power dually conferred by the profits from the drug trade and by the gun. *City of God* presents a hybridised, *globalised* youth culture, combining elements of North American and local or second-order 'indigenous' Brazilian cultures. In its representation of youth gangs and the drug trade in the *favelas* of 1960s and 1970s Rio, Meirelles' film offers a powerful antidote to the Romantic mythology of childhood innocence; an antidote not undiluted, however, by a certain nostalgia conveyed in specific stylistic terms (as will be discussed below). For, even more notable than the graphic depiction of this seldom-depicted world is the manner in which the filmmakers have appropriated specific stylistic tropes and strategies from the current dominant Hollywood model, exemplified (in the late 1990s) by films as diverse as *The Matrix* (Wachowski Brothers, 1999) and *Fight Club* (David Fincher, 1999). [33]

In the words of David Bordwell, 'far from rejecting traditional continuity in the name of fragmentation and incoherence', 'intensified continuity' – the dominant style of contemporary American mass-market film – 'amounts to an *intensification* of established techniques. Intensified continuity is traditional continuity amped up, raised to a higher pitch of emphasis' (2002: 16). Intensified continuity is characterised by four stylistic tactics: rapid editing; bipolar extremes of lens focal length (wide-angle vs. telephoto/zoom lens); close framings in dialogue scenes; free-ranging (i.e. 'un-motivated') camera movement. (To this list I would add the now fully domesticated use of CGI special effects, characterised by the 'virtual camera' effect.) If classical Hollywood continuity style produces cinematic 'realism', then 'intensified continuity' produces a *new* self-conscious 'realism' and the heightened mode of spectatorship this implies:

> The style aims to generate a keen moment-by-moment anticipation. ... Close-ups and singles make the shots very legible. Rapid editing obliges the viewer to assemble discrete pieces of information, and it sets a commanding pace: look away and you might miss a key point. ... TV-friendly, the style tries to rivet the viewer to the screen ... even ordinary scenes are heightened to compel attention and sharpen emotional resonance. (*Ibid.*: 180)

Epitomised in *City of God*, this new style is as much about post-Mulveyan identification as it is a kind of postmodern 'defamiliarisation'. The viewer, it might be said, is sutured into the contradictory gap between spectatorial immersion and the often high degree of self-reflexivity characteristic of such films, all but guaranteeing that any extra-filmic political or historical consciousness will be subordinated anew to story, character and a new brand of 'reality effect'. What more than one critic calls *City of God*'s 'neo-realism' is 'combined with a sense of the image as artifice, the narrative as a fast-moving train of emotions conveyed through elaborate fast edits and computer-created effects' (Xavier 2003: 29).[34] Such effects nevertheless lack the defamiliarising impact of Brechtian *Verfremdungseffekten*, revealing the political neutrality of this contemporary style. For Lucía Nagib, 'none of the self-reflexive techniques used in the film creates a distancing effect' (2004: 249). For example, in his voiceover Rocket dictates 'at whim the freeze-frames, flashbacks and fast forwards, zooms and long shots, thus exposing the mechanics of digital editing. ... At no time, however, is the story called into question' (*Ibid.*). Nor is the narrator's credibility ever in doubt; what Nagib calls Rocket's 'self-reflexive position' in fact *guarantees* the film's postmodern 'realism'. Furthermore (as suggested above), this quasi-godlike control is both motivated and, in effect, justi-

fied, by Rocket's selections as photographer, framing what the viewer sees, as the camera *within* the *mise-en-scene* periodically elides with the film camera's invisible narration from 'outside' the film's diegetic world. In these moments photograph and on-screen image – typically Angelica, his teenage love interest – are commensurate, hypostatising the now classic

Fig. 13 Angelica and her friends on the beach in Rocket's snapshot.

trope of photo-as-memory. The film thus produces its own set of iconic images in these momentary interruptions of the narrative flow that nevertheless grant them their contextual meaning.[35]

To argue that *City of God* epitomises a specifically *Brazilian* inflection of intensified continuity is to draw attention to the degree to which this new vernacular is fast becoming a kind of global cinematic *lingua franca*: one that virtually any 'cineliterate' viewer anywhere could 'read'.[36] As Bordwell implies, the amplified version of classical continuity is suited especially to the bread-and-butter Hollywood high concept action film, which tends to be defined by a relatively high quotient of violence, whether stylised or more graphically 'realistic'. Ironically, intensified continuity's often hyperkinetic cutting in fact lends itself to a highly 'believable', subjective representation of violence in which, in specific scenes, each separate shot is so brief that no single action is shown in its entirety. In this respect, the third section of *City of God* stands alongside such recent Hollywood action fare as the *Bourne* series (Doug Liman, 2002, 2004 and Paul Greengrass, 2007). On the other hand, the representation of violence in Meirelles' film bears distinctively 'Brazilian' features. In Glauber Rocha's aesthetic axiom (responding to the socio-economic situation in 1960s Brazil): 'the most noble cultural manifestation of hunger is violence' (Johnson & Stam 1982: 70). The violence so graphically represented in *City of God* is of course *not* the politically emancipatory or redemptive violence of which Rocha speaks; after all, as a contemporary Brazilian filmmaker, Meirelles is under no obligation to make a virtue out of poverty, backwardness or 'primitiveness'.[37] Nor, obviously, is he guilty of the formerly Brazilian weakness of manufacturing a mere 'imitation' of the Hollywood stylistic model (see Schwarz 2008). What Rocha means by 'violence' could only be read as implicit in the film's language, as the emancipatory potential embodied in its visual style, in its hybrid – but highly legible – aesthetic. Nagib is therefore right in asserting that the 'violence is contained in the *form* of the film, especially in the editing, and for this reason is all the more powerful' (2004: 245; emphasis added).[38] Ivana Bentes critiques the film on this basis, refering to what she calls not its aesthetic but its '*cosmetic* of hunger', promoting a '"spectacularisation of violence" through the association of marginalised themes and characters with modern aesthetics and techniques aiming to conquer the international market' (quoted in Lino 2007: 134).

STYLE AS MEMORY IN *CITY OF GOD*

With the exception of a few scenes shot in Rio proper, or on the beach, the dominant spaces of *City of God* do not exemplify the diasporic chronotope of much transnational cinema (see Ezra & Rowden 2006). Rather, they are the built-up, densely populated and squalid ex-urban spaces of the *favelas* outside Rio, constructed in the early 1960s by the Brazilian government for the express purpose of class-based segregation: physically marginalising people of lower classes, the poor, unemployed and homeless (see Lino 2007). In her insightful comparison of *City of God* and the Paulo Lins source-novel from 1997, Nagib offers a persuasive reading of the film's 'mythical structure', with its '"Paradise", "Purgatory" and "Hell" in relation to the three different phases in the history of the City of God shantytown' (2004: 247). This reading of the tripartite structure (coded in terms of editing, camera work, sound and *mise-en-scène*) accounts for the diegetic presentation of the false utopia of the newly constructed 1960s Cidade de Deus *favela*, seen in flashback in the first section, following the opening framing scene: 'We came to City of God hoping to find paradise', explains Rocket. Nagib's reading also accounts for the visual-spatial disjuncture between the neat rows of subsidised houses of the original ex-urban 1960s *favela* and the subsequent, utterly *urban*, post-1970s in-

Fig. 14 Rocket caught between present and past.

carnation of the Cidade de Deus – what Nagib calls a 'neofavela': a labyrinthine, vertically defined space[39] that 'buries alive the previous rural world': 'The slum had been a purgatory, now it was hell' (*Ibid.*).

Nagib's tripartite socio-eschatological reading is borne out by the complex three-act structure in which each section is separated from the others through clear stylistic choices, a digital intermediate lending each section a distinctive tonality (see Oppenheimer 2003: 83).[40] Paralleling the historical trajectory of the soundtrack music (an effective mix of samba, Western rock and disco, and so forth), the style changes significantly from one part of the film to the next: classical continuity in the 1960s section, while the 1970s and 1980s sections display a gradually intensification of classical style. This stylistic development across the film has important consequences for the classification, representation and valuation of memory. The first section features highly legible editing, smooth and unobtrusive camerawork and virtually the only wide-angle shots in the film. The 'warm, yellow' tonality here also imparts a nostalgic quality to the setting, referencing the classic Hollywood western (*Ibid.*: 84). Nagib calls this the film's 'Golden Age', as much for the prevalent colours of light and setting as for the resulting aura of idealised quasi-rural pastness. This aspect of the first section is ultimately ambiguous, however, in that any spectatorial nostalgia – for Hollywood's as much as Brazil's past – is conditioned by specific intertextual ironies (as will be seen below). Even identification with the 'Tender Trio' – tacitly encouraged on the stylistic level[41] – is ironically destabilised on the intertextual-semantic level. In the second section, the aura of nostalgia is inflected via references in the *mise-en-scène* to already commodified youth subcultural signifiers specific to the period. This is expressed visually through a tonal shift to more vivid colours, favouring blues and greens, as well as post-production effects like split screens; handheld cameras dominate at this point, although camera movement overall 'still respect[s] cinematographic grammar', maintaining the veneer of pseudo-utopian stability that is exploded all the more effectively after Bené's death (*Ibid.*). In the final 1980s section, classical conventions intensify: the camera is almost always moving, often frenetically, favouring close and medium shots, jump cuts and whip-pans; the editing is much faster, flirting with illegibility. This final shift coincides on the diegetic level with the catastrophic introduction of cocaine into the *favela*, and the ensuing struggle for power and all-out gang war with which the film culminates. The tonality is again monochromatic but much darker than in the comparatively idyllic 1960s section.

It must be stressed that the three stylistically distinct sections remain within the purview of a neo-classical style whose grounding aim is not to antagonise but to draw in the viewer through a highly imaginative repertoire of distancing techniques alongside Bordwell's 'intensified' techniques. The three sections also interconnect on the levels of plot and cinematography via recurrent shots, motifs and set pieces. This highly patterned, repetitive structure is effectively masked by the above-mentioned 'realism' of the film's overall style. For example, the film begins and ends with the hold-up of a propane delivery truck, with a very different outcome each time, underscoring the degree of change in the film's representation of violent crime from the 1960s to the 1980s. Each of the three temporal sections ends with the shooting death of a major character: Shaggy, Bené, then both Knockout Ned and L'il Zé. The dream of 'peace and love' (the film's ironic mantra) consecutively invoked by brothers Shaggy and Bené, proves vain in each case, as the film reinforces the irony that the only escape from the *favela* – and thus the cycle of violence – is death. This thematic recursivity is effectively mirrored on the levels of plot and narration. For example, the second and third sections are linked by scenes in which a young man either contemplates or attempts an act of vengeance. Early in the 1970s section (after the third revisiting of the apartment scene), in the flashback that introduces the newly minted L'il Zé, Rocket passes up his chance to kill L'il Zé in revenge for his brother Goose's death – an ironically proleptic 'echo' of the second instance, at the end, when the young Otto kills Knockout Ned to avenge his father's death in a bank hold-up, also revisited in flashback. This last death, along with the Runts' murder of L'il Zé, guarantees the perpetuation of the cycle of violence, even as Rocket's clandestine front-page photo of L'il Zé's bullet-riddled body guarantees him exemption, while bringing L'il Zé (albeit posthumously) the fame he sought outside the *favela*. Finally, this three-act structure is complicated and any potential linearity short-circuited by the film's other major structuring device: the distancing recursivity of Rocket's flashback-narrative (to be returned to below). Far from being truly disruptive, however, this technique remains entirely within the purview of a neo-classical style committed to the viewer's pleasurable experience of the narrative.

FROM STRUCTURAL TO INTERTEXTUAL MEMORY IN *CITY OF GOD*

City of God's frame-narrative conceit means that its story actually begins *in medias res* (as in Homer, right before the climax): from flashback to 'flashforward' (to intermediate past) and back to the opening shot – the temporal transitions achieved through a CGI-enhanced circular trick shot. According to Maureen Turim, 'some flashbacks directly involve a quest for the answer to an enigma posed in the beginning of a narrative through a return to the past'; one type 'is the narrative which employs a flashback just prior to the climactic revelation of the enigma, to provide a missing aspect of the enigma' (1989: 11). The sequence with Rocket caught in the space between the rival forces of gang and police is an excellent example, immediately preceding the story's violent and bloody climax and ironically hopeful dénouement. The shot's much-discussed 'bullet time' appearance was achieved through a combination of a thrice-repeated, simultaneous 'swish-zoom/dolly', and a digital intermediate, in which shot speed was increased and the background dissolve from present to past created (see Oppenheimer 2003: 89).

This arcing shot, for all its self-conscious showiness, established on the micro-formal level the determining pattern of recursivity for the entire narrative, in which memory is an ironically infernal trap or vicious circle from which Rocket longs to escape. It is this desire precisely that drives the narrative forward and, ultimately, back upon itself – even as Rocket's own narrative function is as 'embedded' narrator rather than as protagonist properly speaking. At the same time, this recursivity guarantees the objective 'believability' of Rocket's subjective memory-in-action.

The ultimate elision of 'subjective' and 'objective' in intertextual memory is demonstrated in the ironic appropriation of/homage to *Charlie's Angels* in the film's first third. Broadcast on the ABC network from 1976 to 1981, the original television show post-dates the 1960s historical referent of the film's first section. Obviously not a specifically Brazilian intertext, *Charlie's Angels* is symptomatic of later twentieth-century North American popular culture and, since its initial televisual incarnation, has become part of a multi-media youth cultural matrix.[42] A self-reflexive in-joke, this shot conveys a trans-diegetic intertextual meaning addressed to a media-literate spectator unconstrained by a specific regional-cultural frame of reference. Meirelles and his cinematographer reportedly 'wanted the assault on the gas truck to be like a stagecoach hold-up' in a classic western (*Ibid.*: 84).

Fig. 15 The 'Tender Trio'.

The shot's ironic connotations therefore stem from the transposition of an iconic image from a popular 1970s American television comedy-drama into a cinematic re-creation of 1960s Brazilian hoodlums in an ex-urban housing project holding up a gas truck to help their friends and families. After all, *Charlie's Angels* is famous – as this pose illustrates – for being one of the first network television programs to showcase women in roles traditionally assigned to men.[43] In other words, this shot exemplifies Jamesonian pastiche, symptomatic of the postmodern distortion or erasure of historical consciousness. This is the 'bad' sort of historicity Jameson identifies as typical of this cultural dominant, characterised by an 'indiscriminate appetite for dead styles and fashions' wherein – in the 'nostalgia film' proper – it is not the past that is represented so much as the present in the terms of the past, in the cinematic rendering of the (illusorily) proprietary notion of the ever-present present moment of consumption: the reification and therefore the commodification of the 'past' as image, or of the present in terms of an imagined past.[44] This notion of intertextual pastiche helps explain the nostalgic tonality exploited in *City of*

God, which both is and is not a 'nostalgia film' in Jameson's sense: for, while it evokes a specific Brazilian past through commodified pastiche-images, it generally does not do so in the visual-stylistic terms of that past. (One exception is the film's incorporation of a television newscast in which a simulated interview with Knockout Ned is intercut with authentic footage of the news anchorman, although the footage of the real Ned plays over the closing credits.) As I have argued, *City of God* exploits the contemporary global film vernacular – call it 'transnational intensified continuity' – to represent and comment upon a highly specific past time and place, in a manner unavoidably critical and self-ironic, stylistically defamiliarising but without the carnivalising call to political transformation characteristic of 1960s avant-garde Brazilian cinema.

A more broadly relevant example of this category of cinematic memory comes in one transitional scene in which the film intertextualises famous journalistic photos of the bloodied bodies of dead boy-soldiers in the *favela* drug wars of the 1970s and 1980s.[45] This is one of several scenes that bear out the nihilistic promise veiled by the nostalgic golden hues of the film's first section, with its penultimate shot of Shaggy's dead body, captured in the lens of a tabloid reporter's camera. As indicated above, it is no coincidence, given Rocket's chosen profession, that the film here references iconic images from contemporary media coverage of the *favela* drug wars. In his voiceover Rocket remarks that the *favela*-dwellers got used to 'living in Vietnam' – a cultural analogy concretised via visual pastiche. As Melo argues, however, '*City of God* is not clearly a hybrid. It does not create a truly dialectical tension between documentary and fiction. It does not create space for critical interpretation in this respect, but rather blends both for the sake of a commercial strategy' (2004: 480). The popular, in other words, trumps the political. *City of God* is a 'hybrid' in the other, stylistic, sense however. The examples presented above are two very different, intentional and meaningful instances of intertextual or intermedial images for the recognition of which the media-literate movie-goer must rely on tools – prosthetic memory-devices – like the DVD commentary track, or a website like the Internet Movie Database. Simultaneously, each example reveals, in Canclini's phrase, the film's aesthetic engagement with a peculiarly Brazilian 'multi-temporal heterogeneity' (1995: 3) – glossed by Stam as 'the temporally palimpsestic identity of Latin America, criss-crossed by elements from the constellations of cultures which embroider a harlequinade mix of multicultural elements' (2005: 361). Ironically, it is at this

Glocal

very point that the film risks – but successfully avoids – tipping over into the most banal postmodern self-reflexivity.

City of God is a complex, even contradictory, example of such a cinema, employing the quasi-universal film language of intensified continuity, characterised by what I have referred to as the kind of 'defamiliarisation' techniques inconsistent with the Brechtian-modernist model precisely because in their ultimate function they are not antagonistic to the pleasure-bound contemporary cineliterate viewer. For Brecht, one of the most problematic aspects of conventional classical theatre is precisely the sympathy or empathy potentially generated out of the spectator's engagement with the performance.[46] In filmic terms (and Brecht has never been so relevant, and simultaneously irrelevant, than in the cinema of transnational capitalism), this translates most directly into the question of the relative degree of viewer 'identification' with specific subject positions onscreen. Suffice it to say, in conclusion, that this quasi-universal, intensified style – a *transnational* intensified continuity, as I have called it – in internationally successful films like *City of God*, represents the amplification and validation of this degree of identificatory 'empathy' generated by classical film narratives – reinforcing the 'natural', mythologising dimension of this process. To this extent, therefore, Landsberg's claims about the positive ethical effects of the prosthetic memory embodied within certain mainstream (Hollywood) films become convincing. But again, as implied throughout the foregoing, this position necessitates acceptance of the commodification of the image and therefore the reification and naturalisation of an artificial and collective, indeed 'transnational', memory system. And, while there will always be those who argue that this is only achieved at the expense of individual, regional or otherwise more specific local meanings, especially identities – the ultimate question here is whether narrative film itself, as the basis for what is by now the dominant mode of collective cultural memory, will prove flexible and amenable enough in the future to accommodate within its chronotopes modes of meaningful individual agency and radical difference alike, even as it guarantees its own commercial survival.

NOTES

1 For example, 'global mass culture does not so much replace local culture as coexist with it, providing a cultural *lingua franca* remarked by a "local" accent' (Shohat 2006: 42). See also Robert Stam: 'the ubiquitous presence of Hollywood films as cultural *lingua franca* in Latin America' (2005: 318).

2   See, for example Metz 1974; Prince 2004.

3   See Cook 2005: 1–5.

4   See Turim 1989.

5   As David Bordwell shows, this was a shot dating back at least to Hitchcock's *Vertigo* (2006: 135; 144).

6   See Johnson & Stam 1982.

7   See, for example, Matheou 2007.

8   'With *City of God*, Meirelles joins a distinguished tradition of social criticism and engagement in Brazilian and Latin American cinema that's now being revitalised' as, variously, the Latin New Wave or the New Brazilian film (Neto 2002: 11), following on from the 1960s 'Cinema Novo': Brazil's answer to the various European 'New Waves' (see also: Stam 1982; Andrews 2002; Nagib 2004; Alvaray 2008). Re *City of God* as new *neo*-Realism see Oppenheimer 2003. Cf. Xavier 2003; Nagib 2004; Matheou 2007.

9   Joao Marcelo Melo goes further, claiming that, '[in] a sense, *City of God* is an American film made in Brazil – since its visual exuberance and narrative are influenced by the American gangster genre in films by directors such as ... Scorcese and ... Tarantino' (Melo 2004: 475). Cf. Lino 2007: 134.

10 See Oppenheimer 2003.

11 See also Bordwell 2006.

12 See, for example, Canclini 1995; Sontag 2003; Stam 2005.

13 See, for example, Deleuze 2003; Bordwell 2004; Pasolini 2005.

14 See also Jameson 1991.

15 I owe this observation to Amresh Sinha.

16 Regarding the complications around these designations specific to Latin American cultures, see Canclini 1995.

17 In addition, 'the concept of transnational ... problematises "postcolonialism" as an attempt to maintain and legitimise conventional notions of cultural authenticity' in a 'real world ... defined not by its colonial past (or even its neo-colonial present), but by its technological future, in which previously disenfranchised people will gain even greater access to the means of global representation' (Ezra & Rowden 2006: 5).

18 In Paolo Lins' source novel, the protagonist wants to be a writer. In the film he yearns to become a photographer, 'partially because photography offered more cinematic possibilities' (Oppenheimer 2003: 83).

19 See also Johnson 2003.

20 What Stam, in the context of adaptation, calls 'cinema's variegated chronotopic capacities' (2005: 15).

21 See Berger 1977; Sturken & Cartwright 2003; O'Brien and Szeman 2004.

22 See Spivak 2001.

23 For the best accounts of the history of *ars memoriae* tradition, see Yates 1966; Carruthers 1990.

24 See, for example, Yates 1966; Debord 1967; Crary 1990; Jay 1994.

25 See Turim: 'The cinematic presentation of the flashback affects not only how modern literature is organised and how plays are staged, but perhaps also how audiences remember and how we describe those memories' (1989: 5).

26 See Egoyan & Balfour 2004.

27 See O'Brien & Szeman 2004; Medevoi 2005.

28 Politically, the young men in *City of God* have more in common with those depicted in French-Algerian *banlieue* films (such as Mathieu Kassowitz's *La Haine* (1995)).

29 See also Andrews 2002.

30 But cf. Backstein, who points out that, unlike Marcel Camus' 1959 *Black Orpheus*,

which 'Brazilianises' death as a carnival figure (my term), 'City of God (taken from a semi-autobiographical novel), passes over carnival entirely – and death comes from the barrel of a gun' (2003: 39).

31 The term is from Schwarz 2008.

32 For the best introduction, see Hebdige 1979.

33 The very films and filmmakers invoked by many reviewers. See, for example, Atkinson 2003.

34 See also Nagib 2004.

35 See Draaisma 2000.

36 See, for example, Bordwell 2006.

37 Cf. Oswald de Andrade's modernist Manifesto Antropofágo (1928).

38 Regarding the film's almost classical reticence around the representation of graphic violence and sex, see, for example, Oppenheimer 2003.

39 Re the film's representation of the favela's peculiar spatial organisation, see Lino 2007.

40 See also Neto 2002; Andrews 2002.

41 'Because the younger kids looked at these guys as heroes, we frequently shot the trio from low angles to give them a slightly heroic air' (Oppenheimer 2003: 84).

42 See, for example, Charlie's Angels: The Movie (McG, 2000) and its sequel Charlie's Angels: Full Throttle (McG, 2003).

43 See Read 2004.

44 Susan Sontag had made this point already in the late 1970s; see On Photography.

45 'City of God bears the traits of fiction and documentary. Along with the drama in a stylish and commercial narrative, the film presents journalistic images from the most traditional news programme on Brazilian TV' (Melo 2004: 479).

46 See Jameson 2000.

WORKS CITED

Alvaray, L. (2008) 'National, Regional and Global: New Waves of Latin American Cinema', Cinema Journal, 47, 3, 48–65.

Andrews, N. (2002) 'Anarchy and ecstasy in the ghetto', Financial Times, 30 November, 7.

Atkinson, M. (2003) 'Boys From Brazil: The Young and the Damned', Village Voice, 14 January, 136.

Backstein, K. (2003) 'City of God', Cineaste, 28, 3, 39.

Berger, J. (1977) Ways of Seeing. London: BBC and Penguin.

Bordwell, D. (2002) 'Intensified Continuity: Visual Style in Contemporary American Film', Film Quarterly, 55, 3, 16–28.

_____ (2004) 'The Art Cinema as a Mode of Film Practice', in L. Braudy and M. Cohen (eds) Film Theory and Criticism: Introductory Readings, 6th edn. New York and Oxford: Oxford University Press, 774–82.

_____ (2006) The Way Hollywood Tells It: Story and Style in Modern Movies. Berkeley, Los Angeles and London: University of California Press.

Burgoyne, P. (2003) 'Memory, history and digital imagery in contemporary film', in P. Grainge (ed.) (2003) Memory and Popular Film. Manchester and New York: Manchester University Press, 220–36.

Canclini, N. G. (1995) Hybrid Cultures, trans. C. L. Chiappari and S. L. López. Minneapolis: University of Minnesota Press.

Carruthers, M. (1990) The Book of Memory: A Study of Memory in Medieval Culture. Cambridge: Cambridge University Press.

Crary, J. (1990) *Techniques of the Observer: On Vision and Modernity in the Nineteenth Century.* Cambridge, MA: MIT Press.

Cook, P. (2005) *Screening the Past: Memory and Nostalgia in Cinema.* London and New York: Routledge.

Debord, G. (1967) *The Society of the Spectacle*, trans. D. Nicholson-Smith. New York: Zone Books.

Deleuze, G. (2003) *Cinema 2: The Time-Image*, trans. H. Tomlinson and B. Habberjam. Minneapolis: University of Minnesota Press.

Draaisma, D. (2000) *Metaphors of Memory: A History of Ideas about the Mind.* Cambridge: Cambridge University Press.

Egoyan A. and I. Balfour (eds) (2004) *Subtitles: On the Foreignness of Film.* Cambridge, MA: MIT Press.

Espiritu, T. (2003) 'Multiculturalism, Dictatorship, and Cinema Vanguards: Philippine and Brazilian Analogies', in E. Shohat and R. Stam (eds) *Multiculturalism, Postcoloniality, and Transnational Media.* New Brunswick, NJ: Rutgers University Press. 279–98.

Ezra, E. and T. Rowden (eds) (2006) *Transnational Cinema, The Film Reader.* London and New York: Routledge.

Hebdige, D. (1979) *Subculture: The Meaning of Style.* London: Methuen.

Hoskins, A. (2004) *Televising War: From Vietnam to Iraq.* London and New York: Continuum.

Jameson, F. (1991) *Postmodernism, or The Cultural Logic of Late Capitalism.* Durham: Duke University Press.

_____ (2000) *Brecht and Method.* London and New York: Verso.

Jay, M. (1994) *Downcast Eyes: The Denigration of Vision in Twentieth-Century French Thought.* Berkeley: University of California Press.

Johnson, B. (2003) 'Underworld intrigues', *Maclean's*, 116, 6, February 10, 44.

Johnson, R. and R. Stam (eds) (1982) *Brazilian Cinema.* London: Associated University Presses.

Landsberg, A. (2003) 'Prosthetic memory: the ethics and the politics of memory in an age of mass culture', in P. Grainge (ed.) *Memory and Popular Film.* Manchester and New York: Manchester University Press, 144–61.

Long, J. (2007) *W. G. Sebald: Image, Archive, Modernity.* New York: Columbia University Press.

Lino, S. C. (2007) 'Birds That Cannot Fly: Childhood and Youth in *City of God*', in T. Shary and A. Seibel (eds) *Youth Culture in Global Cinema.* Austin: University of Texas Press, 131–43.

Matheou, D. (2007) 'Life after Death', *Sight and Sound*, 17, 2, 9.

Medevoi, L. (2005) *Rebels: Youth and the Cold War Origins of Identity.* Durham and London: Duke University Press.

Melo, J. M. (2004) 'Aesthetics and Ethics in *City of God*', *Third Text*, 18, 5, 475–81.

Metz, C. (1974) *Film Language: A Semiotics of the Cinema.* New York: Oxford University Press.

Nagib, L. (2004) 'Talking Bullets: The Language of Violence in the *City of God*', trans. L. Shaw, *Third Text*, 18, 3, 241–9.

Neto, A. L. (2002) 'Discovery: Fernando Meirelles', trans. C. Sayad, *Film Comment*, July/August, 10–11.

O'Brien, S. and I. Szeman (2004) *Popular Culture, A User's Guide.* Toronto: Thomson-Nelson.

Oppenheimer, J. (2003) 'Boys from Brazil', *American Cinematographer*, 84, 2, 82–90.

Pasolini, P. P. (2005) *Heretical Empiricism*, trans. B. Lawton and L. K. Barnett. Washington,

DC: New Academia.

Prince, S. (2004) 'The Discourse of Pictures: Iconicity and Film Studies', in L. Braudy and M. Cohen (eds) *Film Theory and Criticism: Introductory Readings*, 6th edn. New York and Oxford: Oxford University Press, 87–105.

Read, J. (2004) '"Once Upon a Time There Were Three Little Girls...": Girls, Violence, and *Charlie's Angels*', in S. J. Schneider (ed.) *New Hollywood Violence*. Manchester and New York: Manchester University Press, 205–29.

Schwarz, R. (2008) 'Brazilian Culture: Nationalism by Elimination', in M. Ryan (ed.) *Cultural Studies: An Anthology*. Oxford: Blackwell, 1334–46.

Shohat, E. (2006) 'Post-Third-Worldist Culture: Gender, Nation, and the Cinema', in E. Ezra and T. Rowden (eds) *Transnational Cinema, The Film Reader*. London and New York: Routledge, 39–56.

____ and R. Stam (eds) (2003) *Multiculturalism, Postcoloniality, and Transnational Media*. New Brunswick, NJ: Rutgers University Press.

Sontag, S. (2001) *On Photography*. New York: Farrar, Straus and Giroux.

____ (2003) *Regarding the Pain of Others*. New York: Farrar, Straus and Giroux.

Spivak, G. (2001) 'Can the Subaltern Speak?', in V. B. Leitch (ed.) *Norton Anthology of Theory and Criticism*. New York: Norton, 2197–208.

Stam, R. (1982) 'On the Margins: Brazilian Avant-Garde Cinema', in R. Johnson and R. Stam (eds) *Brazilian Cinema*. London and Toronto: Associated University Presses, 306–27.

____ (2000) *Film Theory: An Introduction*. Oxford: Blackwell.

____ (2005) *Literature Through Film: Realism, Magic, and the Art of Adaptation*. Oxford: Blackwell.

Storey, J. (2003) 'The Articulation of Memory and Desire: From Vietnam to the War in the Persian Gulf', in P. Grainge (ed.) *Memory and Popular Film*. Manchester and New York: Manchester University Press, 99–119.

Sturken, M. and L. Cartwright (2003) *Practices of Looking: An Introduction to Visual Culture*. Oxford: Oxford University Press.

Turim, M. (1989) *Flashbacks in Film: Memory and History*. New York and London: Routledge.

Vieira, J. L. (1982) 'From High Noon to Jaws: Carnival and Parody in Brazilian Cinema', in R. Johnson and R. Stam (eds) *Brazilian Cinema*. London and Toronto: Associated University Presses, 256–69.

Walsh, M. (1996) 'Jameson and "Global Aesthetics"', in D. Bordwell and N. Carroll (eds) *Post-Theory: Reconstructing Film Studies*. Madison: University of Wisconsin Press, 481–500.

Xavier, I. (2003) 'Angels with Dirty Faces', *Sight and Sound*, 13, 1, 28–30.

Yates, F. (1966) *The Art of Memory*. Chicago: University of Chicago Press.

TRAUMATIC AND ALLEGORICAL MEMORY

5. IMPOSSIBLE MEMORY: TRAUMATIC NARRATIVES IN *MEMENTO* AND *MULHOLLAND DRIVE*

BELINDA MORRISSEY

The brain is an enchanted loom where millions of flashing shuttles weave a dissolving pattern. Since the mind recreates reality from the abstractions of sense impressions, it can equally well simulate reality by recall and fantasy. The brain invents stories and runs imagined and remembered events back and forth through time.

– Edward O. Wilson (1978; cited in van der Kolk & van der Hart 1995: 171)

Memory is treachery.

– Leonard Shelby's tattoo, *Memento*

Cinema has an indissoluble link with memory. Indeed, whether it attempts to represent cultural experience, or to mediate personal memory systems, cinema can never evade memory. Yet, while memory is the bedrock of cinematic representation, allowing us to 'see' that which we could never and have never seen; it remains a most unsatisfactory foundation for any sort of understanding. For memories lie even when 'telling the truth', refuse to look even when supposedly witnessing, hide while apparently revealing all, and confuse when claiming only to explain.

Some films do not even bother to pretend that through memory we can follow a life narrative, take a ride on someone else's journey of discovery, or solve a mystery. Christopher Nolan's *Memento* (2000) and David Lynch's *Mulholland Drive* (2001) are two of these. Both films use representations of the memories of their protagonists, whether faulty because they contain too little information or because they

Fig. 16 Leonard Shelby (Guy Pearce) using the photograph as one of his (false?) memory prostheses.

contain too much, to tear sense apart and, in doing so, to expose and destroy our faith in memory as the basis of a story. In *Memento*, Leonard Shelby has suffered anterograde amnesia during an assault and is unable to make any new memories from the time of the injury. He can recall memories from before that time, but, as he has chosen to surround himself only with people he did not know before the attack, his memory is constantly compromised and he has no way of knowing whether to believe anything he sees and hears. Hence, as his memory is lacking entirely in veracity, there is precious little possibility that the audience will ever discover any sort of reliable narrative. Indeed, it is almost self-evident, that any such thing would be absurd. *Mulholland Drive*, on the other hand, provides the audience with so many competing narratives, some of which are plausible and some fantastic, that we are, once again, forced to confront the impossibility of memory ever allowing for any kind of 'truth function'. Certain characters seem more sympathetic to the idea of coherent storytelling (such as Betty, and even Adam), but the stories they tell quickly become as absurdist as those of the less 'reliable' characters, who suffer from amnesia (Rita) or from depressive hallucinations and homicidal rage (Diane).

Memory, according to these films, is not to be trusted. Rather, as Leonard insists, memories don't matter, only 'facts' are important because memories equal interpretation. Yet, he knows only too well, as indeed do the characters from *Mulholland Drive*, that only through memories do 'facts' become accepted as 'facts', even though, because of the fallibility of memory, 'facts' are never entirely factual in the first place. Reality is up to memory, but memory can never be reality. Here lies the impossible paradox which both these films brilliantly portray: we can never trust memory, yet memory is *all* we have to trust.

Memento and *Mulholland Drive* use representations of narrative and traumatic memory systems in challenging memory as a way to make sense of the world. The distinction between these two kinds of memory is axiomatic in modern trauma theory. It was first developed by Pierre Janet in 1928 in an attempt to understand how personality develops. Janet considered narrative memory a uniquely human capacity, and thus, quite different to the 'habit' memory common to all sentient beings. For humans have the capacity to make sense out of their numerous experiences through the creation of narratives in which they understand and analyse their experiences, and place them within a time frame and a social and historical context (see van der Kolk & van der Hart 1995; Flanagan 2002). However, certain violent, fearful or disturbing events are, at least initially, incapable of any such integration into comforting narrative. Instead, those who have experienced such events develop what Janet called a 'traumatic memory', in which they are unable to recall key features of the trauma itself, yet are tormented by the constant reengagement with the emotions in their psychic lives and enactments in their bodies, through symptoms such as intrusive flashbacks while awake and nightmares when asleep. In essence, traumatic memory is dissociated, unable to be expressed through socially conventional narrative pathways, and is rather 'literally "etched" in the mind and acted out through the body' (Flanagan 2002: 387).

The current and most common response to traumatic memory from those working in psy-complex is to follow Janet's original suggestion and aim for eventual integration of the trauma within a narrative so that the person can resolve the event and stop endlessly living within reruns of it. To make a complete recovery, in Janet's terms, a return to the original trauma, either through hypnosis, simulation or through psychotherapeutic discourse to recover or reconstruct memories, is required (see Laney & Loftus 2005).[1] However, the notion that somehow remembering the event in its totality will allow it to be seamlessly integrated into one's life narrative both demands too much from any therapeutic process, and, more importantly, retains a naïve belief in the 'truth' of the life story. For memory, especially in narrative form, is exceptionally malleable and suggestible. As Anna Madill and Patricia Holch point out 'memories may be accurate, metaphorically true, or false' (2004: 306), and at the very least they are adaptive to the needs of the one telling the narrative and those of the one listening. There is no 'truth' in narrative, only endless multiplicity and interpretation. Integration of traumatic memory into narrative memory may come at too great a cost, then, for spurious benefit.

Memento and *Mulholland Drive* expose the dangers of narrative in the healing of trauma. Both films contain characters who have 'lost' themselves, either due to amnesia of some kind, or to depression and dementia. In *Memento*'s case, Leonard Shelby is desperate to perform an act which will both allow him to avenge his wife's murder and which will be so shattering for him personally that, although he suffers from anterograde amnesia, he believes he *will* remember. However, Leonard's story is entirely unreliable in the present because he simply cannot remember anything for longer than ten minutes, and due to the nostalgic overtones of his narrative memories that do still exist, he may well be simply fantasising his past as well (see Parker 2004). As Matthew Prins observes, *Memento*'s primary theme is 'the clash between our need to trust ourselves and our inclination to tell ourselves only what we want to believe' (2001: 33). Leonard cannot trust himself or anyone else, so he resorts to relying on 'facts' printed on paper, photographed in Polaroids, tattooed on his body. Yet these 'facts', this prosthetic narrative memory he attempts to create, lead him only in circles, and no closer to any sort of resolution to his dilemma to avenge his wife *and* remember doing so.

Mulholland Drive begins with the tale of an amnesiac who cannot remember who she is, but who can make new memories and so engage in a search to discover herself and her traumas. Calling herself Rita, after a Rita Hayworth poster she chances to see, she tumbles out of her 'real' life and into that of ingénue Betty, who becomes enchanted with the idea of finding out her life story. Yet Rita, who cannot remember her past, seems to have enough sense not to want to go looking for it, and she is dragged rather than leads the way into the solving of her own mystery. Rita suffers all the symptoms of the trauma victim, but the drive towards narrative ends only with her complete disappearance and that of Betty, as the need for a story swallows them both. Diane, as the flipside to the Betty character, appears at this point and seems to provide the answers to many of the questions of the first part of the film detailing the search of Betty and Rita. Yet, as Diane is deeply suicidal and homicidal, her story can hardly be trustworthy either, and indeed it finally destroys her.

The search for identity of both Rita and Leonard does not, and cannot, pay off in these films because it is driven by a confusion of selfhood with a coherent life story. Narrative memory cannot substitute for self, and nor can it heal traumatic memory, according to these films. Instead, we are left interrogating our relationship with our own narrative memories, wondering how often we've simply lied to ourselves to avoid unpleasant revelations, or told other tales about our lives that bear a resemblance only to fantasy, and what sorts of people we have fabricated from ourselves along the way. Memory here becomes impossible: we cannot trust it, but we cannot deny it either.

Todd McGowan has observed the ways in which the psychoanalytic concepts of desire and fantasy connect with the concepts of narrative and traumatic memory. He points out that the world of the solely desiring subject, and that of the traumatised one, is inherently atemporal, circulating endlessly around the object of desire. However, because this 'object' is not the goal of desire, but its cause, desire really circulates around a lack (2004: 86): the traumatised person is possessed by the trauma, even to the extent of acting it out through bodily symptoms, yet the trauma is not the object they seek, rather it is a *lack* – of memory – they desire yet cannot have. According to psychoanalytic theory, one cannot remain an endlessly desiring subject, because to desire that which is permanently lacking means to deny life, and thus to ultimately destroy the self. On the other hand, the world of fantasy and that of narrative are closely entwined. Indeed, as Slavoj Žižek has stated, 'fantasy is the primordial form of narrative' (1997: 10–11), and delivers us from the endless repetition of desire and traumatic memory. For fantasy provides temporality, and that produces coherence: it takes a small piece of experience and explains it in terms of its historical and social contexts, just as narrative does. Fantasy, then, becomes reality for us through the narratives we tell of our experience of that reality.

Given these psychoanalytic concepts of desire and fantasy, and their correlation with traumatic and narrative memory systems, it is clear where the belief in the healing of trauma through its integration with a narrated self comes from. After all, the traumatic event is that which remains unassimilated. It isn't even repressed, as such, and therefore able to be retrieved, whole and pristine, later. Instead, it appears that trauma actually damages the neurobiological processes responsible for 'recording' events for later narrativisation (Flanagan 2002: 387). This occurs because traumatic events rip away the shields of narrative and fantasy that usually protect us and force us to confront the terrifying Lacanian 'Real' directly. Our immediate reaction under these impossible circumstances is to refuse to register parts of the event, to allow, instead, a void to form at the heart of our psyches so that our horror never be confronted at the time, left only to recur belatedly when it breaks through unexpectedly and devastatingly (see Caruth 1995). Traumatic events lead then only to what Dori Laub calls a 'collapse of witnessing' (1995: 65).

Nevertheless, the traumatised person is encouraged to believe that if they can only integrate the terrible tale into a life narrative, it will lose its power to harm. This is a highly problematic strategy, for, as our narrative memory correlates with fantasy, it remains a chimera, plagued always by its inherent instability, unreliability and propensity for suggestion (see Grainge 2003). We remember what we want to and can stand to remember, and we don't even keep these memories in timeless vacuum. Rather, as Madill and Holch point out, 'we constantly weave our new perspectives into the past, enriching and reinterpreting our experience' (2004: 300). Memory, as Walter Benjamin (1969) observed, is the domain of the story-teller, who tells multiple life stories tailored for multiple audiences. Further, some of those selves will be speechless or engaged in endless re-petitive re-enactments of events they cannot face. 'Integration' of trau-matic encounters with the 'Real', then, seems as far fetched as many of the narratives designed to 'contain' them. Nowhere is this more evident than in the films chosen for analysis in this essay. For *Memento* demonstrates the false promise of 'integration', while *Mulholland Drive* cures its audi-ence of any belief in a unitary narrative. It is to these most chastening of representations that I now turn.

Memento's primary lesson is that traumatic memory is a structure in and of itself; that it is not, and indeed, cannot, be available for integration into narrative memory structure. Rather, this film proposes and displays the ways in which traumatic memory exists alongside narrative memory, in its own parallel world. Any 'integration' with narrative is likely to be unreli-able at best, and positively false or even dangerous at worst. The film is composed of two narrative threads, comprised of a colour segment that de-picts individual scenes, each of which moves the story backwards in time, while themselves moving forward following classic narrative structure; the second thread is in black and white and is also composed of individual scenes, which this time move forward in a linear pattern. The first thread uses each scene to build on the one before it by showing the viewer what happened to cause the action in one scene after it has already played out. The second thread is a narrative told in flashbacks which both help explain and comment on the action in the first thread. Towards the end of the film, the two threads join up in what director Christopher Nolan has described as a 'hairpin turn' (cited in Parker 2004: 246), where the chronological second thread suddenly switches around and goes backwards, colliding with the first thread. In effect, then, the film is well described, as indeed is the structure of *Mulholland Drive*, as a Möbius strip, where when we reach the end of the film, we have really only realised its actual beginning (see Johnson 2001a; Parker 2004).

The colour thread depicts the activities of Leonard Shelby, who is at-tempting to avenge his wife's murder. However, due to his anterograde amnesia, we, as the audience, are reduced to living within his own per-sonal hell, constantly surprised and bewildered, as we enter scenes which have no meaning for us, or for Shelby. Eventually, as this thread winds its inexorable way back in time, and because we have memories, we can begin to make the links Leonard is never able to, and we can start to construct some chronology to this thread as we watch. The black and white thread depicts a story within a story from Leonard's past as an insurance assessor, and which uncannily mimics Leonard's own situation in the present. As Leonard can remember the past, this part of the tale is easily followed, and is used to critique Leonard's condition and his past actions prior to the attack in which he became amnesiac. This complex structure beautifully demonstrates the 'break' in Leonard's memory and with his own life narrative received via his assault. The film is effectively broken into a pre and a post, but the link between the two is entirely obscured until the final, unreliable, scenes. We simply do not know what happened to Leonard in the assault, or what he did after, until he shows up in colour on our screens approximately a year later. The black and white thread only illuminates his even more distant past, while the colour thread keeps us as confused as he is, and as uncertain about whom to trust, including himself.

Memento's structure has been described as embodying a memento, a souvenir, in itself, in that the two threads 'stimulate, but do not satisfy, nostalgic longing for a prelapsarian truth' (Little 2005): the colour thread promising understanding if we can only hang in there and keep making reverse sense until we arrive at the causal scene; the nostalgic black and white narrative teasing the viewer with its equally false promise of a representation of the 'real' Leonard, pre-amnesia. Neither thread gives us what we want, of course; Leonard's anterograde amnesia puts paid to that dream. Equally, however, both have souvenir qualities, reminding us of *that* moment when something made sense, *that* time in Leonard's life when his actions appeared to have meaning; *that* place we can only remember well through the fragments we have brought back to remind ourselves that we were there, we did do this and we have even made our own special stories in commemoration. These threads are souvenirs of Leonard's life, remnants of who he was and who he has become, but they cannot explain the terrible, traumatic gap in the middle because this rent in consciousness cannot be sutured.

Yet Leonard's entire *raison d'être* is precisely to effect integration, even though his anterograde amnesia will always make this impossible as even if he does manage to place his traumatic experience within a narrative, he will remember it only for ten minutes. Furthermore, he does not want integration into any story, but only integration into a particular story. He's not interested in alternative scenarios to the one he believes: that John G. raped and murdered his wife, and that he must now find him and kill him. As his 'friend'/master manipulator, Teddy, states: 'I guess I can only make you remember the things you *want* to be true.' Here lies the crux of the paradox that this film explores so well: integration of traumatic memories into narrative memory is much more complex than the psychoanalysts would have us believe, for it always involves integration into a story, and that story has to be acceptable to the traumatised person. So, integration is, at base, a highly subjective process, having little or nothing to do with veracity and far more to do with finding the most appropriate fantasy to cover the void of desire which traumatic memory makes too real.

Leonard attempts to paper over the gap in his memory, and the continuing problem of forgetting, using devices to stimulate other kinds of memory which allow him some control over his frighteningly bewildering existence. During the brief intervals when his memory works, he finds ways of capturing the information so that when he inevitably forgets, he will have clues, or as he calls them 'facts', to work from. To this end, he writes notes on post-it stickers, he takes Polaroid pictures and write captions beneath them, and the 'facts' he considers most important, he tattoos on his body. This information allows Leonard to draw, to a limited extent, on 'prospective' memory – remembering to do things in the future – which then permits him to have a future at all, instead of the endless present in which he is trapped (Parker 2004: 243). He also uses his intact long term memory to understand his amnesia and to use conditioning strategies that take the place of 'procedural' memory, which carries the knowledge of certain skills or tasks (*Ibid.*: 244). As he observes very early in the film, habit and routine make his life possible. However, these very means of memory pretence are also the clearest signals that he will never recover. For they indicate that Leonard is stuck at the place of the trauma and can never develop past it.

Indeed, Leonard does not have a clue about anything *but* his condition: he lives and breathes it, turns himself into a souvenir of it, searches for himself as the missing person he is. He tattoos any fragment he feels he *must* remember in order to continue the quest that defines his life; as Teddy points out, the quest is everything and Leonard does not really want it to end because then there would be no focus for his moments of life. This is particularly apparent in that he does not tattoo his *own* actions; he does not tattoo 'I killed John G.' even when he has killed, because that would be to put a permanent end to his quest. Instead, he takes Polaroids of them, which, while hard to destroy, can always be re-interpreted, re-captioned, in a way that tattoos cannot. He becomes an exoticised souvenir; a testimony to his own inability to witness not only his wife's murder but his own murders that follow; a memento of the loss of his own character (see Little 2005). For, as Janet observed of severe amnesia patients, their inability to remember their trauma causes an inability to assimilate any new experiences since that time: 'It is … as if their personality has definitively stopped at a certain point' (cited in Meares 2000: 54). Leonard is forever caught in the moment of his wife's death and all his imaginative 'solutions' to his own missing person status will never allow him to escape it.

Forgetting is absolutely vital to Leonard Shelby, much as he thinks he wants only to remember. As Ruth Perlmutter has noted, amnesia allows the development of a new identity, conveniently blotting out 'guilt, trauma, and therefore, grief and mourning' (2005: 130). This is most evident when Leonard burns some cherished belongings of his wife, in the sure knowledge that he has probably 'burnt truckloads of your stuff', and mourns that his biggest problem is that: 'I cannot remember to forget you.' Her continued presence in his life acts as a thorn that disallows any blissful sinking into a brand new identity; his stubborn memory of her death is the only thing still making him Leonard Shelby. Even Teddy notices this, arguing with him that he is no longer that person; he's 'become someone else'. So remembering is really Leonard's problem, and the reason for his disastrous situation in the present. He cannot remember enough to let go, yet he can remember too much to move on.

Leonard's dreams, in particular, give away this eternal paradox. In his dreams, Leonard is again one with his wife; the tragedy has not occurred. However, as soon as he wakes he must once again go through the horror of losing not only her, but his own memory. He re-experiences these terrors every time he wakes because he moves from a time when he was 'Leonard Shelby, insurance assessor' to his current confusing position as a man on the run from his memory while trying to avenge it at the same time. He attempts to assuage his sense of loss through using the old psychoanalytic trick of recreation. He hires a prostitute to play his wife, and has her wake him with a sound in the bathroom, just as his wife had on the night of her murder, only this time, he is able to rescue her, as he was too late to do in life. Needless to say, this technique does not work. Instead, it leads only to Leonard having a more vivid dream of his inability to save her when he finally dreams all the way to his discovery of her body and his own assault.

In this instance, he manages to emulate both Freud's and Lacan's theories of the purposes of dreaming, showing the complicated world he inhabits as that which Cathy Caruth has called a 'failed survivor' (1996: 103). On the one hand, as Freud argued in *The Interpretation of Dreams* (1899), the dreamer dreams in order to go on sleeping, so as not to have to deal with the trauma of awakening to the intolerable situation. In dreams, the dead loved one is with the one who grieves, and there is still hope that life may continue. On the other, Lacan claims that the function of the dream is, indeed, to wake; that the dream itself is structured so that the dreamer cannot help but wake, once again, too late to avert the death. This awakening is part of the process of responding to the trauma of the death. For Leonard, awakening reminds him time and again of his responsibility to avenge his wife's death, giving purpose to his life, providing an identity when all is lost. To wake up, as Caruth notes, 'is thus to bear the imperative to survive' (1995: 105). Yet thanks to the amnesia Leonard always fails at this task of bearing witness; he always only discovers anew his inadequacy, his failure to see, his inability to get there in time.

Leonard is, quite literally, trapped in the deadlock of his own desire throughout this film. He cannot simply cast his quest aside and begin again. Instead, he is bound, as he says to Jimmy before his kills him, to seek the impossible, answering Jimmy's age-old question of desire: 'What do you want?' with the response, 'I want my life back.' His world is the incomprehensible world of desire, where the audience knows as little as he does about what is happening and why it does. Further, he reveals himself as the quintessential desiring subject by his complete inability to really say *who he is*, despite his arrogant claim at the start of the film that: 'I know who I am, I know all about myself.' *All* he is, is his quest; they are indivisible as Teddy realises, and to *stop* killing John G.s would be to destroy his own world. So, even though, as Natalie points out, when he gets revenge he won't remember it, and thus the quest is really a cruel, pointless joke, he cannot give up on it, for it has become him.

The usefulness of the quest as a focusing point for Leonard does not, however, mean that either we, or Leonard, are ever in the possession of some truth. Indeed, no-one can be trusted in this film. The other characters in the film lie to Leonard, to each other and themselves, just as Leonard also lies to himself and to them. We are never sure whether Leonard's memories of the time before the murder of his wife are true or not; we don't know whether the story within a story, involving Leonard's assessment of Sammy Jankis who also had anterograde amnesia, is real or a self-serving fantasy that he has constructed so that he won't have to face his own violence; we are left in the dark about Teddy's real role in his life throughout the film. Indeed there are at least seven possible scenarios we could consider plausible enough to 'explain' the action and there are few clues as to which one is most likely.[2]

The sheer multiplicity of these narratives, regardless of their credibility, demonstrates clearly that traumatic memory can be integrated into narrative memory only through a brutal displacement of the veracity of memory itself. Leonard does not believe that memory will save him, he appears to believe only in 'facts', and he does not seem to care that they are manipulable as long as he can go on trusting them. As he says, 'we lie to ourselves all the time'; what matters, is what we *choose* to believe. Traumatic memory, then, must exist alongside whatever kind of narrated existence he can create for himself via his mementoes, his 'facts', his 'police file'. Indeed, integration may not even be wise, given some of the possible scenarios and the potential harm the truth may cause. Here, narrative memory would, in itself, become traumatic. In some part of his being, Leonard also knows this, observing that 'we all need mirrors to remind ourselves who we are', but being clever enough to choose to look in only the most flattering ones.

Mulholland Drive makes the slipperiness of narrative even more apparent than does *Memento*. For this film presents the incredible variety of narrative memories, from the adaptive ones to the wish fulfilment variety, and demonstrates that it is not in proliferation that we will find either healing or veracity. There is no refuge from trauma through narrative in *Mulholland Drive*, and indeed, attempting to 'heal' trauma through its integration into narrative is shown to be capable of literally driving one mad, if one follows the most common reading of this complicated film.

Equating trauma with desire (and hence, with lack), and narrative with fantasy, *Mulholland Drive* shows that while in desire we can never have what we seek, and that only through fantasy can we obtain resolution, this is nevertheless a false bargain. For the realisation that the fantasy/narrative is indeed our own construction can be as traumatic as the desire and loss that necessitated its production. This lesson is learned by no less than three of the main characters: Diane, Rita and Betty. Diane is the most obvious example of the three, wherein, under one reading of the film, her fantasy construction comes crashing down with her eventual recognition of her own involvement in the death of her love object, Camilla, and precipitates her own suicide. Rita and Betty, however, can be seen to experience this realisation as well, if one reads the film differently. For, in undertaking a search for Rita's identity, they construct their own fantasy narrative in which they form a relationship but are incapable of surviving their own traumatic contact with the Real, in the form of the dead body of a different Diane, and literally disappear once they realise their explanation of this horror is no more 'true' than the singer's voice at the mysterious Club Silencio. Indeed, silence for all three seems more hopeful than the chattering narratives which ultimately destroy them.

The film illustrates the impossibility of narrative in its very structure. This has been variously described as a spiral: 'a series of unexplained pulsions that blur and destabilise traditional concepts of intellectual sense' (Hudson 2004: 17); and a series of Chinese boxes, incorporating three plots: the first a discontinuous narrative that opens to a second unitary one that finally opens to a third one that 'is intransigent in its multiplicity' (Andrews 2004: 38). Incorporating at least eight story lines, *Mulholland Drive* nevertheless allows for some conventional sense-making through its use of linear plots (even if these are multiplied), and its Möbius strip back to front stories which pair the egos and alter egos of six of the characters (Betty/Diane, Rita/Camilla and the two Adams).[3] Yet, cleverly this technique also serves to only confuse us further, even while we attempt to sort out who did what, when and to whom.

We are never given the opportunity to really know which of the stories these characters tell is, indeed, *the* story; instead, we are left only with the understanding that understanding does not matter. The film and its characters, as David Roche points out, are 'image crystals that, because of their many reflections and their many unsolvable mysteries, multiply subjectivity to infinite' (2004: 51). To attempt to 'interpret' this film in a unitary fashion, then, is to deny the integrity of the film, to force it to become 'rational' in the face of its own, carefully preserved, irrationality. For this film challenges us to come to terms with the real nature of narrative memory, which is to remember things the way we would *like* to. The only veracity of narrative memory, then, is how well it fits with the subject's desire to create their own reality to serve their own needs.

The most common interpretation of the film, dubbed the 'oneiric' reading, incorporates the concept of the fantastic nature of narrative memory, recognising that, only in fantasy, can the irreconcilable demands of desire be met (see McGowan 2004), while at the same time, insisting upon a unitary narrative that explains everything. This reading asks us to consider that the entire film takes place in Diane Selwyn's head; that, in fact, the lengthy and relatively cohesive first part of the film is Diane's wish fulfil-ment fantasy dream, while the 'real' story takes place only in the second part of the film, when Diane awakes, confronts her murder of her lover, and finally suicides. In its very early scenes, we are shown the image of a sleeper, who lies in a room that is very similar to the one later seen con-taining a sleeping Diane. The shot dissolves into the pillow and the 'film proper' begins.

Diane's dream initially introduces us to Rita, who is involved in a car accident while about to be murdered. Rita loses her memory, wanders into the parkland off Mulholland Drive, and eventually ends up sneaking into an apartment at the bottom of the hill. Rita continually falls asleep, beside a bush, under a table and eventually in a bed. She awakens to find Betty, a young ingénue actress, in the apartment with her, who becomes intrigued by her tale of loss and who offers to help her locate her iden-tity (as Rita is not even her name), and the reason for her retrograde amnesia. Betty is considered in this reading to be the wish fulfilment fantasy figure of Diane herself, while Rita is the alter ego of Camilla Rhodes, Diane's 'real-life' lover and victim. Betty has come to Hollywood to be a 'star', and is a talented ac-tress, while Rita is disinter-

Fig. 17 Diane (Naomi Watts) encourages Rita (Laura Harring) to remember her story so that she can help her solve the mystery of her identity.

ested in the business, and in the scene depicting her helping Betty prepare for an audition, shows herself to be an appalling actress.

Diane's dream also contains the story of the unfortunate Adam Kesher, who manages to lose control of the film he is directing to the 'mob', is forced to cast a different, blonde 'Camilla Rhodes' in favour of far better actresses, loses his wife, house and money, and who finally falls hopelessly in love with Betty. Rita and Betty, however, fall for each other, and start a passionate affair. Despite Rita's reservations, Betty insists on continuing their search for her identity, and they eventually wind up at the home of a 'Diane Selwyn', who looks nothing like the later 'Diane', and who is found dead in her bed, having apparently committed suicide. This shock propels the two to the mysterious Club Silencio, where they listen to a woman lip-synching to a Spanish version of the Roy Orbison classic 'Crying', are told there is no band and that nothing is real, and eventually return home after discovering that Betty has found the blue box that matches a blue key Rita had on her person. Upon opening the box, both women disappear and part two begins.

In this, much shorter, section, we learn that Betty is really Diane, Rita is really Camilla, that the two have indeed been having an affair, but that Camilla has recently called it off to marry the very successful film director, Adam. Camilla is the 'star' now, while Diane is reduced to begging Camilla to get her bit parts in the films in which she leads. After various humiliations at Camilla's hands, Diane becomes obsessed with hurting her and eventually hires a hit man, after inheriting some money from her aunt (whose apartment Betty stays in during the first part of the film). The hit man tells her that Camilla will have been murdered when she received a blue key as a signal. Diane wakes, remembers Camilla's last visit to her when she breaks off their relationship, finds the key on the table, falls to pieces and finally shoots herself. The second part of the film is chaotic and confusing as it descends into Diane's world of desire. Unable to continue to comfort herself through sleeping and wish fulfilment dreaming, Diane cannot face the reality she has created through her murder of the object of her desire. Fantasy, here, equates with narrative, and is shown as the only resolution of desire, but ultimately an inadequate compensation. For nothing can help Diane once she realises she has destroyed her own desire (see also Lentzner & Ross 2005 and Vaida & Wildman 2005 for examples of this oneiric reading).

Although this reading is remarkably inclusive, and manages to integrate almost all of the various narrative threads running through the film, it is at heart reductive, ignoring a host of other possible story lines, and trivialising the character development of virtually every other character than that of Diane Selwyn in the second part. Most particularly, it dismisses the troubling, supernatural elements that always invade David Lynch's films (see Andrews 2004). Moreover, it simply cannot account for several occurrences in any legitimate way.

The first of these is that Diane apparently confronts her own corpse in the midst of her wish fulfilment fantasy, which makes no sense given the adaptive nature of the narrative. The second is, as David Andrews notes, that there is more than one sleeper in the story (2004: 33). Rita, for example, sleeps all over the place and in doing so could be read as creating her own narratives in her dreams, including the police investigation into her accident; the weird scene at Winkie's diner involving a young man confiding to his psychotherapist that a terrifying apparition resides at the back of building whom he then confronts and, in doing so, dies himself; the story of the mobsters looking for 'the girl', who then turn up later to harass Adam Kesher and, some have argued, the whole Betty narrative as well.

Rita sleeps in the hope of bringing her memory back, but instead appears to create only a variety of possible stories whose plausibility is tentative to say the least. Rita's sleep is just as 'real' as Diane's in the second part; and her character development as an amnesiac is as nuanced as Diane's depressive, homicidal, suicidal personality. Further, Rita could have 'dreamt up' Betty as a wish fulfilment character to aid her in her quest for identity and to comfort her in her fear and anxiety. This is by no means an impossible scenario; as Betty says herself, she inhabits a 'dream place'.

Rita's desire for meaning can then be allied with that of Leonard Shelby in *Memento*: as a retrograde amnesiac she is a *tabula rasa* in a way that Leonard, as an anterograde amnesiac, is not. For Leonard can remember 'who he is', or thinks he can, and his earlier memories provide context and focus to his current, confusing existence; Rita, on the other hand, does not even know her own name, and is only aware of enough of the trauma which created her condition to feel a nameless dread. Betty then has a similar role in her life to the one Natalie poses in Leonard's: they both help the amnesiacs with their journey towards self-knowledge, yet deflect the final confrontation with the 'truth' – Betty through literally disappearing, Natalie through developing a comforting sexual relationship with Leonard that we imagine continues after the credits roll. Neither Leonard nor Rita are capable of really coping with the trauma that created them; the idea of integration into narrative memory is simply absurd in both films, and the function of both Betty and Natalie is to make certain they never need to face this horror alone. Even though this interpretation does not explain as many elements of the film as the oneiric reading, it nevertheless, opens out new possibilities, thereby undercutting the grand narrative, as Andrews observes (2004: 34).

One of these possibilities involves taking Betty's character more seriously. Ruth Perlmutter (2005) has suggested we could read Betty's story as that of an actor in a retro-noir thriller who plays the role of the jealous, homicidal Diane, and that in doing so, she, in effect, *becomes* Diane. This interpretation would allow for her to discover 'Rita', determine that her identity is really that of Camilla Rhodes, fall in love with her, be humiliated by her and eventually kill her, although whether Betty herself actually engages in any of these actions would be a moot point, as we could never be sure whether Betty was playing herself or merely role-playing noir character, Diane.

Another possible narrative could revolve around the supernatural components of the film, especially the strange character behind the Winkie's restaurant. After all, as Andrews notes (2004: 34), we are told near the beginning of the film, in this very sequence, that this 'Terrifying Bum', in his terms, is 'the one who's doing it', and he may very well be manipulating the entire film to his own bizarre ends. If this were the case, then rationality would become a very low priority within the filmic structure, and the entire story would revolve around his successful mission to destroy Diane's sanity through her dreams, causing her to believe that she took action against Camilla when, in fact, she was incapable of doing so, and this then leads to her suicidal crisis upon awakening.

Yet another narrative, involving Adam Kesher and the mobsters, seems like a paean to Lynch's own relationship with Hollywood, depicting exactly and unsympathetically the sacrifices one must make of one's integrity and honour in order to succeed in such a place (see Perlmutter 2005). Indeed, Adam could be having his own wish fulfilment dream in the second part of the film, where he has the success he craves without the untenable capitulations to the 'system'.

Mulholland Drive considers the ramifications of two different types of trauma and its relationship with narrative. Firstly, the traumatic realisation that the fantasy narratives we construct to make our world more tenable are indeed constructions is at the centre of this complex film. All the narratives, whether minor or monolithic, come back to this single point: no character can face the knowledge that the narratives they tell themselves so they can get by are utterly malleable. Secondly, the actual traumatic events that some characters face, such as Rita and Diane, cannot be resolved through narrative integration; indeed, such activity simply accelerates breakdown. Narrative is far too unstable to bear the weight of the traumatic experience. For trauma forces us to face a 'Real' that renders us speechless and inarticulate for the good reason that experiencing trauma teaches us that there is *nothing to say*. Instead the film paradoxically, given its innumerable narratives, praises the value of silence and the acceptance of the incoherent, the inchoate, the unreasonable. Even the most carefully developed of the various interpretations, the oneiric reading, teaches us that explanation is a mirage. Indeed, narrative is shown to allow us to evade veracity through multiplicity, and to be as traumatic as traumatic memory precisely because it fills in the gaps that traumatic memory exposes, rather than allowing us the comfort of not knowing.

Memory is indeed rendered impossible in *Memento* and *Mulholland Drive*. Narrative memory is made absurd, while traumatic memory, with its impossible remembrances, is conceived as the only 'truth' any of us are ever likely to know. Reality is up to memory, but memory can never be reality, because it cannot include that which cannot be spoken. Instead, as Leonard Shelby so succinctly puts it, 'memory is treachery', and to give in, to narrate the details of one's experiences, is to agree to live a compulsory lie.

Using a postmodern aesthetic, these films approach this conclusion from opposite perspectives. *Memento* demonstrates the constant reinvention Leonard Shelby must undertake every morning in his search for the unitary narrative he believes will set him free: he will kill 'John G.' and he *will* remember. Leonard's task is driven entirely by trauma: he must exorcise his demons in order to reclaim his traumatic memory. However, it is precisely because of trauma that he will always already have failed, for he can never 'fill in' the gap in his memory: the neural pathways have not been laid down and there is no way they can ever be. All he can hope for is a coherent narrative which obscures the damage. Yet even this is impossible for Leonard because, even if he wrote the story down, he would be unable to follow it, as he cannot keep whole narrative threads in his mind at any one time. Moreover, he is entirely untrustworthy as a narrator: we are never sure if we are hearing what 'really' happened, or a version of it, or a fantasy, or someone else's tale entirely. Leonard's search for a 'seamless narrative' turns out to be a search for the only narrative he can stand to hear.

Mulholland Drive, on the other hand, makes no pretence at searching for a unitary narrative, although some of its characters, especially Betty, seem to believe in them. Instead, due to the multiplicity of possible narrative threads, and the various characters' need to process experience through the 'distortions of symbolic and linguistic representation' (Flanagan 2002: 387), the film makes very evident that we will 'never know' the truth, and that searching for any kind of unitary narrative is a furphy as storytellers adapt their stories to their own needs and that of the audience. The film is so full of unfinished narratives, made up stories, delusions, allusions and illusions, that sorting through them becomes a thankless and worthless task.

Memento and *Mulholland Drive* use trauma as the catalyst for narrative, and both show, one through a *lack* of narrative and the other through a *surfeit*, that narrative memory is an utterly insufficient holding vessel for traumatic memory. Rather, traumatic memory must continue to function *alongside* narrative memory. It can never be integrated within it. For it is only through trauma that we ever encounter the 'Real'; such as when Leonard finally sees in his dream that he was too late to save his wife and would always be too late, or when Betty and Rita confront the dead body of 'Diane Selwyn' and flee the apartment in horror. Given the impossible nature of these experiences, we *must* leave them forever unassimilated for our own sanity. The fantastical veils of narrative are perfect for screening us from the everyday, but the abyss at the heart of traumatic memories is absolutely vital for preserving us from our terrors and our desires. As Teddy observes so wisely to Leonard: 'So you lie to yourself to be happy. Who cares if there's a few little details we'd rather not remember?' *Memento* and *Mulholland Drive* teach us that those rents in our consciousness are there for good reason, and that to sew them up with neat narratives is both dangerous and false.

NOTES

1   Yet, of course, this is not possible for all sufferers of trauma; for some, this technique may only allow the person to manage their trauma a little more successfully through learning strategies to enable some retention of knowledge that their horrors are at least momentary, not permanent. For others, according to a variety of critiques, the results may be far more devastating. Steven Gold has summarised it as 'retrieval of traumatic memories is likely to strip away an essential form of protection provided by keeping this material from awareness ... As a consequence, functioning tends to dramatically deteriorate rather than improve' (1997: 989). For many, in Joseph Flanagan's terms, 'History is itself inherently traumatic' (2002: 387), and to be forced to relive it is akin to torture.

2   a) Leonard did see his wife killed; Teddy has been manipulating him to kill 'John G.s' since that time, and lies at the end where he says that the Sammy Jankis story is made up. Hence, although Teddy may or may not have killed Leonard's wife, he deserves to die anyway for the cruel manipulation.
b) Leonard did kill his wife, as Teddy claims. She did not die during the rape, but was killed by Leonard later due to the anterograde amnesia he suffered after his assault. Teddy knows this, but manipulates him to kill anyway, because he can. Sammy Jankis is not real, but is invented by Leonard so he will not have to face his own actions.
c) The Sammy Jankis story is Leonard's invention to prevent himself having to face the

truth that he killed his wife through insulin injections, and Leonard himself was really injured in a car accident. Teddy is still in the role of manipulator. (This story seems less likely than some of the others, except for a scene where we see Leonard in bed with his wife and his body is tattooed at that time, when presumably, it should not have been.)

d) Leonard's story regarding his amnesia and the rape and murder of his wife remain the same. Teddy is lying about manipulating Leonard to kill numerous John G.s. He wanted him to kill only Jimmy G. for the drug money.

e) Leonard's story regarding his amnesia and the rape and murder of his wife remain the same. Teddy is John G. who raped and murdered Leonard's wife, and has been playing with Leonard ever since.

f) Leonard is faking the whole thing and is as corrupt as Teddy, whom he ultimately kills for supremacy. Leonard learnt how to fake anterograde amnesia from watching Sammy Jankis. Leonard also killed his wife, although in this scenario, it is not clear why he did.

g) Leonard may have escaped from an institution, such as the one we see Sammy in, and Sammy is not real at all, but once again, a fantasy narrative for Leonard. Leonard escapes to kill 'John G.' and is then manipulated by Teddy because he suffers from anterograde amnesia, but it isn't clear here how he developed this condition.

3   a) Rita's story as the amnesiac, desiring subject.

b) The 'Terrifying Bum' vignette.

c) The mobster narrative – where they are looking for 'the girl'.

d) Betty's narrative – ingénue arriving in Hollywood who gets involved in Rita's search for identity.

e) Adam Kesher's bad day story – intersects with the mobster narrative.

f) Bungling Hitman narrative – connected to the mobster narrative.

g) Diane's narrative as the depressive, homicidal, desiring subject.

h) Adam Kesher's success narrative – connected to the Diane narrative.

WORKS CITED

Andrews, D. (2004) 'An Oneiric Fugue: The Various Logics of *Mulholland Drive*', *Journal of Film and Video*, 56, 1, Spring, 25–40.

Armstrong, R. (2005) 'Somewhere in the Night: *Memento*', *Screen Education*, 41, 119–23.

Benjamin, W. (1969) 'The Storyteller: Reflections on the Works of Nikolai Leskov', in *Illuminations: Essays and Reflections*, trans. H. Arendt, New York: Schocke, 83–110.

Browne, I. (1990) 'Psychological Trauma, or Unexperienced Experience', *Re-vision*, 12, 4, 20–34.

Bruner, J. (1991) 'The Narrative Construction of Reality', *Critical Inquiry*, 18, 1, Autumn, 1–21.

Caruth, C. (1995) 'Introduction', *Trauma: Explorations in Memory*. Baltimore: Johns Hopkins University Press, 3–12.

_____ (1996) *Unclaimed Experience Trauma, Narrative, and History*. Baltimore: Johns Hopkins University Press.

Flanagan, J. (2002) 'The Seduction of History: Trauma, Re-memory, and the Ethics of the Real', *CLIO*, 31, 4, 387–91.

Gillard, G. (2005) '"Close your eyes and you can start all over again": *Memento*', *Screen Education*, 40, 115–17.

Gold, S. N. (1997) 'False Memory Syndrome: A False Dichotomy Between Science and Practice', *American Psychologist*, September, 988–9.

Grainge, P. (2003) 'Introduction: memory and popular film', in P. Grainge (ed) *Memory and Popular Film*. Manchester: Manchester University Press, 1–20.

Hudson, J. A. (2004) '"No Hay Banda, and Yet We Hear a Band": David Lynch's Reversal of Coherence in *Mulholland Drive*', *Journal of Film and Video*, 56, 1, 17–24.

Johnson, B. (2001a) 'Dreams ... Just a Kiss Away', *Maclean's*, 114, 45, 11, 5.

_____ (2001b) 'Narrative Extremes', *Maclean's*, 114, 14, 4, 2.

Lacan, Jacques (1981) 'The Unconscious and Repetition' in Jacques-Alain Miller (ed) *The Four Fundamental Concepts of Psychoanalysis* Alan Sheridan (trans.) New York: Norton, 17-65.

Laney, C. and E. Loftus (2005) 'Traumatic Memories are Not Necessarily Accurate Memories', *Canadian Journal of Psychiatry*, 50, 13, 823–8.

Laub, D. (1995) 'Truth and Testimony: The Process and the Struggle', in C. Caruth (ed.) *Trauma: Explorations in Memory*. Baltimore: Johns Hopkins University Press, 61–75.

Lentzner, J. R. and D. R. Ross (2005) 'The Dreams That Blister Sleep: Latent Content and Cinematic Form in *Mulholland Drive*', *American Imago*, 62, 1, 101–23.

Little, W. G. (2005) 'Surviving *Memento*', *Narrative*, 13, 1, January, 67–83.

Madill, A. and P. Holch (2004) 'A Range of Memory Possibilities: The Challenge of the False Memory Debate for Clinicians and Researchers', *Clinical Psychology and Psychotherapy*, 11, 299–310.

McCormick, P. (2001) 'Memory loss', *U.S. Catholic*, September, 46–8.

McGowan, T. (2004) 'Lost of Mulholland Drive: Navigating David Lynch's Panegyric to Hollywood', *Cinema Journal*, 43, 2, 67–89.

Meares, R. (2000) *Intimacy and Alienation: Memory, Trauma and Personal Being*. London: Routledge.

Miller, L. (1994) 'Civilian Post-Traumatic Stress Disorder: Clinical Syndromes and Psychotherapeutic Strategies', *Psychotherapy*, 31, 4, Winter, 655–64.

Paquette, M. (2003) 'Real Life and Reel Life', *Perspectives in Psychiatric Care*, 39, 2, 47–8.

Parker, J. A. (2004) 'Remembering the Future: *Memento*, the Reverse of Time's Arrow, and the Defects of Memory', *Kronoscope*, 4, 2, 239–57.

Perlmutter, R. (2005) 'Memories, Dreams, Screens', *Quarterly Review of Film and Video*, 22, 125–34.

Prins, M. (2001) 'Unreliable memories', *Christian Century*, 6–13 June, 33.

Radstone, S. (1995) 'Cinema/memory/history', *Screen*, 36, 1, 34–47.

Roche, D. (2004) 'The Death of the Subject in David Lynch's *Lost Highway* and *Mulholland Drive*', EREA, 2, 2, 42–52.

Telotte, J.P. (1998) 'Rounding up "The Usual Suspects": The Comforts of Character and Neo-Noir', *Film Quarterly*, 51, 4, Summer, 12–20.

Vaida, J. C. and V. H. Wildman (2005) 'Mulholland Dr.', *Psychoanalytic Psychology*, 22, 1, 113–19.

Van der Kolk, B. and O. Van der Hart (1995) 'The Intrusive Past: The Flexibility of Memory and the Engraving of Trauma', *Trauma: Explorations in Memory*. Baltimore: Johns Hopkins University Press, 158–82.

Žižek, S. (1997) *The Plague of Fantasies*. New York: Verso.

6. MEMORIES OF A CATASTROPHE: TRAUMA AND THE NAME IN MIRA NAIR'S *THE NAMESAKE*

AMRESH SINHA

> What does one call thus? What does one understand under the name of
> name? And what occurs when one gives a name? What does one give then?
> One does not offer a thing, one delivers nothing, and still something comes
> to be, which comes down to giving that which one does not have... (Derrida
> 1995a: 30)

INTRODUCTION

At the end of the last millennium, starting in the early 1990s, the experiences of migrant and displaced populations around the globe began
taking on an unprecedented urgency in the critical discourse of diaspora
and memory in the works of many of the South Asian filmmakers of
Indian origin, especially women filmmakers, such as Mira Nair, Gurinder
Chadha, Deepa Mehta and Pratibha Parmar. Their films, made in both
North America and Britain, have been primarily engaged with the notion
of 'the diaspora as a mode of cultural production': a place of contestation
and negotiation for the production of cultural identity in a globalised world
(Hussain 2005: 6).

The politics of identity in the South Asian diaspora is strategically
employed by these transnational filmmakers in their numerous films.
By emphasising transnational identities that are mostly invisible or
sublimated in the dominant culture, Mira Nair and others have successfully managed to decouple the discourse of diaspora from its uncritical
allegiance to the *essentialist* dogma of the homeland and have returned to
narratives that primarily engage with the marginalised and racialised politics of the nation-state of the host country. Their deconstructive strategy
signals the end of the symbolic vestige of Indian 'national consciousness',
a consciousness predicated upon the emergence of the nation that views
itself symbolically in eternal terms.

Nair's quest for a proper cinematic representation of the naming of the
diasporas in exile and minority groups, especially the politics and language

of multicultural identity but not necessarily limited to a stable South Asian identity, persists throughout her *oeuvre*, from *Mississippi Masala* (1992) (Indian diaspora displaced from Africa to Mississippi) and *The Perez Family* (1995) (Cuban refugees in Florida) to *Monsoon Wedding* (2001) (homecoming of Indian transnationals). *The Namesake*, adapted from the novel of the same name by the Pulitzer Prize-winning writer Jhumpa Lahiri, represents the complex saga of intergenerational trauma and (trans)nationalism of an Indian Bengali family, the Gangulis, who have transplanted themselves from Kolkata to Cambridge, Massachusetts. The husband, Ashoke Ganguli (Irfan Khan), a professor at M.I.T., lives with his newlywed pregnant wife, Ashima (Tabu). Ashoke belongs to a generation of Indian immigrants educated in India but due to heavy unemployment and poverty in the 1960s left mainly for England or America for better employment opportunities.[1]

The Indian transnational diasporic community, historically speaking, has not been subjected to the same level of racism and violence in America as the South Asian diaspora in England (where the migratory process began in the 1950s) – well documented in *My Beautiful Launderette* (Stephen Frears, 1985), *Sammy and Rosie Get Laid* (Stephen Frears, 1987), *The Buddha of Suburbia* (Roger Mitchell, 1993) and *My Son the Fanatic* (Udayan Prasad, 1997). In the US it has been mostly defined – which is to say, named – by the difference of its rich cultural and linguistic heritage. The persistent lack of power of the South Asian diaspora to name itself within its own multiplicity and diversity is further compounded by the dominant (American) cultural institutions that resist the insertion of the unpronounceable names of the Indian bourgeoisie in the mainstream culture. 'As a minority community in a foreign nation, the Indian immigrant bourgeoisie experiences the loss of its power of ex-nomination. Where once it stood for the no-name universal in the nation of its origin, it now perceives itself (and is perceived) to be in a position defined by difference. It now risks being named' (Bhattacharjee 1998: 165). The immigrant would rather sink in the darkness of anonymity in which the tenuous relationship with his/her own identity and past shall never be revealed. The motto is: No need to draw attention to oneself. The dominant ideology hails (to use an Althusserian image) the model immigrant thus: 'you are granted permission to stay here as a model immigrant, but you will never be really one of us – so stay on guard and on display as an approved, tokenised prototype, for other potential and future immigrants to model themselves after' (in Dayal 1996: 50).

The film mostly avoids the usual juxtaposition of Indian diaspora and the antagonistic host culture in which the latter continues to marginalise the former. Though there are some racial tensions in the film between the South Asian migrants and the local racist elements, the film does not make that as its essential theme. The second generation immigrants, in some sense, occupy a space of culture more fraught with their own identity crisis (hyphenated or hybridised), in which home and the world are no longer separate entities but are united in their opposition. Unlike the first generation of transnationals, who live in one space in absence of the other, as 'naturalised' citizens, the second generation in the United States has rights of citizenship that far exceeds the civic rights of his/her transplanted first generation parents. The first generation lives at home deprived of the world, shunned from outside and hermetically sealed off. Outside in the world, the home exists in its complete absence, having no cultural space of its own except in the marginalia of the diaspora.

In more than one way, Nair contests the essentialist notion of Indianness, that is, 'ontologising of the conceptual', as a form of identity that transcends all the regional, religious and linguistic differences (Schalkwyk 2000: 179). What is particularly relevant here is the understanding that instead of magically uniting under the banner of 'Indianness', the individual identity, whether it is defined by the name of 'expatriate', 'immigrant', 'transnational', 'postcolonial', 'second generation' and so forth, should not be 'ex-nominated' for the sake of a collective, hegemonic national identity. Similarly, it can be said that the 'politics of identity' in *The Namesake* is not completely wrapped up in the nationalist politics of the Indian bourgeoisie, either here in the diaspora or back at home. Instead of girding in Gandhi's 'loin cloth', the Indian immigrant, the educated bourgeois, is expressing his identity by wrapping himself in Gogol's 'overcoat'.

TRAUMA, MEMORY AND NAME

The novel begins with an epigraph from Gogol's famous short story 'The Overcoat': 'The reader should realise himself that it could not have happened otherwise, and that to give him any other name was quite out of the question.'[2] The premise of the story is based upon the decision of Gogol's parents, Ashima and Ashoke, to postpone the decision of naming their first baby. The decision to name later is due to a simple fact that they are awaiting a letter from the baby's great-grandmother which contains two names, one for a boy and the other for a girl. These names have not been revealed to anyone. In Ashima's family, it is a tradition for the grand-mother to choose the name of the newborn in her family. Thus, Ashoke and Ashima decline to fill out the birth certificate form in deference to the letter that was supposed to arrive soon. The hospital, however, will not allow the release of the patient and the baby without the couple signing the name of the baby on the birth certificate. Despite their protestation to the hospital staff that they are waiting for the baby's name to arrive from India and thus they cannot name him yet, they are forced to give him a name, and Ashoke, the father, chooses Gogol, his favorite Russian author.

The Naming Ceremony, *Namakaran Samskara* in Sanskrit, absent in the novel and in the film (like all cultural loss in a foreign land), is replaced by an absent letter.[3] Unlike Derrida's *la carte postale*, Ashoke's grandmother's letter that contains the secret name(s) of the baby does not arrive until the end of the film. Instead something of an extraordinary nature takes place in *The Namesake*. The father or the father's law, or name, crystallised in the name of Gogol, is privileged over the (grand)mother's law, the mother's name. The relationship between the law and the name, the logogram, the letter or symbol that represents the word, the name, is deferred, delayed, in its arrival. How do we read this letter, sort of providentially delayed, mysteriously absent, forever traveling and never reaching its destiny? Just like any other word which can never reach or exhaust itself in only one meaning? The infinite possibility of names in this letter is a threat to the father's legacy, which has acquired a completely transformed meaning. The father and son trade a secret in the form of a covenant to which the name of Gogol bears both testimony and responsibility. The fact that the 'letter' never comes to its proper destination as opposed to the forgotten 'book', the gift, that is eventually found and accepted by the son, clearly establishes the destined role of a father's command.

One must also take into account as to how the philology and etymology of the proper noun of Gogol appears in figural as well as referential (i.e. peformative) terms. The name of Gogol is presented as an overarching metaphor, like the bridges (Hawrah Bridge in Kolkata and Queensboro Bridge in New York) in the film, that spans the two continents. As a marked and loaded signifier, this 'ur-phenomenon' – Gogol – is both the name and the story. The traumatic moment (a near fatal train accident experienced by Ashoke) marks the presence of the book (literally a lifesaver) whose author's name stamps its signature on this terrifying moment that will haunt him for the rest of his life. The struggle is explicitly formulated upon the consequences of a name that a father gives to his son.

The son, Gogol (Kal Penn), now in college where he is forced to confront his namesake in a literature class, finds his own name eviscerating ('each time the name is uttered, he quietly winces' (Lahiri 2003: 91)),

Fig. 18 Ashoke reading 'The Overcoat' in the train just prior to the accident.

thoroughly humiliating, for it reminds him of his namesake, who starved himself to death in self-exile. 'It dismays him that his parents chose the weirdest namesake. Leo or Anton. He could have lived with. Alexander, shortened to Alex, he would have greatly preferred. But Gogol sounds ludicrous to his ear, lacking dignity or gravity. What dismays him most is the irrelevance of it all' (*Ibid.*: 76). To him, the name not only signifies the utter ridiculousness of his existence as someone who he is not ('that's not really me'), but also denies him the possibility of assimilation and anonymity because of the constitutive difference, that is, the inferential and referential claims, of his proper name from any other common noun. To a young and impressionistic Gogol, his name sounds ridiculous, idiotic, and perhaps even marks the end of any possibility of future romantic entanglements. He can only blame his parents for afflicting him with a 'weird' name (signifying absolute otherness) that he cannot bear to bear. The conflict, the generational conflict, which is also the conflict of cultures within a culture, is played out in the struggle for the son to accept his father's heritage which is symbolised in the name. The name Gogol, therefore, signifies both displacement and trauma, yet it also has a provisional status of a 'pet name' that has become permanent, and it cannot be subsumed by the 'good name' that one inherits from the traditional *Namakaran* (Naming Ceremony) ritual deeply rooted in Hindu culture.

In the Hindu/Bengali tradition the identity of an infant is not necessarily officially established until the child enters social life, i.e. school. The naming process in Hinduism is both culturally and sociologically different from most European and American cultures in which the infant's name is officially consecrated in the birth certificate. In India, the author Lahiri writes, 'names can wait' (2003: 25). Most parents normally take their time before naming their children.

It wasn't unusual for years to pass before the right name, the best possible name, was determined ... Besides, there are always names to tide one over: a practice of Bengali nomenclature grants, to every single person, two names. In Bengali the word for pet name is *daknam*, meaning, literally the name by which one is called by friends, family and other intimates, at home and in other private, unguarded moments. Pet names are a persistent remnant of childhood, a reminder that life is not always so serious, so formal, so complicated. They are a reminder, too, that one is not all things to all people. They all have pet names ... Every pet name is paired with a good name, a *bhalonam*, for identification in the outside world. Consequently, good names appear on envelopes, on diplomas, in telephone directories and in all other public places ... Good names tend to represent dignified and enlightened qualities ... Pet names have no such aspirations. Pet names are never recorded officially, only uttered and remembered. Unlike good names, pet names are frequently meaningless, deliberately silly, ironic and even onomatopoetic. (*Ibid.*: 25–6)

The Namesake traces the journey of the pet name Gogol – a provisional or supplemental name – as it is transformed into the 'good name' and to the ultimate revelation 'that to give him any other name was quite out of the question', as Nikolai Gogol wrote of his protagonist Akaky Akakyevich in 'The Overcoat'. But the political aspect of Lahiri's novel comes from her effort to wrest the power invested in the American culture to nominate, to name, the other as unnamable in its irreducible singularity. She names her protagonist Gogol, a name that signifies, to many, the very logos, the patronym, of modern literature. 'Remember, we all came from Gogol's Overcoat', reminds Ashoke to his son, the namesake of Gogol, on his birthday, lest he forgets 'the defining power of the name'.[4]

What is peculiar about the process of naming in *The Namesake* is that the name, a surname, has a certain disruptive potential within the normative naming process.[5] Now here instead of place or the name of the father or the place of the father's ancestry we have a supplanting/transplanting of Gogol that jettisons the first name with the surname. The first name has no authority, but it would be obviously impossible to designate a name like Gogol simply as *a* name, a pet name, given to a child. The supplanting of the legitimate paternal origin by the name of literary origin is the very act of subversion that the novel and the film are trying to perform. The name Gogol is a global sign of the events gathered around a singular crisis, a marking of the archetypal trace, from which both the film and the novel derive their sustenance. All beginnings and endings are ultimately realised, given a meaning and solace, in Gogol's name, in the name of Gogol. For Ashoke, every critical moment, every crisis, can be understood by thinking of Gogol and 'The Overcoat'. As if the answer to the trauma lies in the trauma itself. This trauma that is named after Gogol is the naming of the trauma, which leads to its own annihilation in memory. In other words, the significance of naming and narrating cannot be exaggerated in the discourse of memory, especially in the film.[6]

Nair's film is an exemplary cinematic adaptation of Lahiri's novel re-presenting a rich cross section of themes, issues and characters in the Indian diaspora, although some crucial details of Gogol's young adult life are missing in the film. Taking the name as the source of the narrative, the film depicts the problematic and vexed relationship between the first- and second-generation Indian immigrants struggling to maintain their independent cultural identity while at the same time being told to become invisible in the dominant culture. For example, when the furious son, Gogol, wants to confront local racists who have defaced his family surname Ganguli on the mailbox by spray painting it to 'Gangrene', while the family was away holidaying in India, the father, Ashoke, tells him to take no fur-ther notice. Complaining about such racially motivated action, in Ashoke's mind, would simply draw more attention to their already precarious and marginalised existence in the diaspora.

The film incorporates in itself some of the major problems and issues that are directly related to the South Asian population in the diaspora. It foremost engages with the difference between the immigrant experiences of first and second generations which can no longer be simply governed within the normative logic of homogeneity in the diaspora. The primacy accorded to the ontological connection, to the place of origin, defines the first order of immigrant, whose identity is rooted in the cultural and lin-guistic milieu of his/her home country. But that unity is radically ruptured by the arrival of the second generation whose continuity depends on this very separation from the country of origin and integration into the host culture of the first generation (see Hussain 2005).

The first generation of South Asian immigrants have not found it reason-able or even essential to assimilate within American culture. Their refusal to assimilate is not a sign of an ingrained prejudice against other cultural values, but is simply a matter of their preferring their own identities as

Indians and maintaining a closer relationship with their national culture and values. Apart from professional relationships in the workplace and in limited social spaces, American and Indian cultures remain blissfully apart. These moments are crucially highlighted in scenes of parties thrown in the traditional style by the Ganguli family which are mostly attended by an assortment of South Asian friends from MIT. Gogol's fiancé Maxim (Jacinda Barrett), an American, is completely left out and is baffled by the Indians sticking to their culture in her own country. What appears as a benign and playful curiosity, for Maxim, will soon be overcome by abject frustration and cultural isolation. She cannot fathom what Nikhil (Gogol's new adopted name) finds so intimate and close to him in this bizarre display of cultural difference.

The cleavage or lack of relationship of social and cultural form between the Indian diaspora and American society has changed in the last decade or so as many transnational generations of Indians, who are born and brought up in the United States, are now completely assimilated and yet not fully integrated into American society until they form matrimonial alliances with the latter. The easiest way for an Indian to enter the socio-cultural sanctum of an American family is through marriage. This is seen as a threat to 'authentic' Indian identity, a kind of mythology deconstructed in *Monsoon Wedding*, when an Indian woman teases an Indian NRI (Non-Resident Indian) living in Australia, who has fallen in love with her, by reminding him that she did make him into an 'Indian' after all. For Indians, matrimonial alliance with people from another country and culture is looked upon with a great sense of remorse and loss. It signifies a loss of identity and capitulation or seduction to the other as opposed to having remained faithful to one's own cultural and social values. This is clearly evident in the behaviour of Gogol's parents.

Devoid of history and identity, Ashoke (named after the great Mauryan King who ruled India from 273 to 232 B.C., and also a Sanskrit word meaning 'a man without mourning or grief') and his wife, Ashima (a name that signifies 'without borders'), live a life amidst an atmosphere of acute cultural isolation devoted to the fervent remembrance of the family and country left behind. The idea of assimilation only increases the fervour to never forget the family members and friends left behind, to continuously dwell in the memory of the happiness of life, the prelapsarian phase of life, before the catastrophe. One should realise that space and time intrude into a transnational life in a manner that is profoundly afflicted by the pain of separation from the loved ones now in a distant land, not because one was connected before being uprooted, but because uprootedness forges the strongest bond between the transnational subject and his/her history, which has now congealed and frozen into a memory closer to nostalgia.

Ashoke, it appears, neither belongs to the moment of the catastrophic memory before nor inherits the life after. His life signifies a cleavage, a tear, from the past into the future, where the present simply becomes a domain of memory. There are two things, or two kinds of traumas, to be specific, that we need to take into account: the fact that Ashoke is a diasporic subject, which entails a physical or spatial separation that defines the condition of an immigrant, and that he is also a victim of temporal loss that occurred after his accident. So, Ashoke is traumatised both spatially and temporally, whereas Ashima remains a disconsolate figure due to her traumatic separation from her parents rooted exclusively in the spatial dimesion and not the temporal loss. The father's secret trauma assumes an overt shame for his son in this complex interplay of intergenerational trauma. Gogol 'detests' the name that means everything to his father. An incident – in fact an accident, dedicated to the name of the renowned Russian writer – inexplicably surfaces in the form of intergenerational clash between the father and the son, between the name-giver and the named. Who has the authority to name the other? And what this intergenerational struggle among the transnationals reveals is a breach in identity of a self named after a memory and the lack of memory in the one who is named after the memory.

The name Gogol, in Nair's *The Namesake*, however, redefines the language of identity of the transnational community of the Indian diaspora in the United States in a manner that challenges the traditional mode of identification reserved for foreigners in an alien society. It signifies an irreducible otherness – the 'individual names are sacred, inviolable', says Lahiri (2003: 28) – because it is neither a Bengali name nor an American name, thus it names the very condition of the possibility of the second-generation immigrant who is neither an Indian nor an American (see Peaco 2004: 581). This condition, 'neither-just this/nor-just that', is often referred to in the contemporary discourse of disaporic studies within the framework of 'double consciousness', a term first coined by W. E. B. Du Bois in the *Atlantic Monthly* in 1897.[7] It has now been re-inscribed by postmodernist and cultural critics like Stuart Hall, Homi K. Bhabha, Paul Gilroy and James Clifford to denote a specific type of consciousness that aspires to move beyond essentialising notions such as 'ethnicity' and 'race' in order to celebrate the notions of hybridity, heterogeneity, identity fragmentation and (re)construction, double consciousness, fractures of memory, ambivalence, roots and routes, discrepant cosmopolitanism, multi-locationality and so forth (see Baumann 2000).

Could the name Gogol be also taken as a sign of a 'double consciousness' that 'rejects the "ontopology", "axiomatics" that conflates the ontology and topology and biology', as Derrida defines it, the mundane and facile discourse of cosmopolitanism?[8] Is it not the irreducible foreignness of the name – Gogol – in the American/Western hegemonic culture that exceeds the discourse of identity so commonly held in the narratives of origin and displacement, race, ethnicity, sexuality, and so forth, which cannot be synthetically or dialectically resolved? Gogol, divided into English 'Go', to move, and 'gol', in Hindi and also in Bengali, meaning 'round', as in the earth or the planet being round. In other words, the name Go-gol, as a hyphenated and hybridised word, could also mean to go around the world. 'See the world … you will never regret it' were the last words uttered by the Bengali businessman Ghosh, whose name easily rhymes with 'ghost', a revenant who spoke reverently of England and America on the train to Ashoke, just before the fatal accident. Ashoke's real departure from India began the day he commemorated his life to Gogol in both figurative and literal senses. Ashoke identifies with Gogol on multiple levels and feels 'a special kinship with Gogol'. Aside from being his favourite author and the saviour of his life, he finds in Gogol a reflection of his own exilic life. 'He spent most of his adult life outside his homeland. Like me', asserts Ashoke when confronted by his son.

Being at home does not always mean truly being at home. Gogol is not at home in his name. But by *cutting* his name from himself, he becomes more attached to it. Ironically, this act binds him even more to the name than before. Like the cinematic 'cut', the name is marked on the body as both presence and absence. Gogol's identity, too, belongs more firmly to the name he 'cuts' loose with the stroke of a pen. The newly adopted name, Nikhil, the foreskin of his new identity, seems as unreal to him as his new life without his old name. What he misses now, after he has legally changed his name, is the former life, a life that he shared with his family. With the arrival of the new name, the old name has simply become a memory of his old life that he cannot access. As he cuts himself legally adrift from his original given name, Gogol, he is more drawn to it in its absence, much like the transnational who pines for the country that s/he has voluntarily left behind. The parallelism cannot be more acute.

In many senses the novel/film challenges the idea of name changing, a right that Lahiri admits is the 'right of every American citizen'. So what is the falsehood in our true identity if the name by which we are known is replaced by another? Does one become another person after the name change? Should we take it for granted that Gogol does not exist after he has been officially and authoritatively replaced by Nikhil? The banishment or exile of Gogol sets the intergenerational trauma of transnational historical subject in play. Gogol's identity is inherently linked to the name by which he is identified by his family (in which the roots of his father's identity are secretly buried). By casting his name Gogol out of his life like an old worn-out overcoat out of embarrassment, reciprocating Akaky Akakyevich's embarrassment and shame toward his tattered overcoat, Gogol symboli-cally banishes his father's sign from his signature.

The postcolonial (with or without the hyphen) multicultural identity in Nair's film works from within the logocentric patricidal logic (phylo-genetic model in Freud) of the literary and filmic narrative that attempts to de-centre and thus re-place the symbolic father (Gandhi, Nehru and oth-ers) by the signifying father (Gogol). The *neme* of Gogol in *The Namesake* is governed by a 'sign creating activity' that produces multiple resonances and textual readings. Displacement and patricidal forces operate here: the logos of natural father, symbolised in primal father figure (represented by Gandhi, symbolising the ancient, or Nehru, symbolising the modern, India), is replaced by the ghost (once again we must remember 'The Overcoat') and its trace, the signature, the haunting, of the literary father, the exilic father. As opposed to symbolising a mythical consciousness enshrined in the image of eternal India, the name, in *The Namesake*, as a 'sign creating activity', aligns itself to a thinking memory that 'thinks in name', as Hegel reminds us:

> The name is ... the thing (*Die Sache Selbst*) ... In the name, reproductive memory has and recognises the thing, and with the thing it has the name, apart from intuition and image. The name, as giving an existence to the con-tent in intelligence, is the externality of intelligence to itself; and the inwar-dising or recollection of the name, i.e. of an intuition of intellectual origin, is at the same time a self-externalisation to which intelligence reduces itself on its ground. The association of the particular names lies in the meaning of

the features sensitive, representative or cogitant – series of which the intelligence traverses as it feels, represents or thinks. Given the name lion, we need neither the actual vision of the animal, nor its image even: the name lion alone, if we understand it, is the unimaged simple representation. We think in names. (1971: 219–20)

NAME AND MEMORY

In his classic essay, 'Sign and Symbol in Hegel's *Aesthetics*', Paul de Man introduced us to Hegel's thought, in *Encyclopedia of Philosophical Sciences* (1830), on the relationship between the name and memory. The importance of the name for Hegel remains consistent with his pedagogical theory of learning and especially learning by heart. In thinking through the name, we must also not lose sight of the sign-creating activity which produces words and names. Name, first of all, is the synthesis of content and meaning – intuition and idea – and is unfolded in the sign.

Hegel devotes sections 452–4 of *Encyclopedia* to recollection (*Erinnerung*) and sections 461–4 to memory and remembrance (*Gedächtnis*). The middle sections, from 455–60, deal with imagination, with general representations of ideas and images in terms of signs. The first stage is referred to by Hegel as recollection or *Er-Innerung* (inwardisation), as he sometimes writes it with a hyphen, which is often translated as 'interiorising memory' that 'consists in the involuntary calling up of a content which is already ours' (de Man 1982: 772). This stage of *involuntary* recalling or *Erinnerung* in Hegel is, according to de Man, 'rather like' Proust's *mémoire involontaire*. And since de Man equates *Erinnerung* with *mémoire involontaire* in Proust, it is natural that *Gedächtnis* is similarly identified with *mémoire volontaire*. For Proust, we must acknowledge, the significance of *mémoire involontaire* is definitely of a higher order than *mémoire volontaire* in aesthetic representations. De Man's argument consists in establishing that memory in the name of *Gedächtnis*, which he explains as 'thinking memory', is always in relation to the future, whereas recollection (*Erinnerung*) maintains itself within the confinement of the past

The dialectical relationship of inside and outside, of *Gedächtnis* and *Erinnerung*, of thinking memory and interiorising recollection, for Hegel, is performed within the insignia of the name. *Gedächtnis*, the thinking memory, which functions more or less like a technique or machine, as *tekhnè*, is regarded a higher form of memory than its counterpart *Erinnerung*, the memory that is normally associated with subjectivity, the interiorised memory in which the other is made a part of us, the 'metonymic' form of memory. Memory as the name – within the Hegelian dialectic – is primarily directed against *Erinnerung*, that interiorisation of memory which cancels what is outside of memory – which in the name of memory is always already in advance, 'in memory of' – and preserves what is already inside.

The distinction between recollection and memory in Hegel can truly be appreciated in the light of his most important distinction between sign and symbol. Hegel aligns recollection with symbol, while the latter, he explicitly announces, forms the transition to memory. For Hegel, the symbolic, the natural, the allegorical are 'subjective elements' which give themselves 'over to the objectivity in the image and thereby authenticate' themselves (1971: 212). And this 'subjective element' is still conditioned by the relatively less free symbolic imagination because of its grounding in natural and anthropological elements. The sign, on the other hand, has a privilege of not having a natural or subjective correspondence to its signification, but rather, must be constructed or 'learned' from the very beginning. In the general economy of the sign-producing activity, one learns by 'deleting the connotation which properly and naturally belongs to it, and conferring on it another connotation as its soul and import' (*Ibid.*: 213). The 'sign-creating activity' is aptly named by Hegel as 'productive memory', which in ordinary life is often used as interchangeable and synonymous with 'remembrance (recollection)'.

The true relationship between name and memory reaches a point, in Hegel, where the distinction between the two, which we initially surmised to be sign and symbol, is determined by the activity of thinking which closely resembles the functioning of a machine. According to Hegel, the distinction between meaning and name is abolished in mechanical memory because intelligence or thought is 'at once that external objectivity and the meaning' whereas the latter 'no longer has a meaning', i.e. a meaning that is independent of objectivity. Memory is that which is bereft of itself, a 'memory without memory', as Derrida calls it (1989: 65). It is the highest stage of remembering (learning) by names or rote, where the word and the meaning are no longer separate but united in the 'function of *thought*, which no longer has a *meaning*, i.e. its objectivity is no longer severed from the subjective, and its inwardness does not need to go outside for its existence' (Hegel 1971: 223). In thought meaning no longer has a meaning, because it is the meaning. Similarly in mechanical memory there is no interiorising memory, there is no recollection, for the names are already bereft of any significations.

'We *think* in names'. *Gedächtnis*, the thinking memory, which thinks, as Derrida says, in 'the name of memory' and [in] the 'memory of the name' forms the basis of some of Derrida's most profound interrogations of this subject, in works such as *On the Name*, *Acts of Literature* ('Aphorism Countertime') and *Memoires for Paul de Man*, to name only a few. In 'The Art of Memoires', Derrida tells us that '"memory" is first the name of something [which] preserves an essential and necessary relation with the possibility of the name, and what in the name assures preservation. It has to do with the very *possibility and preservation* of names' (1989: 49). Similarly, in this case, Gogol, too, functions as a name that preserves the memory of the catastrophe (the interiorised (*Erinnerung*)/terrorised memory, the traumatised memory) and, at the same time, it is also a form of *Gedächtnis*, the 'essence' of remembering, that it, the name, signifies in the future. Thus Gogol at once is both the sign of the trauma and recollection of the trauma that negates or voids the interiorised and subjectivised memory of the past by sublating (*aufhebt*) it in the memory that opens up to the future in which all events are recalled: 'in memory of'.

The ineradicable alterity of Gogol's name cannot be ruptured by a disavowal for it contains the deepest semblance of mourning that all names strictly represent. In a profound sense, the name reminds us that each invocation of the name is inexplicably related to the anteriority of mourning and memory. We remember in name what cannot be truly present in real life (death marks an absence); the latter in its infinite scattering and fragmentation can only be inadequately and provisionally re-membered in the name. One only comes back to oneself through a detour; in Gogol's case, this detour is already symbolised in his father's choice of his name that traces the detour of memory: to be named after someone, to be that someone who bears the name.[9] The name as a trace, a memory, of what he lost and what he never indeed even had, his own name came to him via the detour of his father who named him after his favourite author, which has now acquired a larger significance in his life for it is now both the name and the memory of the name. This double helix of name, the double bind of language that all names conceal and reveal, constitutes the primacy and anteriority of response and responsibility to the name. The name lives leaving death behind, and is always responsible, i.e. performative, to its name. The name continues, it goes on, it 'survives' the bearer, but it also reminds us that, as Derrida says, it is always from the outset 'in memory of'; 'we cannot separate the name of "memory" and the "memory" of the name; we cannot separate the name and memory' (1989: 49).

Gogol's identity crisis begins with his name, a name that inscribes otherness in its very presence. The film/novel is about Gogol ultimately coming to terms with his name, i.e. his irreducible otherness. It is a search for an identity that begins with an accidental pet name that is rejected by the bearer only to be mourned later in his life as his true identity. At the end of the film Gogol accidentally finds the hardbound volume of 'The Overcoat', a birthday present from his father, as a testimony of memory to the debt of memory. The thinking memory, the memory that thinks in name, *Gedächtnis*, leads to the thinking of the name in terms of his father's memory and thus becomes indebted to it. It leads to his origin via this detour of remembering through the act of reading that joins him to his father's memory; it becomes the memory of his father. His name Gogol is now fully realised because it is now both a name and a memory, both *Gedächtnis* and *Erinnerung*. The father's journey was interrupted by the near fatal railway accident and the trauma of the accident that continued throughout his life; this traumatic journey will ultimately be given a proper name in his son's journey through his own life that will be ultimately commemorated and remembered in the name and the memory of the name of the other. It is only after Gogol has achieved the tracing of his father's life in his name that his name signifies the memory of his father. Without knowing the secret of his name as a trace of his father's memory, a catastrophe, Gogol unwittingly separates his existence from his family's and embarks on a life with few reminiscences of his childhood and his parents' struggle to come to terms with a world that refuses to allow their memories to be a part of the socio-cultural narrative of the United States. As long as Gogol is alienated from his memory he will also be alienated from his family.

What begins as a 'gift of death' in the past becomes the 'gift of life' in the present. What leaves the body of the nation comes back in the name of memory of a catastrophe, the returning that is forever deferred but always a possibility. There is a memorable scene in the film; it follows a rather awkward domestic moment, the primal scene of culture clash (the Indian mother notices Gogol's American girlfriend Maxim holding hands with him, just a glance that speaks voluminously of the cultural schism) between Maxim and Gogol's Indian family. The father, Ashoke, asks his son Gogol to accompany him to buy ice cream from a store. As they are driving, Ashoke reveals the story of his accident, shown to us in a flashback (the supreme trope of memory in film) to Gogol, the origin of his name.

> Ashoke: 'I want to tell you something.'
> 'What?' Gogol asks.
> 'It's about your name.'
> 'My name?'
> 'Gogol. There is a reason for it, you know,' his father continues.
> 'Right, Baba. Gogol is your favourite author. I know.'

And then the father narrates in exquisite detail the story of the night that almost took his life. We see a hand clutching the title pages of the Gogol book, whose rustling was overheard and noticed by a rescue team who untangled his body from a mass of steel and brought him to the hospital. 'Is that what you think of me?' Gogol asks him. 'Do I remind of you

Fig. 19 Ashoke to his son Gogol: 'I want to tell you something'.

of that night?' 'Not at all.' His father says eventually. 'You remind me of everything that followed' (Lahiri 2003: 123–4).

THE GIFT OF NAME

It is perhaps tempting to approach the film from a psychoanalytical angle by describing the accident as a primal scene in the life of the protagonist. But it does not hold water. Somehow reading Freud into in this context seems improbable. The film resists Western theoretical frameworks pertinent to its discourse, which requires a different set of approaches, based on Indian cultural context. But the theory behind trauma is not a space- and culture-bound phenomenon, for it is a condition that happens in both collective and individual lives. That by revealing the secret behind Gogol's name the father is somehow wishing to absolve himself of the guilt of his own survival is a possibility that cannot be completely ruled out in this case. But this moment of revelation for Gogol that he is named after an event which is intrinsically linked to the moment of his father's almost death and resurrection can only be grasped by him as a moment of great horror and terror, of death. The fact that he is linked to his father through a memory that haunts the latter forever is a disclosure that the son cannot truly comprehend. Thus he asks in the film, 'Is that what I remind you of? Of your death'? Ashoke's reply is not only enigmatic but a declaration of life embedded in his son's name, Gogol. In the film Nair improvises the scene by making Ashoke say that everyday since then has been a 'gift'. The conversation leads to the defining moment of Gogol's existence, which in a way is handed down to him, a gift of life from his father, who himself received it from the pages of Gogol's 'The Overcoat'.

The giving of the name exceeds the circulation of a gift that negates itself in return. It imposes itself as a double bind, a name that comes from a name, the originary and improved 'sign' in Hegel, but an iterable 'signifier' in Derrida that repeats itself with a difference, and the name that one gives in the name of the other is a non-returnable name to its origin. 'What is given – and this would also represent a kind of death – is not something, but goodness itself, a giving goodness, the act of giving or the donation of the gift', writes Derrida in *The Gift of Death* (1995c: 41). But this act of giving, this goodness of the gift, the source of it must remain 'inaccessible' to the donee. It is a gift that cannot be returned. The name, for Derrida, most of all signifies the primacy of response. One responds to one's name in responsibility to the other, in mourning to the other, who is no longer with us, and who can no longer respond but only in the 'other' way, in its name.

In Gogol's name lives the other, which he cannot bear to identify with. This is the continuous source of his trauma and until the other is banished from the self the self teeters on self-destruction. But ironically, after Gogol has dispelled the ghost of his name who had snatched his identity like his namesake's overcoat, he starts to feels an uncanny melancholia for the loss of his name much akin to the loss of a dear one; he begins to mourn the loss of his name. Reading the book, Gogol's last act in the film, is an act of countersignature, which itself can only be understood in terms of a response that articulates itself in the double affirmative that says 'yes' to the work, and again 'yes this work was there before me, without me' (Derrida 1992: 70). The iterability of the name makes the possibility of the necessary repetition entailed in any word that can be 'experienced as meaningful', which is also at the same time a condition in which the name can never be exactly repeated, 'since it has no essence that could remain unaffected by the potentially infinite contexts ... into which it could be grafted' (*Ibid.*).

In a slightly different but similar context, the name Gogol is a word whose iterablilty is always already preconditioned by the possibility of changes that keeps it open, a condition necessary for it to undergo in the infinite repetition that each 'countersignature', that is, reading, testifies to in the presence of writing, of name.

The very condition of the possibility of the gift is intricately related to some secret. If there is a secret then by its very nature it cannot be intuited in the Kantian sense, it cannot be revealed to the 'squinted gaze' (Derrida 1995a: 30). For the very nature of a secret, as Derrida reminds us, depends on the fact that it is disclosed as a secret. A secret never disclosed is no secret. Whereas a gift known is a gift returned (re-gifting, for instance); it is only when the gift is a secret that it is seldom acknowledged or returned. Thus Derrida says that 'a gift that could be recognised as such in the light of day, a gift destined for recognition, would immediately annul itself. The gift is the secret itself, if the secret itself can be told' (Derrida 1995a: 29–30). Ashoke, just prior to his death, reveals the secret of his son's name, the source of his name, that the name Gogol constitutes his existence more than any other name, that he cannot be separated from his name.

Gogol's self analysis begins after his father's death. For Gogol, the death of his father breaks the specular narcissism of his self in search of a memory that is bound with the secret of his name, in the patronym of Gogol. The significance of his name now seems to have absolute bearing to his father's death, and a loss that can only be recovered by going back to the source of his trauma and memory, to the 'The Overcoat', to his namesake. The name, a proper noun, is a word, 'pure language', or 'untranslatable', that differs from itself through the 'spacing', in its iterability, by a trace, of what comes before, the name, and of what comes after, memory.

This 'spacing' of the transnational is constantly repeated and recalled into being through the narratives of 'journey' and 'separation' in the cultural production of differences, in the novels and films of diasporic writers and filmmakers like Lahiri and Nair. It is impossible to mourn what is simply inside as interiorised memory. But *Gedächtnis*, the thinking memory which 'thinks in name', in the exteriority of 'sign', is the other name of writing, as Derrida has demonstrated in countless pages of his writings, associated with both exile and forgetting. Without the anteriority of forgetting, 'the forgetting of forgetting', there will be no remembering.[10]

The last scene of the film partakes in the poetic discourse of prosopopeia by presenting (through Gogol's double flashbacks of his father) the absent father addressing his son via a command 'to remember this day'. De Man has described the figure of prosopopoeia in the allegory as 'the very figure of reader and of reading' (1979: 33). By taking up the book of Gogol in the end, the son, Gogol, acknowledges the metonymic relationship to the memory of his father; the book is part of his father's memory which is passed on to the son in an allegorical mode as opposed to the historical mode privileged by the other discourse of transnationalism: the discourses of neo- and postcolonialism that I am unable to pursue here.[11] The story of 'The Overcoat', therefore, not only stands in an allegorical/metonymic relationship to the memory of his father's story but is also a part of Gogol that Gogol must realise in the otherness and outsidedness of his being, in the 'exteriority' of his name. Gogol's return to his cultural roots signifies a return to the origin of the name – the translation of 'nameless in names; a translation of the mute into sonic' – to the trauma, and not a place (Benjamin 1978: 325). For the purpose of human language is to call things by their appointed name, because, as Benjamin tells us, 'language itself is not perfectly expressed in things themselves'; things are imperfect because they are 'denied the pure formal principle of language – sound' (*Ibid.*: 321). Through sound, by translating the 'mute into sonic', man establishes an immaterial, symbolic community with nature which is communicated through the name.

'The name vanishes in sound', says Hegel. The thinking memory, the Hegelian philosophy of memory, functions more efficiently and deliberately when inwardising (*Erinnerung*) fails to materialise. Gogol's memory of his father is no longer an inwardising memory, the symbolic grasp, that keeps the other in us, inside us, as a part of us, a part of our history, an interiorised mourning, but a thinking memory (*Gedächtnis*) that is open to the outside, that is bereft of memory.

CONCLUSION

One of the tasks of this essay has been to trace how the name of Gogol dwells in the margin, in the supplement, and in the trace of a father's life that the son will discover only after he has forfeited the appellation for a more acceptable 'anglicised' one (although not too far an echo of the celebrated Russian author's first name, Nikolai). Nikhil (a classic Indian or Bengali name) – or Nick, for short – is exchanged for Gogol. By legally changing his name from Gogol to Nikhil, he severs his present life from its transnational roots in favour of an assimilated existence that also marginalises his intimate horizon of family and friends. As Gogol becomes the hybridised 'Nick', he embarks upon a life that takes him away from his transnational family into an American arena where his past has no consequence. His family is simply a family like any other family, as all families are in America. The traumatic existence of his parents and their struggle not to assimilate and remain different (the struggle of the first generation), which is to say remain identical to themselves, in the host country loses its historical significance and becomes more or less an ever present source of embarrassment to the second generation. The intergenerational clash of culture opens up a broader and more heterogeneous formulation of the meaning of the word diaspora.

The Namesake is dedicated 'to the memory of' Mira Nair's parents, and to all parents who sacrifice their lives for their children. But most importantly it is dedicated, consecrated, to the name of Gogol, the storyteller. 'The man who gave you his name, from the man who gave you your name' reads the annotation on the title page of the hardbound volume of *The Short Stories of Nikolai Gogol*, a gift from the father to his son on his birthday. The

Fig. 20 Ashoke's annotation on the title page of *The Short Stories of Nikolai Gogol*.

father gave the son a name that he himself received from the other.

So what is in this giving of what one does not have? The name signifies the power of language whose secret can only be disclosed through its creative possibilities. Who can forget Benjamin's musings on the power of divine language which is communicated to us through the incantation of names?[12] The film is devoted to the creative and restorative power of the name. Nair closes the film by taking recourse in the allegorical (by emphasising the constitutive category of temporality, i.e. human finitude), the irreconcilable and inconsolable sign forever adrift and always already displaced, like the grandmother's letter that never arrives at its destination, to mourning and prosopopoeia, as opposed to the symbolic totality of the historical fable, which it nonetheless is, for what is story but a way of telling the story that some people do and the others do not?

NOTES

1 This phenomenon of educated youth leaving their country for jobs abroad is known in India as the 'Brain Drain'. A great number of highly educated Indians – doctors, engineers, professors, scientists, and so forth – left India for the United Kingdom or the United States in the late 1960s, a period of intense unemployment and economic stagnation, although the fact is that a very marginal, miniscule percentage of Indians have settled in America, a mere 4.3 per cent of total graduates in India (checked in year 2000). The perception indicates that it has a huge impact on the Indian psyche.

2 The epigraph is absent in the film.

3 *Namkaran* is the traditional Hindu practice of naming the baby child. *Nama* means 'name' and *karana* means 'to make, to effect'. The naming ceremony depends on the culture, religion, rituals and education of the family; the *Namakaran* is thus an important *Samskara* (rite) in the life of a Hindu, and people consult elders and priests for naming their baby.

4 See the dust jacket of the book *The Namesake* (Lahiri 2003).

5 There are various arts of permutation and combination that signify the presence of a surname in the selection. In some instances, people coin a suitable name from a combination of the parents' names. In certain communities, the first child is named after the paternal grandparent; in others, the first son is given the same name as the father. Sometimes, the baby is named after the *nakshatra*, or star, of its birth. The child could also be named after the family deity or guru. The father leans towards the baby's right ear and whispers its chosen name.

6 For a brilliant reading of the relationship between memory and narration, see Caruth 1996b: 25–6.

7 The concept of 'double consciousness' first made it appearance in an article by Du Bois, 'Strivings of the Negro People', in 1897 in *Atlantic Monthly*. He defined it as 'this sense of always looking at one's self through the eyes of others, of measuring one's soul by the tape of a world that looks on in amused contempt and pity' (1995: 2).

8 Cited in Dayal 1996: 46.

9 'To name and to cause a name to disappear is not necessarily contradictory. Hence the extreme danger and the extreme difficulty there is in talking about the *effacement* of names ... very often to inscribe the name is to efface the bearer of the name' (Derrida 1995b: 390; emphasis added).

10 See Sinha 2005.

11 Postcolonial theory, on the other hand, implies that 'colonialism' is over. It emphasises hybridity, ambivalence and mimicry, the state of being in between. It explores the spaces of subalternity and feminism. Yet postcolonial theory, in emphasising the post-, risks obscuring 'the deformative traces of colonialism in the present' (Shohat & Stam 1994: 40). See also Williams & Chrisman 1994.

12 See Benjamin 1982: 318.

WORKS CITED

Baumann, M. (2000) 'Religions in the Disenchanted World', *Numen*, 47, 3, 313–37.

Benjamin, W. (1978) 'The Task of the Translator', *Illuminations: Essays and Reflections*, trans. H. Zohn. New York: Schocken.

_____ (1982) 'On Language as Such and on the Language of Man', in *Reflections: Essays, Aphorisms, Autobiographical Writings*, trans. E. Jephcott. New York: Harcourt Brace Jovanovich, 314–32.

Bhattacharjee, A. (1998) 'The Habit of Ex-Nomination: Nation, Woman, and the Indian Immigrant Bourgeoisie', in S. D. Dasgupta (ed.) *A Patchwork Shawl: Chronicles of South Asian Woman in America*. New Brunswick, NJ: Rutgers University Press, 165.

Caruth, C. (1996a) *Literature and the Enactment of Memory (Duras, Resnais, Hiroshima mon amour)*. Baltimore: Johns Hopkins University Press.

_____ (1996b) *Unclaimed Experience: Trauma, Narrative, and History*. Baltimore: Johns Hopkins University Press.

Dayal, S. (1996) 'Diaspora and Double Consciousness', *The Journal of the Midwest Modern Language Association*, 29, 1, 46–62.

De Man, P. (1979) *Allegories of Readings: Figural Language in Rousseau, Nietzsche, Rilke, and Proust*. New Haven, CT: Yale University Press.

_____ (1982) 'Sign and Symbol in Hegel's Aesthetics', *Critical Inquiry*, 8, 4, 761–75.

Derrida, J. (1989) *Memoires For Paul de Man*, trans. Cecile Lindsay, Jonathan Culler, Eduardo Cadava, and Peggy Kamuf. New York: Columbia University Press, 65.

_____ (1992) *Acts of Literature*, David Atridge (ed). New York: Routledge.

_____ (1995a) *On the Name*, ed. T. Dutoit, trans. D. Wood *et al.* Stanford: Stanford University Press.

_____ (1995b) *Points...: Interviews, 1974–1994*, trans. P. Kamuf *et al.* Stanford, California: Stanford University Press.

_____ (1995c) *The Gift of Death*, trans. D. Willis. Chicago: Chicago University Press.

Du Bois, W. E. B. (1995) *The Souls of Black Folk*. New York: Penguin Books.

Gogol, Nikolai V. (1992) *The Overcoat and other short stories*. New York: Dover Publications.

Hegel, G. W. F. (1971) *Encyclopedia of Philosophical Sciences* [1830], trans. W. Wallace. Oxford: Clarendon Press.

Hussain, Y. (2005) *Writing Diaspora: South Asian Women, Culture and Ethnicity*. Hampshire: Ashgate.

Lahiri, J. (2003) *The Namesake*. New York: Houghton Mifflin Company.

Peaco, E. (2004) '*The Namesake* by Jhumpa Lahiri', *The Antioch Review*, 62, 3, Summer. Online. Available at: http://www.jstor.org/stable/4614714 (accessed 20 January 2009).

Schalkwyk, D. (2000) 'Derrida, Apartheid, and the Logic of the Proper Name', *Language Science*, 22, 2, 176–91.

Shohat, E. and R. Stam (1994) *Unthinking Eurocentrism: Multiculturalism and the Media*. London: Routledge.

Sinha, A. (2005) 'Forgetting to Remember: From Benjamin to Blanchot', *Colloquy: text theory critique*, 10, 22–41. Online. Available at: http://www.colloquy.monash.edu.au/issue010/sinha.pdf (accessed 10 January 2009).

Williams, P. and L. Chrisman (eds) (1994) *Colonial Discourse and Post-Colonial Theory: A Reader*. New York: Columbia University Press.

7. THE FUTURE AT ODDS WITH THE PAST: JOURNEY THROUGH THE RUINS OF MEMORY IN ALKINOS TSILIMODOS'S *TOM WHITE*

WARWICK MULES

Tom White (2004) tells the story of a white, middle class man's mental breakdown through disillusionment with the aims of life under corporate capitalism, and his subsequent journey of self-discovery, told as a kind of morality play that prophesises a future built out of the ruins of memory. In the allegorical mode, the film prefigures its future by showing us the trajectories that will and will not be taken through a series of vignettes in which Tom (Colin Friels), the film's hero, is tested for his worthiness as a human being and his potential as a 'new man'. This requires a complete re-evaluation of the ground on which life – not just his life, but life in general – is based; a *forgetting* that makes him live again, but in a new, affirmative way, rather than in the self-seeking mode of his past life. In showing us Tom's journey, the film enacts a series of dialectical images, to use Walter Benjamin's phrase, which crack open the smooth surface of corporate culture, exposing modern forms of capitalist production to the ruins that it leaves behind and upon which its projects are built. Memory in *Tom White* is not a theme but a mode of appearing inhabited by potential otherness. The non-resolvable dialectical structure of the narrative reveals a further level of filmic imagery in which the film gestures to its origin in silent film through the tableau scene. *Tom White* is thus a remembering of film's own pastness – its embeddedness in earlier film technology which is both present and erased in the very gesture of the film image. In this essay I explore this potential in *Tom White* (and by implication in all film) as film's allegorical presentation of its own materiality.

FIGURAL ANALYSIS

In its capacity to represent things and events, film offers an audiovisual world composed of figures unfolding in time and space, usually but not necessarily organised according to the causal logic of narrative. Gesture, action and speech are understood in terms of narrative teleology: what does this gesture, this action, contribute to the 'ends' of the film considered in terms of the way it 'represents' a state of affairs of the audiovisual world in the broadest possible terms?

Time and space are represented in terms of this state of affairs whose reality exists elsewhere, as if the characters and actions that we see on the screen have no motility or force *in themselves*, but simply provide a way of presenting something else – a fantasy world somewhere else, at some other time. This way of understanding film elides film's specific presenting of itself *as film*: its expression of audiovisual material as a configuration of filmic 'essence'.

To understand film in its filmic presentation is to engage in the figural economy of film. A figure is not a character, but a material element that obeys the logic of the film's material 'becoming'. As William Routt has indicated in his commentary on the film criticism of Nicole Brenez, figural analysis is concerned with the 'complex bundles of sense' that appear in the 'figurative economy' of the film, including characters not as individual agents of narrative action, but as bearers of a prefiguration that needs to be fulfilled: 'the figure's fulfilment ultimately dictates all of its prior existence. The figure is constructed by its unknown future, not motivated by its past' (2000).

Figural analysis is not concerned with the causal logic of narrative, but with transformations of figuration that produce the story world as a matrix of prefigured filmic material. Causality implies retrospective knowledge of cause and effect built up through the articulation of images that accord with a predetermined totality. I can make sense of the actions of a character, if I already know what that character is like from other scenes, and where she fits in the overall plot. The spectator needs to *know* this through retrospection. Causality is a matter of human cognition involving categories of time and space in the mind of the cognising agent. However, transformation is a different matter altogether. Transformation is not related to causality, but to the process whereby one thing becomes another. In film, one image constantly dissolves into another, in a continual becoming of the space-time of film. Henri Bergson has proposed that human consciousness is itself cinematic, composed of a series of visual retentions and protentions through time, an idea taken up by Gilles Deleuze in his materialist concepts of the movement-image and the time-image, as pre-cognitive perceptions of 'flowing-matter' (1986: 59).[1]

The transformations seen in film are not narratives but exchanges of stored audiovisual material between anterior and posterior phases of an ongoing trajectory of becoming. This trajectory is not inside the narrative. Rather, it *is* the film as immanent figuration. In this case the transformation of images does not accord with a predetermined totality known through a retrospective cognition, but is itself the totality in the very act of its being presented, in the unfolding process of the audiovisual event that the film is. The spectator does not cognise a totality through reading causal events retrospectively; rather the spectator is *shown* the whole as the prefiguring of parts prospectively, as the foretelling of the future.[2]

It should be possible to follow the chain of audiovisual transforma-tions throughout films as a series of figurative becomings. Embedded in this trajectory are myriad gestures, rhetorical expressions, theatrical devices, fetish objects and modes of visual display which owe nothing to the narrative action. Rather they belong to a rhetorical scheme or 'system of figuration' felt as the 'bodily "palpitation"' (Schefer 1995: 26; 28) of their enigmatic presence within and beyond the narrative. Figural analysis thus has a hermeneutic dimension in the sense that it involves the reading of one thing in terms of another – as a prefiguring of what will come. As Routt (2000) reminds us, figural analysis is a form of hermeneutics involving the historical relation between signs and events, between the text's present condition of meaning and its capacity to draw on and summon forth the past through the power of signs. The figural opens up the historicity of the film text so that the event's past is also its 'coming to presence'. Reading the fig-ural is to read the past in the present; to read with the 'pastness' of the text as a prefiguring of something beyond what the text says in its normative, denotative mode of signification. All texts have figures, since all texts have a past, or at least point to a past as the very materiality of their signification.

The task of figural analysis is not limited to describing figures in film texts. Rather, it concerns the mapping of an abstract machine: a machine for writing in images, composed of various historically defined elements drawn synthetically into particular arrangements and assemblages that make film happen in the way that it does. Here, I am not referring to 'context', but to a genealogical tracing of the lineages and interconnectivi-ties between older and more recent image technologies, and their hybrid formations through time. Any given film text will exhibit interconnections with pre-existing modes (even if those modes have been pronounced obsolete), which define and control the potential that the film undertakes to make happen.

Figures foretell the future by the very fact of what they are, in the acts that they do and in the gestures that they make. From this perspective, films have to be read as allegories of their own futurity: they foretell what will happen by virtue of the very figurations that take place at the figurative level of the film. All films can be read in this way. Some films, however, signal their allegorical status in more obvious ways than others. In so doing, they provide ready access to the figurative economy of film as well to the exposed level of filmic material – the technological essence of film – carried forward and expressed in each and every film.

TOM WHITE

In turning to *Tom White*, the hollowness of life in corporate Australia is spelt out in the early part of the film. Tom is a draughtsman employed by a large project building company in Melbourne. The company is constructing an ultra-modern housing estate for wealthy Australians, but built over a toxic rubbish tip. Fed up with the company's lack of public virtue in selling the estate to unsuspecting buyers, Tom has a mental breakdown that releases a kind of critical vision where he sees through the contradictions inherent in the project, causing him to rebel against the company and his own complicity in the corporate vision that perpetuates false ideals. For instance, on his way to work (his last day, the day of his crack-up and sacking) Tom briefly visits an oriental pagoda in his backyard where he refills a bird feeder, looking hopefully to the sky for absent birds. Later in the film, Tom's wife logs on to his computer and comes across a giant Sim City-style image of a suburban environment covered with menacing bird-like figures. Apparently Tom has been spending his spare time working obsessively on this doom-laden image of simulated nature, as a rebellion against the work assigned to him by his company. This dystopic image of corporate vision taken to the extreme is juxtaposed with the hope that real birds will eventually arrive in Tom's own life: a prefiguring of the future through omens.

Tom's obsessiveness leads to violence. In one scene we see Tom confront a younger rival at the construction site office surrounded by huge piles of bulldozed dirt and puddles of muddy water. The violence of this confrontation, where Tom assails his rival with rolled up plans and verbal abuse, is inversely symptomatic of the violence inherent in the corporate world more generally, which exploits people through false promises and excludes those who do not fit in. In an ironic gesture, the film *shows* us the source of this violence, through the contradictory image of the ruined landscape juxtaposed against the name of the project 'Clearwater Springs' seen on a billboard at the entrance to the building site. These are 'dialectical images' as described by Benjamin. A dialectical image is, in fact, not one but two images juxtaposed in such a way that their contradictions clash violently, releasing an experience of absolute openness – a messianic sense of the future as absolutely other.[3] Absolute otherness cannot be experienced in terms of the same; it is not the end result of a prediction or calculation, but the dissolution of the same in the materiality of otherness experienced as ruination.

Tom is precipitated into the *demi monde* of the city, where society's cast-offs struggle to survive in a world of street hustling and welfare dependency, and where identity is no longer based on the possession of credit cards, but on social security numbers. Tom's life has reversed itself. He is no longer a member of the aspirational class for which the corporate elite builds dream houses, lifestyles and wealth; instead he has become part of the *detritus* of that very world. The violence implicit in the corporate world through exploitative practices becomes explicit in the mean streets of Melbourne where life is lived under the constant threat of the sinister forces of the black market, drug dealing and other forms of petty criminality that emerge when people are excluded from the main avenues of wealth creation.[4] Tom's journey is not that of an individual seeking his own self-identity, but that of an everyman whose identity as part of the dominant culture is exposed to 'bare life' (Agamben 1998: 4) in the struggle to survive. This world is not *nice*, but driven by violence, fear and suspicion. But in it are the seeds of wisdom, which Tom, in his journey, is required to learn.

On this journey Tom is *tested*, the true role of a mythic hero. We are told this obliquely through the allegorical structure of the film, which is signalled in various ways through a visual framing of elements that freezes the narrative action into a visual configuration, flooding the scene with figurative meaning. For instance, as Tom departs on his journey into the mean streets of the city, he walks under a railway bridge at exactly the same time as a train carrying his wife and children passes over it. At this moment the film configures the contradictory destinies of Tom and his wife, gesturing towards the future at odds with the past. Here, any sense of a conventional realist narrative is displaced into the allegorical mode, where the film prefigures its future by showing us the trajectories that will and won't be taken.

TABLEAU

The freezing of narrative action into a figuration in the 'train' scene and many others throughout the film indicates the work of a tableau structure. Tableaux are visual freezes of narrative action that point to meanings at another level. A brief digression into the early days of film is warranted here. In the stage melodrama of the nineteenth century, tableau images were composed by the actors freezing into complex gestures that pointed to some more general idea that the play was trying to convey. In their study of stage and film melodrama, Ben Brewster and Lea Jacobs describe the tableau as 'the literal embodiment of the idea that situations should take the form of pictures' (1997: 29). For instance in D. W. Griffith's early Biograph film *A Corner in Wheat* (1909), a tableau is formed, as Roberta Pearson writes, 'at the moment when the poor line up to buy the overpriced bread and become perfectly motionless' (1992: 39). This stillness contrasts with the 'frenzied activity' of those who control the production and distribution of wheat, a dialectical rendering of the contradictions between the powerful and the powerless in the social order. In this way, silent films were able to *show* the logic of power struggles directly to their audiences in film-specific terms rather than have it invoked through spoken dialogue.

Not all film tableaux are dialectical. But all films carry tableaux as part of their image repertoire. This can be traced historically, when film incorporated the stage gestures of melodrama in the silent era, and then, when film began to incorporate a style of visualising events by reflecting on the photogram, or the still image that lies at the heart of all photographic film.[5] In his concept of the 'third meaning' of film, Roland Barthes (1977) has indicated the presence of the stilled image spreading transversally throughout the film that resists and exceeds narrative action.[6] Seemingly minor elements of a scene (for instance, in Eisenstein's *Ivan the Terrible: Part One* (1944), the particular curl of an old woman's hair, the incongruously long nose of a young courtier) indicates the operation of a third or obtuse meaning in film, exceeding the communicative and symbolic registers of signification. Insofar as these elements do not contribute to the narrative but serve to arrest the eye, drawing it back into the material insignificance of the film, the third meaning is an asignifying trait of the capacity of film to appear as a technological achievement. Barthes calls this *signifiance*: the way the film signifies what it does through *direct* audiovisual presentation of filmic materiality (but perceived indirectly as an 'obtuse' meaning). At this level, the signifier – the material mark of the sign – neither communicates nor symbolises. Rather, it *reveals itself* as material expression that, in its very significance, resists signification. As the 'founding act of the filmic itself' (1977: 65) *signifiance* is the stillness of the photogram in resistance to movement and narrative teleology. This is, in effect, an *image of time* manifested directly by the film – the *arkhé* trace of the film's original instauration *as* film.

The figurative economy of film relies on an exposure of film to its third meaning, as a potential to regress into a still image. Through this potential, the moving image has the capacity to gesture against the grain of the narrative, as a stilled image of time. This capacity provides scope for filmmakers to enrich their narratives with images that obey their own logic of transformation. The film can then be stitched into its own skin through the repetition of images and image repertoires drawn from various sources (from other films, from art and photography and from within the same film) in such a way that they are not simply illustrations of what the narrative requires to explain its causal logic, but entirely independent visual and audiovisual transformations threaded through the film.[7]

We can see this borrowing from other image sources taking place in *Tom White*. In a striking novelty, the film draws some of its tableau images from the paintings of contemporary Australian artist, Stewart MacFarlane, whose neo-noir images of modern life have almost single-handedly reintroduced male desire into contemporary debates about sexuality and the human condition. One scene stands out in particular. Tom wanders into a fairground, passing by a carousel and various stalls selling drinks and confectionaries. Two young men fight over an air gun from a nearby shooting gallery, while the crowd passes by. This scene bears a striking resemblance to MacFarlane's painting *The Fair* (see overleaf) in the same way that D.W. Griffith's images of farmers sowing wheat in *A Corner in Wheat* (1909) borrows from Millet's *The Sower* (1850).

In this image, a worried young woman appears in the foreground with her hand to her head. In the background we see the usual iconography of the fair, including a Ferris wheel, dodgem cars, tents and stalls. A man stands waiting to be served at one of the stalls, while behind him two men are lifting an unconscious body (or are they in the middle of a bashing and robbery?).

Fig. 21 Stewart MacFarlane, *The Fair* (1990–92);
oil on canvas. Photograph supplied by the artist.

Immediately to the woman's right a man lies unconscious or asleep, arm extended towards a half-crushed drink can. Just behind the woman, a man in silhouette strides off with a clenched fist. Here we see the stilled image of violence as part of everyday life.

This image is picked up in an equivalent scene in *Tom White* and extended into an entire scene. The worried woman becomes ex-prostitute and drug addict Christine as the shooting gallery attendant and Tom's future lover, *confidante* and damsel in distress who Tom fails to rescue from the clutches of her former pimp (one of a series of failures, the consequence of Tom's inability to fully understand the singularity of their lives and the simple values that make life meaningful for them). The link between the MacFarlane painting and the film scene is made even more explicit when the camera holds on Christine standing in front of the Ferris wheel a little later in this episode, her concerned face duplicating that of the worried woman in the painting. From time to time Tom's particular pose and look bears a striking resemblance to the male figures in MacFarlane's paintings – a haggard, upright demeanour, face staring straight ahead with longish hair swept back – emphasising rigid masculine isolation. More generally, the *chiaroscuro* imagery of MacFarlane's paintings are paralleled by the visual style of *Tom White*, which bathes the mainly night time images in a fantastic aura of light and shadow. This is not the world of psychological realist drama, but the spectacle of good and evil played out in dramaturgical gestures.

The potential for film to freeze itself in its very movement – to stop itself in its tracks *while still moving* – is the ground of the film; its vanishing into material insignificance. The grounding of film in its own materiality is its figuration as a surface of *signifiance* – the very basis upon which film builds itself into narrative structure. All films display figuration at some level, however some films position themselves within the movement of figuration as the basis of storytelling. These films become allegories of their own materiality in a decisive manner. The story they tell is told through the structure of their own becoming as films.

MEMORY

In its allegorical drive to show the redemption of a good man through a series of trials and ordeals, *Tom White* also shows a debt to the filmic past. This debt is not acknowledged in terms of a retrospective gaze that seeks to recover something in the past that has now been lost. Rather, it is reinvested in a hermeneutic gesture where the past is brought forward as a material prefiguring of the future. *Tom White* is thus a film not about memory: how one remembers the past as a solution to the troubles and problems of the present, but about an absolute forgetting in which the relation between the present and the past is collapsed, thereby clearing an entirely new space in which to build a future. The film enacts forgetting, not as the loss of the past, but in terms of an *affirmation* of the collapsed present as prefigured future. This forgetfulness takes place as a *remembering* of film's *signifiance* – its grounding in the stillness of the photogram as a capacity to reveal images.

In *Archive Fever* Jacques Derrida writes of the origin as an *arkhé* or mnemonic archive, a place of remembering by destructive forgetting: 'the archive takes place at the place of originary and structural breakdown of the said memory' (1995: 11). The destruction of memory is not an annihilation but a *revelation* of remembrance in the ruin of self-forgetting; the breaching of memory's closure in forgetfulness, exposing it to an absolute outside as the very possibility of new experience and new memory. In *Difference and Repetition*, Gilles Deleuze writes of memory as a secondary activity of the mind that 'reconstitutes the particular cases as distinct, conserving them in its own "temporal space"' (1994: 71). Thus memory is a kind of forgetting that elides the place of the particular as an immediate retention by the mind, to constitute the particular in another place: 'The past is no longer the immediate past of retention but the reflexive past of representation' (*Ibid.*). The taking place of the particular as a present mental experience can only occur by forgetting its own taking place in favour of a representation that reflects itself into the past. Memory is thus founded on a paradox in which the past can only be reconstituted as a representation of the past from the point of view of a present that is already past. This suggests that time is a chiasmic collapse of anteriority and futurity operating at an *arkhé* level – an originary transtemporal time that *takes place* as an absolute opening. Deleuze identifies this transtemporal time with the past itself, as 'the synthesis of all time for which the present and the future are only dimensions' (*Ibid.*: 82).

The taking place of time is the affirmation of the singularity of the event of time in the absolute opening of futurity. In *Cinema I: The Movement-Image*, Deleuze refers to this opening as 'any space what so ever ... a space of virtual conjunction, grasped as a pure locus of the possible' (1986: 109). The place where this takes place is the archive as *arkhé* trace, as an originary taking place, which takes place not just once in a founding moment in the past, but as the onceness of the singularity of the very possibility of taking place, in each and every possible taking place, now and in the future. This is an affirmation of the taking place of the present time, but as a prefiguring of the future. To access the taking place of *arkhé* memory we need to employ a memory that does not operate by a simple forgetting, but by remembering the very taking place of memory itself as a forgetting of its own taking place. To do this is to expose memory to the ruins of its still-present past: the *signifiance* of the archive as figurative material that allegorises its own becoming.

ALLEGORY

As 'other-speaking', allegories are movements of figuration operating in the ruins of subjective experience opened to absolute possibility. Here we can think in terms of Walter Benjamin's theory of allegory, found mainly in *The Origin of German Tragic Drama*, but spread more generally throughout his writings. Benjamin's development of allegory takes place in terms of a critique of the distinction between allegory and symbol through readings of various writers on this topic (1977: 163 ff). Benjamin shows that the symbol, as a transcendental unifying power, is itself part of a more general allegorical impulse in modern literature, as an immanent materialisation of modern experience. As a consequence, the affect laden qualities of the symbol such as immediacy, contingency, expressiveness and life, are retained as allegorical, while the transcendent qualities such as unity, clarity, beauty, are abandoned. In effect, Benjamin reverses and displaces the theory of the symbol, exposing it to an excessive allegorical structure grounded in an immediate experience of futurity as the 'yet to come'.

For Benjamin, allegories operate in the contingent, disjunctive experience of modern life in terms of the impossibility of an experience of unified self-presence (promised but never delivered by the Romantic symbol). Allegories thus operate in the ruins of memory, as the revelation of an ego incapable of remembering itself, and hence unable to project itself into an already knowable future based on a self-same identity.[8] The motif of ruin is central to the allegory: 'allegories are, in the realm of thoughts, what ruins are in the realm of things' (Benjamin 1977: 178). The ego, or what is left of it, faces the future as 'the *facies hippocratica* [the face of death] of history as a petrified, primordial landscape' (*Ibid.*: 166). Benjamin's rendering of allegory can be seen as a re-working of Romantic irony – the attitude that thought reflects the world around it in the contingency of subjective experience. Benjamin takes this attitude a step further by exposing the contingency of reflective thought to its own materialisation in the absolute *grasped from the contingency of experience itself*. Benjamin thus avoids the Hegelian *aufhebung* of subjectivity into a transcendental mind while retaining a confrontation with the absolute in experience itself – a remembering of its ruination in self-forgetting.

Unlike symbols which aspire to transcend the contingency of linguistic expression, allegories lament the failure of language to do so, and through this limitation, point to something beyond themselves – a not-yet-realised state made possible as a becoming-significant in a yet to be experienced world. Where symbols express the transcendental *idea*, allegories point to a not yet realised *concept*, that, in its very possibility, indicates its present unattainability. In this case, allegories cannot bring about the rescue of the ruined ego through transcendence into a unified synthesis, but can only provide consolation and hope. Allegory thus operates on the presentation of scenes in which ruined experience is presented in absolute terms, leaving the ego suspended in a state of disrepair but with the hope of fulfilment in a future yet to come.

Benjamin writes that at 'the heart of the allegorical way of seeing' is the face as a 'death's head' (*Ibid.*) – the sorrowful face of mourning over the plight of human existence alienated from redemption in transcendental self-unity. At the end of *Tom White*, Tom is shown staring steadfastly ahead, sorrowful concern written all over his face.

This 'death's head' image confirms the allegorical structure of the film as the presentation of remembered forgetfulness — a revelation of self-forgetting as the remembrance of the taking place of memory itself — in its very possibility. This is why the image here is stilled: it holds itself together in a tableau that resists the movement towards closure, but which, coming at the very end, is itself the closing of the film. Thus, the film closes in openness, but not an openness from which one could predict what will happen, since Tom has already eliminated all hope of a reunion with his

family and with his former life. Rather, it ends in the openness of *insight* that comes from an experience of absolute otherness: a sense of unseen futurity, which, in the death's head expression, remains unfulfilled. In this bleak visage, we nevertheless feel a sense of hope for something that *might* come to pass.

Fig. 22 Tom contemplating life at the very end of the film.

That is to say, the film does not so much point to that which will come to pass, but *expresses* the possibility of a coming-to-pass in the death's head image itself, in its fixated moving stillness and visual intensity.

NEW MAN

Tom White can be read as an allegory of the coming of the new man.[9] Tom's identity as a traditional 'old man' — white male, ego-driven masculinity, rationalist in outlook, problem solving through violence — is exposed and ruined through the device of a 'crack up', which plunges Tom into a journey of self-discovery in which none of these virtues is of any help. In fact, Tom does not need to discover anything at all about himself, since there is no self left to discover. Instead, the allegorical structure of the film turns Tom from a self-seeking individual to an everyman whose actions and motivations are not reflected back into his own psychic motivations, but signify more general truths about life. Tom's journey from the ruins of his previous life is a quest for wisdom, not self-identity — Tom has to learn to love life.

The allegorical structure of the film sets Tom's journey up right from the start in the opening sequence in which each of the people that he meets on his journey are presented in a brief vignette. This technique, popular in silent film and early talkies, signals the allegorical mode by prefiguring events which will be fulfilled later in the film. At the end of the film Tom appears to be waiting for something – a promised masculinity that is yet to come. This 'new man' that Tom is not yet, but might be, is signalled throughout the film as a 'coming', in Tom's encounters with others. His initial concern is to rescue these others (the four individuals seen briefly in the *vignettes* at the start of the film) from their plight by applying the kind of reason that worked well in his previous life in the corporate world – the reason of instrumental rationality that sees things in terms of problem solving. However, as he soon learns, there is an underlying meaning to their lives that makes them worthwhile just as they are.

Wisdom comes when Tom realises that he is in fact not helping them, but learning from them. From Matt, the young male prostitute, he is told that 'love is love' and not a calculation of desire for personal gain. From drug-addicted Christine, he learns that love is something to be shared, and not kept to oneself (Christine declares her love for Tom who fails to understand the genuineness of her feelings). From Malcolm, the alcoholic street philosopher, he learns that the pain of love is part of the human condition, to be suffered rather than repressed (Malcolm lives his life mourning lost love, which fills his life with human insight that he tries to impart to Tom). And from Jet, the street boy, he learns that love requires unreserved commitment, encompassing a duty of care to the beloved (having abandoned his own family, Tom is shown up by Jet's father, an unreformed armed robber, who, in the midst of being arrested for his latest heist, still manages to retain a loving relation with his son). Wisdom, or the *love of life* as openness to the other is what Tom must learn if he is to become a new man.[10]

By being open to the other, the self-absorption of ego-identity recedes, and a wise concern for others takes its place. In response to the demand 'have you got any identity' from a pushy social worker, Tom replies sarcastically 'this', pointing to his face. Here we go to the heart of the matter, and to the reason why it's so difficult to call *Tom White* a film about the restoration of lost identity. Tom's gesture is not an attempt to secure identity, but quite the reverse, a refusal of identity. This refusal requires a focus on the body, and especially the face, which figures prominently in the film. The face itself cannot be an identity, unless recognised in terms of a classification.

By invoking the sheer this-ness of his face, Tom is implicitly rejecting the social order that insists on identifying people in terms of classifications that transform bare life into a number or type. The raw 'this' of Tom's face (often shown blotched and reddened in close up elsewhere in the film) resists social classification, and becomes instead the death's head turned to the other in the extreme immediacy of bare life.

Tom's life lies in ruins. It needs to be rebuilt. But how? The coming man proposed in *Tom White* bears no relation to the feminised new man of many recent Hollywood films but to a remaking of the Anglo-ethnic old man from the ground up. At the end of the film, Tom is not reconciled with his family; he does not look forward to a future based on the reparation of identity. Rather, Tom's life has undergone a re-evaluation which has put him on another path, towards a future that cannot yet be seen or known. The film is thus prophetic rather than realistic – an *exposé* of the problems of Anglo-Australian identity in facing the challenges of a world no longer made to suit its demands. The new man that Tom must become must come from the ruins of what he has already been, a re-evaluation of old man values through what might be termed the getting of wisdom.

CONCLUSION

As an allegory of its own becoming, *Tom White* exposes the structure of allegory as temporal disjuncture. By meditating on temporal disjuncture as the finite condition of human experience, allegories point to the future in terms of the insuperable contingency of the present. Allegories do not predict, they prophesise, thus bearing futurity with them in their very prophesising. In bearing the future with them, allegories operate out of the ruins of the past: the still remaining fragments of the past carried forward into the present. Allegories are based not on the time of the continual present emerging fully realised out of the past, but on another time: a transtemporality in which past, present and future are collapsed into an experience of absolute otherness as the death's head memory of ruined pastness that *is* the present in its orientation to futurity. Allegories mobilise a figurative economy in which this predicament is presented as a potential way of 'being other' as becoming. The 'becoming other' involves a movement of figuration where characters bear their future with them in terms of their responses to others, which, in the absence of any real internal or psychic motivation, transforms their deeds and actions into moral gestures of virtue and worthiness.

In *revealing* its figurative economy the allegory manifests a technical operation that makes the figuration happen – a technique in which narrative drive is punctuated with tableaux images as stilled images of time that constitute the very possibility of the allegory being revealed. This is not something that befalls film as an optional extra. Rather it *is* film in its self-revealing. I argue that *all film* is allegorical at its heart – a performance of the filmic 'essence' of film in the stilled image of time drawn from the photogram, constituting the very possibility of a film time that offers an image of the future as absolute, but at the cost of exposing its own technical limits in the finitude of its own *signifiance*: its vanishing into the ruins of its own pastness as the 'founding act of the filmic itself' (to repeat Barthes words); as the material out of which it perpetually comes.

NOTES

1   For Deleuze, perception is not in the mind of the perceiver, but attached to the thing perceived as a quasi-autonomous affect. The movement-image is the way perception is stitched into the apparatus of the film in terms of a sensory-motor link with cognition. The time-image is a decisive break with this link, producing an image of time as pure filmic image. These ideas are worked out in Deleuze's two film books: *Cinema I* and *Cinema II* (1986; 1989).

2   According to Deleuze, parts relate to wholes on the basis of openness. Wholes are thus always parts and parts always whole. This is different from sets which are always closed (1986: 10). It's not difficult to see here a distinction between a whole and a totality. A totality is something calculable (to total something is to add it up). Sets are closed in terms of the totality of its parts. Totalities are composed of a series of closed sets. Deleuze is a philosopher of wholes, not totalities. See Badiou 2000 for a critique of Deleuze along these lines.

3   For more on dialectical images, see Benjamin 1968: 253–64. See also Pensky 2004.

4   The underclass has no lifestyle because its members have no power to consume. They therefore lack the kinds of identity markers necessary to access the money required to consume. However, as Neil Maycroft points out, they do have a life, a life that remains resistively free (2004).

5   The introduction of digital technology to filmmaking is not in itself a decisive break with film's technological origin in the photogram. The digitisation of film remediates the photogram into a pixel set that can be manipulated directly by computer-based tools. As Lev Manovich has argued digital cinema is a form of animation or painting in which 'live footage' has no special status to normalise reality, but becomes material to work with (2001: 302–3). But these modifications are more along the line of enhancements to the existing film paradigm, seeking to gain more intimate control over image style. It would require a truly decisive break with the photogram to make film in a different way, but this would be to produce something that would no longer be recognisable as film. Perhaps this possibility may not be far away.

6   See also Raymond Bellour's (1991) detailed theoretical elaboration of the still image as

the basis of modern cinema.

7 To take just one example from the unlimited range of possibilities, there is a scene in Alfred Hitchcock's *The Man Who Knew Too Much* (1956) where the husband attempts to protect his wife from her own hysterical outburst after learning that her child has been kidnapped, by wrapping his arms and hands tightly around her head in a smothering hold. This is a repetition of the same image appearing at the end of Robert Wiene's *Orlacs Hände* (*The Hands of Orlac*, 1924). This can be read not simply as a repetition, but also as a transformation of the sense of the image within the scope of the signification 'obsessive love'. There is, of course, a massive dissemination of repeated images throughout the history of film, an enriching of film with its own sense, requiring careful genealogical unpacking.

8 We might like to compare this with Heidegger's concept of *ruinance*, as movement in the collapsed nothingness of an essential lack that life *is* in its factical affirmation of its own possibility. See Raffoul 2008 for an examination of Heidegger's idea of *ruinance*.

9 The 'new man' here does not refer to the feminised new man, seen for instance in the feminised aspects of the otherwise hard-boiled sleuth Fitz in the British television series *Cracker* (see Greeber 2002). Rather, it refers to a 'coming man' made out of the ruins of the older masculine type (old man). Unlike Fitz who retains old man characteristics as his core personality, Tom in *Tom White* simultaneously retains and is deprived of old man values, leaving him entirely open and vulnerable to life.

10 The most significant modern philosopher who has written on love as openness to the other is Emmanuel Levinas (1996). Jean-Luc Nancy has also written on love along similar lines (1991).

WORKS CITED

Agamben, G. (1998) *Homo Sacer: Sovereign Power and Bare Life*, trans. D. Heller-Roazen. Stanford: Stanford University Press.

Badiou, A. (2000) *Deleuze: The Clamour of Being*, trans. L. Burchill. Minneapolis: University of Minnesota Press.

Barthes, R. (1977) 'The Third Meaning', *Image, Music, Text*, trans. S. Heath, London: Fontana, 52–68.

Bellour, R. (1991) 'The Film Stilled', *Camera Obscura*, 24, 99–123.

Benjamin, W. (1968) *Illuminations: Essays and Reflections*, trans. H. Zohn. New York: Schocken Books.

_____ (1977) *The Origin of German Tragic Drama*, trans. J. Osborne. London: NLB.

Brewster, B. and L. Jacobs (1997) *Theatre to Cinema: Stage Pictorialism and the Early Feature Film*. Oxford: Oxford University Press.

Deleuze, G. (1986) *Cinema I: The Movement- Image*, trans. H. Tomlinson and B. Habberjam. London: The Athlone Press.

_____ (1989) *Cinema II: The Time-Image*, trans. H. Tomlinson and R. Galeta. Minneapolis: University of Minnesota Press.

_____ (1994) *Difference and Repetition*, trans. P. Patton. London: The Athlone Press.

Derrida, J. (1995) *Archive Fever: A Freudian Impression*, trans. E. Prenowitz. Chicago: University of Chicago Press.

Greeber, G. (2002) 'Old Sleuth or New Man? Investigations into rape, murder and masculinity in *Cracker* (1993–1996)', *Continuum: Journal of Media and Cultural Studies*, 16, 2, 169–83.

Levinas, E. (1996) 'God and Philosophy', in A. T. Peperzak, S. Critchley and R. Bernasconi (eds) *Basic Philosophical Writings*. Bloomington: Indiana University Press, 129–48.

Manovich, L. (2001) *The Language of New Media*. Cambridge, MA: The MIT Press.

Maycroft, N. (2004) 'Cultural Consumption and the Myth of Life-Style', *Capital and Class*, 84, 17, 61–75.

Nancy, J.-L. (1991) 'Shattered Love', in *The Inoperative Community*, trans. P. Connor *et al*. Minneapolis: University of Minnesota Press, 82–109.

Pearson, R. E. (1992) *Eloquent Gestures: The Transformation of Performance Style in the Griffith Biograph Films*. Berkeley: University of California Press.

Pensky, M. (2004) 'Method and Time: Benjamin's Dialectical Images', in *The Cambridge Companion to Walter Benjamin* , ed. D. S. Ferris. Cambridge: Cambridge University Press, 177–98.

Raffoul, F. (2008) 'Factical Life and the Need for Philosophy', in F. Raffoul and E. Sean Nelson (eds) *Rethinking Facticity*. Albany, NY: State University of New York Press, 69–85.

Routt, W. D. (2000) 'For Criticism, Nicole Brenez, De la figure en general et du corps en particulier: l'invention figurative au cinema', parts 1 and 2, *Screening the Past*, March. Online. Available at: http://www.latrobe.edu.au/screeningthepast/current/cc0300.html (accessed 1 May 2009).

Schefer, J. L. (1995) *The Deluge, The Plague: Paolo Uccello*, trans. T. Conley. Ann Arbor: University of Michigan Press.

8. FILMING THE PAST, PRESENT AND FUTURE OF AN AFRICAN VILLAGE: OUSMANE SEMBENE'S *MOOLAADÉ*

DAVID MURPHY

INTRODUCTION

Moolaadé (2004), the final film by the renowned Senegalese director Ousmane Sembene (1923–2007), is set in a remote village in Burkina Faso. Throughout the history of African filmmaking, the representation of village life has played a highly significant and evolving role: sometimes imagined as a timeless source of cultural 'authenticity' – as in Dani Kouyaté's *Keïta! The Heritage of the Griot* (Burkina Faso, 1995); in other cases the village is subjected to a virulent critique as site of superstition and repression, acting as a brake on urban modernity – as in the more recent *Clouds over Conakry* (Guinea, 2005) by Cheick Fantamady Camara. The opening credits of *Moolaadé* provide contrasting images of village life: the depiction of young boys reciting the Koran in the shade of a tree beside the beautiful and other-worldly mosque, the women in their compounds sweeping, bathing babies and preparing food may at first glance suggest the mythical 'timelessness' of African village life – a concept that will be analysed in greater detail below – but, in fact, these images are framed by moments of disruption, both internal and external in origin. The film opens with the arrival of the trader from the city (a character intriguingly known as 'Mercenaire' [Mercenary] who goes on to play a vital role in the development of the narrative), which immediately links the village to the outside world; even more significantly, household chores in the compound are interrupted when four young girls arrive seeking 'asylum', the *moolaadé* of the film's title. They are dressed in the robes of those about to be 'purified' – in the terms of the village elders – or be subjected to female genital mutilation in the terms of opponents of this practice – that is, they are about to have the labia and their genitalia removed as part of an initiation ritual common throughout much of West Africa.[1] The girls' decision to reject the initiation process throws the social order into turmoil, and, moreover, leads to a profound questioning of the community's sense of identity and history. Sembene's representation in *Moolaadé* of a village wrestling at the turn of the twenty-first century with the issue of genital 'excision',[2] allows the director to explore competing notions of time, place and memory, and it is this exploration that will form the heart of this chapter. As Sembene draws past, present and future into a dialogical relationship, the village becomes a site in which the future of Africa is played out; far from a timeless backwater, it is the location of a crucial battle for Africa's right to its own modernity.

TIME, HISTORY AND AFRICAN CINEMA

Moolaadé's depiction of a dynamic, conflictual and evolving village life stands in stark contrast to dominant Western perceptions of rural Africa. In his landmark text, *Time and the Other* (1983), the anthropologist Johannes Fabian writes of the 'denial of coevalness' to which Africa has been subjected by the West, consistently relegated to a less 'developed' moment of human existence. Throughout the eras of slavery and colonisation, Africans increasingly found themselves allocated the status of 'primitive' beings, relics of an earlier or a parallel stage in the development of mankind, who could only reach the standards of 'modern man' through the civilising endeavours of the coloniser. By the early decades of the nineteenth century, no less a figure than Hegel could declare that Africa was a continent devoid of reason and morality, existing outside of both history and culture. Hegel concludes his brief consideration of Africa in his *Lectures on the Philosophy of World History* (first published 1830) as follows:

> The condition in which [the Negroes] live is incapable of any development or culture and their present existence is the same as it has always been. In face of the enormous energy of sensuous arbitrariness which dominates their lives, morality has no determinate influence upon them. Anyone who wishes to study the most terrible manifestations of human nature will find them in Africa. The earliest reports concerning this continent tell us precisely the same, and it has no history in the true sense of the word. We shall therefore leave Africa at this point, and it need not be mentioned again. For it is an unhistorical continent, with no movement or development of its own. (1975: 190)

Regrettably, the shelf life of such racialised tropes and myths of the nineteenth century has proven long. For example, on 26 July 2007 the newly elected French president Nicolas Sarkozy stood before an invited audience of students, scholars, dignitaries and political leaders at the Université Cheikh Anta Diop de Dakar in Senegal and made the following statement as part of a speech dedicated to the 'young people of Africa':

> Africa's tragedy is that the African has largely remained outside of History. The African peasant, who has lived by the seasons for several millennia, and whose ideal is to be in harmony with nature, only knows the eternal cycle of time, which is marked by the endless repetition of the same gestures and the same words. In this imaginary where everything is always repeated, there is no place for human adventure nor for the idea of progress.[3] (My translation)

Although these remarkable comments brought about an immediate response from Africanist scholars – within just over a year of the speech, three books had been published in response to it (Mbem 2007; Gassama 2007; Chrétien 2008) – I would argue that Sarkozy's comments are not exceptional in and of themselves. What is exceptional is the frankness with which the French president expresses ideas that are still commonplace in the West, but that are often expressed in a more insidious or veiled fashion, relating to Africa's underdevelopment, for example. Africa remains for much of the world a continent dwelling in the past, unable to develop modern, democratic, technologically advanced or even 'civilised' societies: essentially, there is a perceived temporal disjunction between Africa and the rest of the world.

Postcolonial Africans' perception of their own continent has inevitably been shaped in complex ways by the legacy of these Eurocentric notions on Africa's position in world history (although my position here should not be confused with arguments that limit postcolonial African thought to an endless recycling and reworking of European thought). This is no less the case in the field of cinema. Early African films of the 1960s and 1970s were, for the most part (but far from exclusively), left-leaning engagements with contemporary urban Africa – see Sembene's landmark early films, *Borom Sarret* (1962), *Mandabi* (1968) and *Xala* (1974) – that were, in part, a reaction against colonial notions of a continent continually turned towards its past (consistently viewed as rural and village-based). As the colonial era receded, and as the promises of a socialist Africa began to prove elusive, a growing desire to engage with the African past finally led to a body of filmmaking in the 1980s that became known as the 'return to the source' genre, most commonly associated with directors such as Gaston Kaboré, Souleymane Cissé and Idrissa Ouédraogo. The 'return to the source' films have been variously lauded and critiqued as either a turn towards a new and more authentically African aesthetic or as an escapist flight into a mythical past. For example, Frank Ukadike includes Cissé's *Yeelen* (Mali, 1987) in a list of African films, alongside Ouédraogo's *Yaaba* (Burkina Faso, 1989) and *Tilaï* (Burkina Faso, 1990) and Kaboré's *Zan Boko* (Burkina Faso, 1988), which are deemed to 'offer meticulous anthropological renditions of African cultures. The films are true to life and do not attempt to re-arrange natural settings or modernise them to look foreign' (1994: 252). On the other hand, Manthia Diawara in his brief assessment of *Yaaba* argues that the film's message of tolerance – 'Don't judge others, for they have their reasons' – is a 'bourgeois humanist conception of tolerance, which is imported from the big city' (1992: 162), and he largely views Ouédraogo's work as a postmodern escapism that rejects the radicalism of Sembene and other predecessors. Whatever one's critical standpoint on this body of filmmaking, it is evident that it placed the village, generally represented as a site of continuity with the past, at the heart of much African cinema, a position it still occupies today.

As I have argued elsewhere, the so-called 'return to the source' genre might in large part be seen as the product of recently urbanised film directors making somewhat idealised films about rural communities (past and present) for a recently urbanised audience, in effect 'staging authenticity' (see MacCannell 1976) for a public physically distant from, but with strong emotional ties to, the countryside (see Murphy & Williams 2007, chapters 5 and 7). In an important recent collection of essays, *Black and White in Colour* (Bickford-Smith & Mendelson 2007), a range of leading historians of Africa cast a critical eye on the engagement with the past in key works of sub-Saharan African cinema. Mahir Saul writes of Gaston Kaboré's *Wend Kuuni* (Burkina Faso, 1982) and its follow-up *Buud Yam* (Burkina Faso, 1996) that their depiction of the pre-colonial African village is an act of 'cultural redemption'. These films are representative of a postcolonial desire for a lost world untouched by colonialism and, consequently, the past is 'created' through the removal of modern, Western objects with little other concern for historical verisimilitude: 'The past is primarily a rhetorical figure of the present, an argument hurled against the ghost of colonialism' (Saul 2007: 21). While some of his fellow historians in the collection view their role in rather limiting terms as one of 'correcting' the historical errors and approximations of filmmakers, Ralph Austen takes the far more productive view that the role of the historian cannot be limited to providing an alternative version to the director's historically 'inaccurate' version, for this is to deny the imaginative process involved in creating a work of cinematic fiction. This is not to reject notions of historical objectivity, for Austen champions historians' ability to 'qualify the claim that any visions of the past can fully transcend the conditions of their own construction' (2007: 40). Essentially, the African historical film acts as an intervention into debates on the construction of a collective historical memory, and for Sembene, as we shall see below, film is a privileged forum in which to challenge dominant accounts of the past.

IMAGINING ALTERNATIVE HISTORIES IN SEMBENE'S FILMS

Sembene is an artist who constantly 'imagines alternatives' both in relation to his society and to his work, repeatedly stressing the importance of thinking through and beyond the different forms that social domination can take (for a more sustained development of these arguments, see Murphy 2000). This 'creative thinking' extends to his cinematic treatment of the past both in terms of collective and personal histories. As will be shown in the analysis of *Moolaadé* below, Sembene rejects the notion that individual memories should be given absolute priority over collective ones. Indeed, rather than viewing the collective and the individual in opposition to one another, Sembene explicitly reveals the complex interrelationship of personal and historical memory. For instance, in *Guelwaar* (Senegal, 1992), Sembene mixes realism with powerful political symbolism in a narrative that uncovers the officially 'silenced' story of a murdered political militant who had denounced African dependence on Western aid and the denial of political responsibility within the African political elite. A largely conventional social realist narrative, the film works on a dual temporality built on flashbacks of Guelwaar's life, which build to a hugely powerful climax at the aid rally where the political activist castigates his audience for allowing themselves effectively to become beggars. This memory of an exemplary moment of courage, of the 'heroism of daily life' (as Sembene termed his incomplete final trilogy of films of which *Moolaadé* was the second part), from the recent past has an immediate effect on the present as the young people, inspired by Guelwaar's message, destroy the contents of a truck carrying food aid.

As for Sembene's explicitly 'historical' films, they are all informed by a desire to counter 'official' versions of the past, which usually promote amnesia regarding controversial events: for example, *Emitaï* (Senegal, 1971) and *Camp de Thiaroye* (Senegal, 1988) both revisit 'forgotten' acts of colonial violence from World War II. *Emitaï* explores the ways in which indigenous religious-cultural forms can both inspire and limit resistance to colonial domination, while *Camp de Thiaroye* represents the awakening of an African nationalist consciousness amongst colonial soldiers from across the continent. However, *Ceddo* (1977) is undoubtedly Sembene's most complex historical intervention, a film that seeks to uncover the violent social and political forces that produced a Senegalese Islam, which was increasingly seen as a 'natural' presence in 1970s Senegal. As David Rosen argues in his highly incisive reading of the film: 'In *Ceddo*, the issue of the nation and its representation is located as a problem of history and its representation. Only in the constructions of its histories will a nation be defined' (1991: 148). Essentially, *Ceddo* acts as a striking example of Sembene's belief in the power of cinema to intervene in the process of constructing and transmitting historical memory, opening a space in which the dominant historical narratives of the nation can be questioned. In interviews, Sembene readily acknowledged the contentious nature of his historical accounts, for what interested him was never historical 'accuracy' *per se* but rather the ways in which he might find in the past models to inspire his contemporary audience. As he stated in relation to *Ceddo*: 'I admit that the film is not historical but it's *my* version' (quoted in Murphy 2000: 235).

As for the moral, ideological and aesthetic value of the village in Sembene's work, it is evident that the director does not view rural Africa as a source of cultural authenticity, an unproblematic link to a mythical past. To take the example of his first two short films, *Borom Sarret* reveals the social divisions and corruption at the heart of the postcolonial African city but its follow-up *Niaye* (Senegal, 1964) is equally scathing about the moral corruption to be found in the decaying villages blighted by poverty and urban flight. Essentially, the significance of the city and the country is always contextually and strategically deployed in Sembene's work. Both are locked in a symbiotic relationship that cannot be portrayed through false dichotomies between past/present, authenticity/alienation, tradition/modernity.

COLLECTIVE AND PERSONAL HISTORIES IN *MOOLAADÉ*

As was mentioned above, *Moolaadé* is for the most part shot in a relatively conventional realist mode and adopts a clear, linear narrative that only becomes muddied with the cryptic 'flash forward' contained in the film's closing image, which will be discussed further below. (The most experimental phase in Sembene's career had come in the 1970s with films such as *Emitaï*, *Xala* and *Ceddo*.) Although sometimes cast as a polemical and didactic director, Sembene in fact created a body of filmmaking that was always incredibly eclectic in style. There is didacticism in his work – see the early sequence in *Moolaadé* in which the girls explain to Collé why they ran away, which at times resembles a public health film – but there is also psychological realism, as in the representation of the hierarchies at work within polygamous marriages, and drama bordering at times on melodrama: for example, Colle's act of bravery in refusing to yield as she is publicly whipped by her husband. Equally, Sembene is not adverse to the deft manipulation of his audience's emotions, as is witnessed by the death of the little girl, Diattou, and her mother's subsequent lament for her. Finally, there is (as always in Sembene's work) comedy: far from playing solely on the pain and tragedy associated with his subject matter, Sembene deploys comedy as one of his most effective narrative devices: for example, the comedy of Mercenaire's endless attempts to bed the local women, or Collé's sharp and biting tongue, which cuts the menfolk down to size. However, perhaps the most significant feature of the film's aesthetic is the manner in which it deliberately operates on a symbolic level. As in so many of Sembene's films, Moolaadé sets in train competing rituals, which represent values/beliefs between which the audience must choose, those of the *moolaadé* (the rite of asylum) or those of the *Salindana* (the women who carry out the act of excision). The tense standoffs between Collé and the *Salindana* framed in the doorway of the compound with just the flimsy red, yellow and black rope representing the *moolaadé* lying between them are not just a human confrontation between individual antagonists. The viewer is in fact witnessing a struggle between rival values, rival interpretations of the past and of the future direction of the village: the struggle for control is mirrored by a struggle to occupy the screen, and it is only in the closing sequence that the *Salindana* and their male supporters are literally sidelined within the frame.

The *Salindana* and the village elders locate the village within an un-

changing mythical frame-
work that inherently sanc-
tions excision and practices
like it as authentic expressions of the village's timeless identity; indeed, their
very status as elders confers
a certain level of authority on
them within the African context, where respect for age

Fig. 23 Collé Ardo Sy front left foreground) confronts the *Salindana* in the doorway to her compound.

remains a strong facet of social life. The *Salindana* are shrouded in menace
and mystery with their red cloaks and headscarves, and the twin-headed
serpent that adorns the staff carried by their leader: in one sequence, they
are even transformed in the eyes of the young girls into malevolent, mask-
wearing spirits looming large in the doorway of the compound. When we
first see the *Salindana* in the sacred grove where the initiations takes place,
the camera at first remains at a remote distance from the action and films
the women from a low angle as they mount the steps to a raised platform.
However, when the camera moves closer for a medium-distance shot of
the group, their sense of mystery is replaced by the more prosaic and present demands of confronting the challenge posed by Collé Ardo Sy and her
invocation of the right to asylum, the *moolaadé*. Sembene's aim in such
sequences, and in the film as a whole, is to drag the practice of excision out
of its timelessness and into the exigencies of the contemporary world.

The elders' conception of the relationship between the present and an
originary past, viewed as the font of all authority, meaning and value for the
village is revealed most strikingly in the long scene in which they hold an
audience with the *Salindana* (which lasts almost eight minutes). Sembene
here captures in close detail the rituals that enshrine and reinforce existing hierarchies within the village, in particular the patriarchalism that
the film seeks to challenge. These rituals act as a physical link to the past;
the repetition of gestures and words deemed 'ancient' is for the elders a
way of constantly reasserting the primacy of what they believe to be the
thoughts and values of their ancestors. The elders, led by their chief (the
Dougoutuigui), slowly parade in file towards chairs laid out in the shade
(although it should be noted that alongside local, carved stools, there are
also modern, deck chairs: nothing is ever as timeless as it seems); as they
walk, they are framed against the monumental structure of the mosque.

The sense of ritualistic performance is reinforced by the echoing diegetic sound of the *griot* who announces the arrival of the great and the good (the *griot* is a complex figure in traditional West African societies: aligned with particular noble families, he/she preserves their history through epic stories and acts as a sort of intermediary in public gatherings conveying the words of the chief to his people and conveying their words to him.) The camera then cuts to the *Salindana* who also arrive in single file from another direction; when they arrive before the male elders, they sit on the ground on cloths laid out for them (they are literally beneath the level of the elders).

As they debate Collé's challenge to the traditional order, they consistently claim that no-one before her has ever challenged 'purification'; it is presented as a universally accepted norm with its roots deep in the mists of time. However, the scene gradually reveals that 'purification' is a ritual carried out on behalf of men but that is policed by women themselves: the leader of the *Salindana* taunts the men by asking if they will now accept to marry *bilakoro* (women who have not been 'purified') and they rapidly proclaim their allegiance to social norms. She proposes to carry out excision on the young girls and also Collé's daughter, Amsatou, which would allow her marriage to the chief's son to proceed within fifteen days. (Amsatou's engagement to the son of the chief is a rather unconvincing element in the narrative. After the furore caused by Collé's invocation of the *moolaadé*, Amsatou's engagement to his son is broken by the chief due to her status as a *bilakoro*, which everyone seems conveniently to have forgotten when they became engaged in the first place.) This prompts the griot to make the lewd joke that 'no man can keep an erection for fifteen days', which leads all present to burst into laughter. Excision is here revealed as being all about men's (perceived) needs rather than women's. (This gender imbalance is strikingly illustrated by Sembene through the character of Fily, the eleven-year-old girl to whom the chief's son, Ibrahima, is married, without his knowledge: she never utters a word and is treated as an object designed to satisfy male needs.)

As the social order is challenged, the elders increasingly turn to violent methods to restore order and bring the women into line. The women's radios are confiscated for they are perceived by the men to have 'corrupted' the women with alien ideas (as we shall see below, for the women, the radios are a voice from outside that breaks the stranglehold of past/place). Collé's husband Ciré is goaded into whipping his wife in public in order to get her to bring an end to the *moolaadé*. And, finally, Mercenaire is murdered off screen for deigning to intervene and bring the assault on Collé to a halt: the men, their faces painted white, chase him from the village carrying torches in what for all intents and purposes is a lynch mob.

However, the opening scene discussed above also reveals the ambiguity of tradition and the selective way in which the past is often interpreted. When the elders discover that Collé has invoked the *moolaadé*, one of their memebers rises to his feet and makes a speech on the significance of this act:

Fig. 24 One of the elders rises and makes a speech about the significance of *moolaadé*.

Moolaadé, you are in this anthill that embodies our first king Yérim Dethié Kodé Ndiak. His people rebelled and he was transformed into this anthill. He had offended the *moolaadé*. His rebellious subjects killed him. After he was buried here, his body was swollen and transformed into this anthill.

The significance of the elder's words here is not deliberated as discussion veers off into a debate on how to get round the *moolaadé* (through the power of a husband to compel his wife to obey him). However, this speech in effect reveals that the *moolaadé* is inextricably (if somewhat obliquely) linked to a popular rebellion, which stands in stark contrast to the elders' constant invocation of the past as the source of unquestioned patriarchal authority. As the *Salindana* troop away at the end of the scene, they pass by the anthill and the image then cuts to a static shot of the anthill, this physical embodiment of the village's past. What lessons from the past will inform the village's present?

A rival account of the past to that proposed by the elders, one at once both personal and historicised, is revealed through the character of Collé Ardo Sy, the middle wife of three to Ciré Bathily. (Collé is played with outstanding presence by the non-professional Fatoumata Coulibaly, a Malian radio presenter and campaigner against female genital mutilation; while Ciré is played by one of the main stars of Burkinabe filmmaking, Rasmane Ouédraogo). When the four girls fleeing the excision arrive in the compound, they ask for asylum; the mythical past of the village is here evoked through the notion of asylum, *moolaadé*. As was indicated above, the precise meaning or value of the *moolaadé* is never explicitly explained to the viewer; rather it is deployed within the film to emphasise notions of care and hospitality in opposition to the pain and subjugation invoked by the *Salindana*. The only tangible presence given to the *moolaadé* is a simple, red, black and yellow rope hung low across the doorway. Throughout the film, Sembene plays on its physical flimsiness in repeated shots of the doorway in which children and animals pass back and forth over or even under the rope but in the confrontations with the *Salindana* (evoked above) the life-and-death nature of the confrontation is made evident. When Collé ties the rope across the doorway, she calls the four children to her and explains that the *moolaadé* has now been invoked and, until it ends, she cannot dismiss them from her home nor can others enter the compound to take them away. She ominously declares that 'anyone who breaks this law will be killed by the *moolaadé*'; the right to asylum and protection are thus given great force within the narrative.

At first apparently reluctant to support the children, Collé soon becomes their ardent defender, as the viewer gradually becomes aware of memories of Collé's own traumatic experience of excision and her earlier decision not to have her own daughter 'excised'. In the early scene in which she asks the children why they have come to her for asylum, Oumy replies: 'We were told you refused to have your daughter cut.' Collé's reponse – 'there is too much gossip at the well' – appears to act as a denial of Oumy's assertion but when she goes to on to state somewhat obliquely that 'purification is one thing and *moolaadé* a different thing', the viewer is given a sense of the struggle between rituals and values that will ensue. When the final child Awa asserts that Collé did not have her daughter, Amsatou, 'cut' and, despite this, she is engaged to the son of the village chief, the symbolic role of Collé's own back story is made apparent: through her lived experience, she has offered an alternative mode of conduct, the memory of which has inspired these children to rebel. (In many ways, the film aligns Collé with the character of Mercenaire. He too has a traumatic past, revealed in the second scene with Ibrahima, which is that of a rebel who spoke out against injustice in the army. For this revolt, he is sent to prison and given a dishonourable discharge from the army. As we see with Collé, the past of an individual can offer hope of new modes of conduct that break with social norms.)

This personal challenge to the social order is deeply shocking to the rest of the village. In the first confrontation between Collé and the *Salindana*, accompanied by the mothers of the children who have fled the initiation ritual, framed against the doorway to the compound, there are repeated efforts to undermine Collé through references to her 'disgraceful' actions of the past. She is accused of wanting their children to be 'unpure' (*bilakoro*) like Amsatou, and she is demeaned for her alleged childhood reaction to her own 'initiation': 'During our purification, you were the only disgraced girl to cry. You peed too.' In the face of this incrimination, Collé retorts to the leader of the *Salindana*: 'Truth be told, you cut me and stitched me twice. Twice, and you also buried my two children.' Collé here refers to one of the potential long-term side-effects of excision, namely damage to the external reproductive system, which can cause childbirth to be highly dangerous for both mother and infant. Standing framed against the doorway in a medium shot, she pulls up her blouse to reveal a long scar across her stomach, the result of an emergency caesarian (conducted by a female doctor who is held up as a model of care for fellow women in opposition to the harm brought by the *Salindana*), which had finally allowed her to give birth to a healthy child. It is her willingness to draw on her own (shameful) past in public that gradually inspires other women to rally to her cause.

The other highly intimate physical legacy of excision is the pain that can potentially accompany sexual intercourse. This is depicted for the viewer in a short sequence half way through the film. The image cuts from Collé alone smoking her pipe to shocking images of a young girl screaming in terror as she is pinned down by the *Salindana*. We then cut back to Collé lying in bed with her groaning, panting husband on top of her; Collé bites on her little finger to take her mind off the pain and prevent herself from screaming out loud. The image cuts back and forth between the two scenes, graphically linking the violence of excision to the denial of sexual pleasure to women; sex is merely equated with pain for Collé. However, this pain brings women together in solidarity: Amsatou bathes her mother the following morning and the first wife Khardjatou soon joins her, their tenderness contrasting sharply with the brutality of the sexual intercourse with the husband.

However, Collé's refusal of excision is not immediately accepted by her fellow women. At one point, even her daughter Amsatou questions the decision not to have her 'purified', as this has led to the breaking of her engagement to the chief's son, Ibrahima. (Note that Amsatou keeps a photograph of Ibrahima in classic tourist pose in front of the Eiffel Tower.

Fig. 25 The women's radios are confiscated.

He is a pristine photographic memory but upon his return Amsatou tears up the photo as present reality has ruined her dream.) It is the men's decision to confiscate the women's radios that really begins to mobilise the women against the patriarchal system in which they are living. As three women pass in front of the growing pile of radios lying in front of the mosque, one of them comments that the men 'want to lock up our minds': the radios are a link to the outside world, a window on to other experiences and ideas. Later the women gather at night at the well where the two girls fleeing excision had drowned themselves, and express their outrage at their husbands' behaviour; a growing sense of female solidarity emerges. When Collé is led before the entire village and whipped by her husband, it is mainly the women, although still not all of them, who take her side. By the end of the film, all of the women bar the *Salindana* are in revolt, partly inspired by what has happened to Diattou, one of the four young girls who had sought asylum with Collé; lured away by her mother, Salba, while Collé was being whipped, she was 'cut' and died from the bleeding. The graphic memory of her act haunts Salba and seems to bring all of the women together in solidarity. As in much of Sembene's work, women are here portrayed as agents of change: their lived experience forces them to challenge traditional wisdom.

The film's long closing sequence in which the women confront the elders and the *Salindana* takes the form of a visual and ideological struggle between competing interpretations of past/present/identity: set against the backdrop of the mosque, the anthill/*moolaadé* and the pile of blazing radios (set alight by the men), the sequence draws together different layers of history and different versions of the village's identity. The anthill represents the animistic origins of the village, which are then overlaid by Islam, which arrived in the nineteenth century, while the radios represent an engagement with late twentieth-century modernity. Collé, accompanied by the female griot who sings her praises as a woman more valiant than the men, relieves the *Salindana* of their knives and lays them before the elders. In response to criticism that 'purification is required by Islam', she responds that the Grand Imam himself has declared this to be false on the radio. This deliberately idealised resolution of communal issues, requires individual moments of heroism from Colle, of course, but also from her husband Ciré (who breaks with the men, declaring 'It takes more than a pair of balls to make a man!'), as well as Amsatou and Ibrahima who dare to face down convention on marriage to a *bilakoro*.

However, Sembene does not conclude with this message of 'hope' or 'heroism'. Instead, the camera tilts upwards from the two young lovers, following the plumes of smoke climbing towards the sky, and focuses on the ostrich egg sitting atop the village mosque (a merging of animism and Islam). Then, in the film's striking closing image, Sembene gestures towards an imagined future in a jarring cut to an image of a television aerial, before the screen fades to black. Sembene here seems to indicate that more change is on the way; those with a vested interest in structures of power may seek to cast their position as predicated on a long and unbroken history but the film reveals that from animism to Islam to postcolonial modernity, the village has been a constant site of change and upheaval. Change is inevitable, although not necessarily positive (despite the posi-tivist claims of the West): what matters is how one deals with it.

In conclusion, Sembene's film demonstrates that this is no timeless village, living out an eternal repetition of the past: on the contrary, it is a place locked in a struggle to determine its relationship to the past and the nature of its evolving present. No matter what Hegel or Sarkozy may think, Africa is not a continent that lives in the past. In depicting the past, present and future of an African village, Sembene carves out a space in which the ongoing project of African modernity can unfold in all of its complexity.

NOTES

1 The information on female genital mutilation in this chapter is largely taken from fact sheets and dossiers prepared by the UK-based Foundation for Women's Health Research and Development (Forward), which were distributed at screenings of the film in London in June 2005.

2 I will use the term 'excision' as a middle ground between 'purification' and 'female genital mutilation', terms that immediately charge the act of excision with specific values and meanings. Although more 'neutral', the notion of excision acknowledges the act of cutting as central to these rites of initiation. It is precisely over the significance of excision that the villagers come into conflict.

3 The full text of Sarkozy's speech can be found online at: http://www.elysee.fr/elysee/ely-see.fr/francais/interventions/2007/juillet/allocution_a_l_universite_de_dakar.79184.html (accessed 10 January 2009).

WORKS CITED

Austen, R. A. (2007) 'Beyond "history": two films of the deep Mandé past', in V. Bickford-Smith and R. Mendelson (eds) *Black and White in Colour: African History on Screen*. Oxford: James Currey; Athens, OH: Ohio University Press; Cape Town: Double Storey, 28–40.

Bickford-Smith, V. and R. Mendelson (eds) (2007) *Black and White in Colour: African History on Screen*. Oxford: James Currey; Athens, OH: Ohio University Press; Cape Town: Double Storey.

Chrétien, J.-P. (ed.) (2008) *L'Afrique de Sarkozy: un déni d'histoire*. Paris: Karthala.

Diawara, M. (1992) *African Cinema: Politics and Culture*. Bloomington: Indiana University Press.

Fabian, J. (1983) *Time and the Other: How Anthropology Makes its Object*. New York: Columbia University Press.

Gassama, M. (ed.) (2008) *L'Afrique répond à Sarkozy: contre le discours de Dakar*. Paris: Éditions Philippe Rey.

Hegel, G. W. F. (1975) *Lectures on the Philosophy of World History. Introduction: Reason in History*. Cambridge: Cambridge University Press.

MacCannell, D. (1976) *The Tourist: A New Theory of the Leisure Class*. Basingstoke: Macmillan.

Mbem, A. J. (2007) *Nicolas Sarkozy à Dakar: débats et enjeux autour d'un discours*. Paris: L'Harmattan.

Murphy, D. (2000) *Sembene: Imagining Alternatives in Film and Fiction*. Oxford: James Currey; Trenton, NJ: Africa World Press.

Murphy, D. and P. Williams (2007) *Postcolonial African Cinema: Ten Directors*. Manchester: Manchester University Press.

Rosen, P. (1991) 'Making a Nation in Sembene's *Ceddo*', *Quarterly Review of Film and Video*, 13, 1–3, 147–72.

Saul, M. (2007) 'History as cultural redemption in Gaston Kaboré's pre-colonial films', in V. Bickford-Smith and R. Mendelson (eds) *Black and White in Colour: African History on Screen*. Oxford: James Currey; Athens, OH: Ohio University Press; Cape Town: Double Storey, 11–27.

Ukadike, N. F. (1994) *Black African Cinema*, Berkeley: University of California Press.

HISTORICAL AND CULTURAL MEMORY

9. 'THE UNQUIET DEAD':
MEMORIES OF THE SPANISH CIVIL WAR
IN GUILLERMO DEL TORO'S CINEMA

JONATHAN ELLIS AND ANA MARÍA SÁNCHEZ-ARCE

Spanish society remains in two minds about the Spanish Civil War. While the generation with memories of the war and its aftermath are nearly always cautious about 'reopening anything', from an archive to an unmarked grave, the grandchildren who cannot remember anything because they did not see anything are desperate to learn more.[1] For many years fictional and non-fictional representations of the Spanish Civil War and its aftermath were largely completed by foreign artists. They include films like *Casablanca* (Michael Curtiz, 1942) and *For Whom the Bell Tolls* (Sam Wood, 1943) and *L'espoir* (André Malraux, 1945), non-fiction works such as George Orwell's *Homage to Catalonia* (1938) and Gerald Brenan's *The Spanish Labyrinth* (1943).[2] Cinema and literature in Spain were necessarily curtailed by both active and imagined censorship during the dictatorship. Although Spanish films like *Bienvenido Mister Marshall* (Luis García Berlanga, 1953) and *Plácido* (Luis García Berlanga, 1961) reflect on the poverty and social inequality of the post-war years, the Civil War itself is not mentioned. This remains the case even in Victor Erice's *The Spirit of the Beehive* (1973), *the* film about the Spanish Civil War for most foreign audiences and a major influence on Guillermo del Toro.[3]

Del Toro has made two films set during or shortly after the Spanish Civil War, *The Devil's Backbone* (2001) and *Pan's Labyrinth* (2006), and they are the cultural equivalent of the grandchildren's gaze. They are as much an attempt to recover Spain's past as to mythologise it. Pam Cook talks about the importance of film in the process of creating national memories:

> The term 'prosthetic memory' has been used to describe the process whereby reconstructions of the past produce replacement memories that simulate first-hand experiences. Such enterprises lay themselves open to charges of lack of authenticity, of substituting a degraded popular version for the 'real' event, and to accusations that by presenting history as dramatic spectacle they obscure our understanding of social, political and cultural forces. The

pessimistic view assumes that the images and stories of the past fed to us by the global media networks produce 'false' memories, or at least memory scenarios whose veracity, or relationship to the real, are impossible to determine. Yet, in the very act of addressing audiences as nostalgic spectators and encouraging them to become involved in re-presenting the past, the media invites exploration and interrogation of the limits of its engagement with history. (2005: 2)

Cook's comments on the value of historical cinema are particularly pertinent in relation to cultural representations of the Spanish Civil War for which there may be few first-hand accounts available. As she acknowledges, 'such enterprises lay themselves open to charges of lack of authenticity' while at the same time encouraging 'nostalgic spectators ... to become involved in re-presenting the past'. In other words, filmic history cannot claim to be the equivalent of so-called historical 'facts' or testimony but it can provoke us into considering why such witness accounts might be missing and where one might go to recover them. During Franco's dictatorship there was no shortage of first-hand experiences of the Spanish Civil War; the problem for contemporary historians is that only the winning side of the story was available. In this sense, Spanish representations of the war and its aftermath were already 'prosthetic' in their origins since Francoist memories and representations were at least partly simulations of events that did not necessarily occur in the way they were remembered. In addition to this, the Republican witnesses who were able to tell their stories were all in exile.

This is where directors like del Toro can help in the psychological rather than the actual recovery of historical memory. Cinematic 'false' memories like those of del Toro would not hold up in a court of law. But they are narratives of what might have occurred, and at least as convincing as many of the myths propagated during Franco's dictatorship which were neither challenged during the Transition nor for the first thirty years of democracy in Spain. As anthropologist Michael Taussig has put it, creative work of this nature 'allows the moral and magic powers of the unquiet dead to flow into the public sphere' (qouted in Graham 2005: 146–7). False memories may eventually summon real ones or at least prompt a fresh engagement with historical documents. Therefore, we could go further than Pam Cook and suggest that a 'prosthetic memory', particularly one that makes viewers aware of its own artificiality, may be the only way to remember the past. An imposed, realist 'prosthetic memory' may indeed pass for historical fact; a self-aware, artificial 'prosthetic memory' will, on the other hand, call into question the very acts of remembering and historicising the past. Del Toro's films set in war-torn and post-war Spain are clear examples of the second type of 'prosthetic memory'.

Del Toro's first film about the Civil War, *The Devil's Backbone*, is conscious of the extent to which memories of the war are artificial. In the film the metaphor of 'prosthetic memory' is literalised in Carmen's artificial right leg. The lost leg which hurts even though it is not physically there is yet another absence as presence. Carmen significantly replaces it with a 'heavy' wooden leg which is nevertheless hollow. It is highly significant that Carmen's false leg is the right one. She has to put on an artificial right limb to walk in the same way that Republican survivors had to fake a belief in right-wing ideology to avoid being executed or imprisoned. The fact that the leg is made of wood like the statues of saints that she decides to retrieve from storage as the Fascists approach is also significant. Carmen is externally unbalanced by this arrangement in the same way that other Republicans felt internally divided between a public mask of acquiescence to the regime and a private sense of revulsion. In both cases, the left and right sides are working at cross purposes.

Del Toro is particularly concerned with the idea of the Spanish Civil War as a memory that is suspended in time. The film begins with the question 'What is a ghost?' posed by Casares, an Argentinean old man who both in appearance and personality resembles the character of Fernando in *The Spirit of the Beehive*:

> What is a ghost? A tragedy condemned to repeat itself time and again. An instant of pain, perhaps. Something dead which still seems to be alive. An emotion suspended in time. Like a blurred photograph. Like an insect trapped in amber.

Casares's voiceover is accompanied by a series of disconnected images that only make sense towards the end of the film when he repeats this passage with the additional information that he too has become a ghost. At the beginning of the film, we see a bomb being released from an aircraft payload, an unconscious boy cradled by another boy, and the same unconscious body sinking through water. As the voiceover ends, these images of war are replaced by the ghostly outlines of an unborn foetus with what looks like an underdeveloped spine in an amber-like solution. Each image narrates a human life either aborted or about to be terminated. For a brief moment, we see atrocities take place in the present before either side has had a chance to narrate or (mis)remember them.

Most of these images take on narrative significance in the film. The boy is later identified as Santi who is accidentally injured by Jacinto, the orphanage's caretaker who then weighs down the boy's unconscious body and throws it into an underground pool. Santi's ghost haunts both the orphanage and many spectators' memories of the film. He attempts to warn the other children of their eventual fate while at the same time requesting revenge on his own behalf. Del Toro never makes it clear whether we are meant to interpret Santi as an avenging angel, some kind of evil spirit, or an innocent victim forever in limbo. Like most liminal characters, he has both a material and supernatural presence. While his body looks as if it is decaying, his injured head continues to shed blood. This blood is also mixed with water which brings to mind the sufferings of Christ. Santi is later seen standing on water in a clear reference to Christ. Santi's name is a shortened version of Santiago, the patron saint of Spain. If Santi *is* Spain, the Spanish Civil War is seen as a conflict in which dying children leave blood everywhere, a red trail that eventually catches up with the murderers as well as the victims. It is also a conflict where the losers, the 'unquiet dead', whisper. Santi is known by the children as 'the one who whispers'.

In Del Toro's film, burying (or sinking) past crimes leads not to their disappearance but to their 'suspension in time'. These events are 'condemned to repeat' themselves 'time and time again'. The pain does not subside either; it is merely deferred. As the caretaker sinks underwater, Santi's ghost still looks at us with open eyes. Casares is the only adult left to help the children. In coming back to life as a ghost, he appears to have struck some kind of deal with the devil as suggested by the flies that accompany his resurrected body. Like Santi, who is also surrounded by flies, Casares is surely condemned to remain at the orphanage forever. The film's final shot depicts him watching the children's departure from the open door of the orphanage. Just before this last shot, the rectangular doors of the orphanage frame the children walking towards the horizon. The composition of the image looks like a cinematic still or group photograph, an effect emphasised by Casares' voiceover which speaks of 'a blurred photograph'. The children look less like real people and more like abstract figures or allegorical shapes. One of the children actually appears to appreciate this as he looks over his shoulder, as if already aware of the past being frozen in amber. The children's sombre outlines are reminiscent of the shadow cast by another lonely-looking child in Giorgio de Chirico's painting, 'Mystery and Melancholy of a Street' (1914). Del Toro makes us aware of the artificiality not just of this particular story but of any narrative device. This does not take away film's potential to entertain, move and even educate its spectators. On the contrary, an awareness of the extent to which images are cropped and framed for narrative and symbolic effect can often help us to notice such manipulations when they are less obvious. *The Devil's Backbone* does not end with the painterly image of children, however, as Del Toro's gaze backs away from the harsh light of the Spanish plain. Instead, the film's final point-of-view stays in the dark with Casares, the adult-ghost. This aligns the audience with the historical past too. While the children stumble forward into the future, we can only watch them disappear. Are we ghosts as well? Certainly we are condemned to remember the Spanish Civil War not as an event we have lived through ourselves but as a series of painterly images and shadows that can both obscure and recover what occurred. In other words, del Toro makes us think about film as a memory generator at the precise moment the film is coming to an end.

Fictional frames are equally at issue in del Toro's next film about the Spanish Civil War, *Pan's Labyrinth*. As Paul Julian Smith (2007) points out, the film contains several allusions to Spanish art and cinema, particularly Erice's *The Spirit of the Beehive* but also Diego Velázquez's aesthetic of elderly women preparing food as seen in a painting like 'Old Woman Cooking Eggs' (1618). In addition to these intertexts, del Toro also creates a fictional book within the film, *El libro de las encrucijadas*, or Book of Crossroads, which in Spanish alludes to the Cross and therefore to choice and, in the Christian tradition, sacrifice and resurrection. The Book is given to Ofelia by the Faun so that she can learn what tasks she is expected to perform. It predicts what is going to happen and memorialises it in advance, only for its pages to be erased, ready to be written upon the next time that Ofelia opens it. It also fulfils the narrative function of the fairytale which, much like Ofelia's (and del Toro's) favourite reading matter, gives textual authority to that which would otherwise be seen as folk tales. The Book is thus a powerful reminder of del Toro's own fascination with the act of storytelling as well as a comment on the extent to which Spain and the rest of the world were at a historical crossroads in 1944.

The Book's stories are written before the events they describe have actually happened. Ofelia can see herself performing the tasks that she will only carry out after reading about them. As in the Bible, the Word comes before anything else. Yet *Pan's Labyrinth* does not offer a sacred text to the viewer but a text which is always open to interpretation. For example, just before the second task the illustrations show Ofelia inserting the key into the central door whereas in fact she opens the one on the left. Were Ofelia to have taken the illustration and the fairies' advice at face value she would have failed the task. We cannot be sure if the Book relays a version of events, a prediction of the future or a rewriting of the past. The Book's unreliability thus casts doubt on the truthfulness of any historical accounts, however fixed they seem.

The function of *Pan's Labyrinth* as a comment on memory is even more apparent in the circular frame of the story, particularly the initial scene which acts as a spatial and temporal nexus. The first shot of the film corresponds to Ofelia's death although this is not necessarily clear on first viewing. The image is uncanny because of the reversal of time and the disorientating camerawork. The blood that has already trickled down Ofelia's nose returns back to her body as a nursery rhyme places the viewer firmly in the timeless world of the fantastic. The nursery rhyme is in fact Ofelia's last link to the real world since it is Mercedes who sings it to her as she dies.

Fig. 26 Ofelia (Ivana Baquero) lies dying at the centre of the labyrinth.

The camera moves from right to left on the screen but this disguises its vertical movement from the centre of the labyrinth to the ground where Ofelia lies having just been shot by Captain Vidal. This is the viewer's introduction to Ofelia who looks directly at us as if imploring our intervention and sympathy. It also recalls a similarly haunting image in *The Devil's Backbone* when Santi's open eyes stare at us through water. Whereas Santi's blood in this film keeps flowing freely as a sign of an open wound, Ofelia's is magically restored thus hinting at either a healing process or a process of forgetfulness. In *Pan's Labyrinth*, del Toro's camerawork highlights the sacrifice that Ofelia makes on her brother's behalf. She looks as if she is being crucified with her extended left hand bleeding into the fountain at the centre of the labyrinth like Christ's on the cross. This may be a comment on the metaphorical sacrifice made by the immediate generation of children after the Civil War. It is Ofelia's left hand that the camera concentrates on just as Franco focused on punishing the children of the left in the post-war period.[4]

Spatial inversions and temporal twists place the spectator's point-of-view after Ofelia's death has taken place, moving back in time to recover and remember her life. The film begins in the present but the past is accessed not by travelling in a linear fashion but through ascent disguised as lateral movement and circularity. Memory of the past does not so much resurface from below since it is always there waiting to be found. It is not the past which is buried and lost but ourselves who are in the dark, as in the final moments of *The Devil's Backbone*. This conception of the present as moving away from the past is heir to pre-Judeo-Christian (linear) ways of thinking about time. We begin *Pan's Labyrinth* in the same place, down there, in a Platonic Cavern of forgetfulness, out of which we are given the chance to come out. The past is there, like Ofelia, looking at us straight in the eye. As the Faun says at the end, Ofelia leaves behind 'small traces of her time on earth, visible only to those who know where to look'. But we have to make an effort to return the past's gaze, to acknowledge that it is part of the present.

Pan's Labyrinth is a representation of memory loss and memory recovery on several levels from Ofelia's role as a princess 'who forgot who she was and where she came from' to Vidal's attempts to live up to other people's memories of his own father's heroic death whilst denying that same heroic death. Above and beyond this, the film also comments on the enforced forgetting of the Spanish Civil War, both during and after the dictatorship. The film counters this historical drift towards amnesia in part through its memory of Spanish art, cinema and literature that did engage with the legacy of the conflict. Del Toro's employment of two clearly defined worlds, the real world and the Underground Realm, is perhaps an allusion to the familiar trope about two Spains, the most well-known example of which can be found in Antonio Machado's poetry. However, the concept is certainly older than Machado and goes back at least as far as the nineteenth-century Spanish satirist Mariano José de Larra and Machado's contemporary, philosopher Miguel de Unamuno. The protagonist of *Pan's Labyrinth* has a dual identity too as Ofelia and Princess Moanna. Although Michael Atkinson believes that 'visually, del Toro makes no great transitional distinction between the countryside, gore-soaked and seething with secrets as it is, and the Gothic netherworld' (2007: 52), this distinction is expressed visually by the film's use of colour. The real world, in line with the realist Spanish film tradition of directors like Juan Antonio Bardem, Luis Garcia Berlanga and Carlos Saura, is mostly mossy green, grey and brown. Subdued natural colours and spectral light drain the characters and *mise-en-scène* of life. The underground world, on the other hand, is normally characterised by vibrant reds, golds and dazzling light. In *Pan's Labyrinth* the underground world appears more alluring and sensual than the drab, rain-drenched naturalism of 1940s Spain, a naturalism that harks back to seminal films such as Saura's *Raise Ravens* (1975), a labyrinthine film about a young woman's memories of her childhood.

Pan's Labyrinth encourages us to share Ofelia's wish to go underground. This might seem a rather peculiar desire for a young girl, yet it is perfectly in keeping with the way colour was seen to represent illusion during the dictatorship. As Alejandro Varderi points out:

> In Franco's Spain, intent on hiding the modernist colour of Gaudí's and Domènec i Montaner's architecture under black religious processions that 'purified the streets', Hollywood Technicolor as seen on the screens of local cinemas was the only way to escape misery and fear. (1996: 66; authors' translation)

Ofelia's love of illustrated fairytales and her desire to travel elsewhere, even if that elsewhere involves monsters at least as terrifying as those aboveground, reflect a preference for fantasy over reality. The subterranean colours and spaces of *Pan's Labyrinth* represent this cinematic world of rich possibility. Ofelia literally draws herself into the underground world with a piece of chalk. Her imaginary cinema is anywhere she goes.

Although these colour schemes are broadly adhered to, the fact that some characters move between the two worlds inevitably causes some overlap. For example, the first magical creature that Ofelia encounters is a stick-insect that transforms itself into a fairy after seeing a drawing of one in Ofelia's book. It is thus curiously both part of the forest and part of the story, part real, part imaginary. The film as a whole is a similar hybrid. The Faun is a particularly obvious creature of two domains. He looks like a tree or one of the abandoned statues that litter the forest and labyrinth, his dark, mossy colours indistinguishable from the real world, but as the film progresses he becomes more silvery. At the very end of the film, he is bathed in the golden light of the Underground Realm. The Faun is also physically protean. He becomes younger the closer Ofelia comes to completing her tasks and as a consequence 'revealing her own spirit.' The Faun is thus

Fig. 27 The Faun (Doug Jones) demands the sacrifice of Ofelia's brother.

a barometer of Ofelia's transformation, of her double coming of age as a human character and as a supernatural princess of the underworld.

Like the Faun, the film moves between these different spatial and temporal worlds without fully separating them. This is not to say that both worlds are given equal status. The underground world certainly has some of the most memorable images but they are framed by and understood in relation to events aboveground. The film is a palimpsest where layers of images and writing interact with one another in unpredictable ways just as memories are modified and perhaps even forgotten as they are narrativised. Paul Ricoeur refers to this process in *Memory, History, Forgetting* when he states that:

> Could there then be a measure in the use of human memory, a 'never in excess' in accordance with the dictum of human wisdom? Could forgetting then no longer be in every respect the enemy of memory, and could memory have to negotiate with forgetting, groping to find the right measure in its balance with forgetting? And could this appropriate memory have something in common with the renunciation of total reflection? Could a memory lacking forgetting be the ultimate phantasm? (2004: 413)

For Ricoeur it is human to forget and to misremember while it is 'monstrous' never to 'forget anything' (*Ibid.*). The only characters who never seem to forget anything in the film are the King, the Faun and Vidal. Might the three characters be in fact related? Certainly their ability to remember everything appears monstrous in a film in which the most humane characters are all female and forgetful at some stage. Ofelia, for example, forgets her clothes in the rain and more importantly, the Faun's command not to eat from the Pale Man's table. Mercedes also forgets that she is not supposed to have a key for the storeroom. The only human father in the film has already died and is actively being forgotten by Ofelia and her mother. He is never named in the film and only referred to in relation to his occupation as a tailor. Vidal even usurps the title, 'father', from him. Ricoeur's argument is true in relation to individuals and nations, both of whom attempt to create an 'appropriate memory' they can live with, yet what seems understandable and perhaps desirable for individuals becomes monstrous itself in terms of national history. For who decides where the 'right measure' lies and what is the 'appropriate' historical memory?

Captain Vidal embodies the rhetoric of the dictatorship when he talks about wanting his son 'to be born in a new, clean Spain'. He is in charge of cleansing the land of enemies of fascist Spain. By 1944 Franco had been in power for five years but there were still pockets of resistance, particularly in inaccessible terrain and near the border with France. Vidal's mission is to cleanse the forest of *maquis*, usually anarchist, communist, socialist or Republican-leaning soldiers who kept fighting fascism well into the 1950s, sometimes with help from exiled political leaders. Many of these soldiers fought in Spain and on the Allies' side in World War II and later on returned to Spain to fight the fascists again. The *maquis* hiding in the mountains were thus seen by the fascists in much the same way that the toad is described in the Book. They were underground fighters who were accused of making Spain ideologically and morally ill just as the toad is killing the tree.

Del Toro's monsters represent many things. If one accepts Philip French's interpretation that the film is 'an allegory about the soul and national identity of Spain' (2006: 14), then Ofelia's first task of purging the toad's stomach in order to rid the tree of its unwelcome guest can be interpreted alongside Vidal's cleansing of the land. The *maquis* were not just a problem for the political right. They were also a historical inconvenience for the Allies and for the left in Spain who were all too ready to leave them to their fate. The *maquis* have thus been triply erased, first by Franco, second by the Allies, and third by their own political leaders during and after the dictatorship.[5] Secundino Serrano has commented on how Spain's Communist party systematically erased the *maquis* from its official history. He also draws attention to the failure of the Socialist party, in power for thirteen years after the Transition, to acknowledge the contribution of these fighters. Serrano suggests that politicians of the left are uncomfortable associating themselves with an enterprise that failed.[6]

Del Toro does not deal with these issues directly in *Pan's Labyrinth*, but his mythologising of the *maquis* could be seen as an attempt to retrieve their memory, however romanticised his portrait. The film shows the *maquis'* belief that the Allies might help them to remove the dictatorship, a hope that in early 1944 was still alive as the Allies were beginning to win the war. The fact that the *maquis* are able to kill Vidal at the end of the film appears to suggest that they were capable of securing a larger victory over Franco's forces. In fact, their fate was as uncertain as that of the orphan children at the end of *The Devil's Backbone*. The Allies never came south and the fascists regrouped and eventually defeated them. The only traces of their presence in Spanish forests and villages nowadays are the unopened graves 'visible only to those who know where to look'.

The toad does not only stand for the *maquis* and Republicans, however. It is also a figure of greed and degeneration connected with the dinner party and its guests. At Vidal's party the main agents of repression during Franco's time (policeman, mayor and priest) proceed to gorge on a sump-tuous feast whilst discussing rationing for everyone else. The comparison with the toad is perhaps too clearly spelt out by del Toro's editing which has the dinner party scenes straight after Ofelia's task and by the motif of the key which links the task to the key used by Vidal to lock up food in order to control the villagers and act as bait for the *maquis*. The film also comments on the ideological brainwashing that accompanied rationing, particularly in a scene in which a Civil Guard is seen to distribute bread whilst shout-ing: 'This is our daily bread in Franco's Spain … The Reds lie, because in a united Spain, there's not a single home without fire or bread.' Fascists appropriate the language of the Lord's Prayer to place themselves in the position of God and the role of provider. Food is crucial to the functioning of del Toro's real and fantastic worlds. This is appropriate in a film set in Spain during the 1940s, a decade known as *los años del hambre* or 'Years of Hunger'.[7] This was a period in which old men would wait by schools to beg for children's unfinished breakfast and many people died of hunger.[8]

Pan's Labyrinth also reflects the belief popular in folk tales that one should not eat or drink anything whilst in fairyland lest one risk never being able to return to the human world. In both worlds food is used as bait and succumbing to temptation has dire consequences. The toad dies after eating the amber stones hidden under insects. The *maquis* successfully steal food from Vidal but at the cost of several lives and blowing Mercedes' cover. Ofelia is nearly eaten during the second task for daring to eat a couple of grapes from the Pale Man's table. Only the fairies' sacrifice prevents her being killed like other children before her. This is explicitly shown in the paintings on the apse behind the Pale Man and in the accompanying sound of children's cries that can just about be heard as the camera pans over the paintings following Ofelia's gaze. It is thereby suggested that Ofelia is imagining what has happened and is actually bringing the paintings to life. The paintings depict the Pale Man's murder and consumption of a child while two other children look on in horror. In the first painting, the Pale Man appears to be biting the child's head off. In the second, he dangles the same child upside down in front of him whilst stabbing him in the chest with a dagger similar to the one Ofelia will steal. This is yet another example of del Toro playing with narrative time to show the corrosive effect of witnessing traumatic events. As in the opening scene, the camera's movement from right to left signals the mind's journey from present to past.

The position and theme of the paintings bring to mind the biblical massacre of the innocents and also Francisco Goya's famous painting, 'Saturn

Fig. 28 The Pale Man (Doug Jones), disfigured by marks of fascism.

Devouring One of His Sons' (c. 1819–23). The Pale Man is another version of Saturn, eating generations of children to preserve himself. Significantly, the Pale Man also looks like Jesús Gris, the modern vampire in del Toro's first film, *Cronos* (1993). Both Gris and the Pale Man evade mortality and transcend time.

Cronos means time and is also another name for Saturn, the God of time who ate his children to avoid his own predicted demise. This also evokes Vidal's own killing of his step-daughter and his obsession with time (symbolised by his father's watch) and leaving a legacy. The fact that del Toro houses such a monster in a place that looks like, or may in fact be, a hellish church, supports the thesis that the Pale Man is not only Saturn or Time, but also the institution of the Church. The Pale Man sits at the head of a table of riches but he does not allow anyone to partake of this feast. His white skin makes him look like a vampiric version of the Pope, just as his stigmata mark him out as a Christ-like figure, albeit one who sacrifices others for his own survival rather than the other way round. This inversion of Christian dogma turns the Pale Man into an Anti-Christ dressed in the iconography and symbols of the Church. The Catholic Church was guilty of at least two 'sins' during the Spanish Civil War and immediately afterwards, siding with Franco against the legitimate Republican government during the war and subsequent repression and ignoring the persecution of Jews across Europe during World War II.[9] The Pale Man cannot see anything unless it affects his well-being. This is why his eyes are idle on a plate in front of him, the pile of children's shoes at the side of his table an obvious reference to the Holocaust.

In addition to representing the Church, the Pale Man is disfigured by the marks of fascism. When he spreads his hands in front of his face in order to see, his fingers resemble arrows bunched together. These ten outstretched fingers are reminiscent of the symbol of the Falangist movement in Spain which consists of five arrows and a yoke. The Falangists take their name from the Greek word for finger. The Pale Man is, in other words, a monstrous hybrid of Catholic Church and fascist state in 1940s Spain. The Pale Man's banquet is made up of red food as if literally of blood. The fascists called the communists and Republicans *los rojos*, or Reds. The food stands not only for Spain's hunger and deprivation, but also for the censorship of certain political ideas (most of which were figured red). Red food is forbidden because of its ideological significance. Ofelia does not seem to realise that eating such food is almost synonymous with death. This is not Ofelia's first ideological blunder. She also offers her left hand to Vidal on their first meeting.

Ofelia's left-sidedness is only one aspect of her deviance from the 'norm'; the other one is her gender. She is about to become a woman in a patriarchal society which values masculinity above all else. This is best seen in Vidal's certainty that Carmen is carrying a son rather than a daughter and also in his failure to spot Mercedes as an informant. Even after Vidal has captured Mercedes he still underestimates her and tells his subordinate to leave, commenting that 'she's just a woman'. Mercedes' reply reflects not just Vidal's prejudice against women but that of society as a whole: 'That's what you've always thought. That's why I was able to get away with it. I was invisible to you.' Mercedes takes on the role of surrogate mother to Ofelia whilst Carmen is ill. The two adult women represent Ofelia's existing choice between two models of femininity: on the one hand, the acceptable, conventionally beautiful and passive victim embodied by Carmen, on the other, the unacceptable, resilient and active womanhood represented by

Mercedes. Carmen schools her daughter in the language of romance as seen in her sentimental account of how she met Vidal. She dresses Ofelia to look like John Tenniel's illustrations for the 1865 revised version of Lewis Carroll's *Alice's Adventures in Wonderland*, but she does not want her to use them for real adventure. In relation to Ofelia's own identity as a daughter unwilling to become like her mother, one might also see the toad that she confronts during the first task as a figure for the pregnant female body, becoming immobile and overweight to conceal and protect something precious (in the toad's case, the key; in the mother's case, Ofelia's brother). In both cases neither toad nor the mother survive the expulsion of the valuable object inside them. The toad's limp body is forgotten about by Ofelia as she reaches into the toad's vomit, an abject yellow mound that looks something between reconstituted fat and a gigantic jelly. Peter Bradshaw comments rather unfairly that *Pan's Labyrinth* is little more than 'a series of four or five brilliant images, like illustrative plates from a Victorian volume, or frames from a graphic novel' (2006: 10). The toad's destruction is certainly one of the film's most memorable images. It exists, as the best cinematic images do, outside of any narrative logic. As del Toro observes: 'Fairytale logic is not linear, it's random' (quoted in Brooks 2006: 9). Ofelia does not have to do much to bring about the toad's demise. She simply has to wait for its self-destruction. We can certainly see this moment in the film as a fairytale version of Ofelia's own feelings of fear about motherhood. She sees pregnancy as the bodily degradation of the mother and childbirth as quite literally the end of her. Del Toro admitted in creating the film to being 'obsessed with images of stillborn things' (*Ibid.*). The toad's vomit is surely one of these 'stillborn things'.

Carmen spends most of the film in bed or in a wheelchair. Her main purpose, at least for Vidal, is to remain alive long enough to bear his son. Vidal is obsessed with his own image and having a son is part of this. In addition to cleaning and polishing his boots with the clinical efficiency of every other cinematic sadist, Vidal also spends a remarkable amount of time gazing into the shaving-mirror, at one point slashing at his own reflection in frustration. This is partly explained by an anecdote another soldier relates of having met Vidal's father in Morocco. At the moment of death, his father crushed his fob watch to commemorate forever his heroism. Vidal is haunted by his father's ghost and the pressure to hand on a similar legacy of bravery to his own son. In addition to cleaning and recalibrating the watch, he also appears to be preparing his face for the moment of death. It is as if Vidal spends his whole adulthood waiting to re-enact his father's death. Yet at the same time, he seems desperate for his son to witness this. Thus, a memory that he never possesses, that has been passed on to him via strangers, possesses him anyway.

Vidal has several people attend Carmen, including Mercedes and two different doctors. But she appears fated to die from the moment she arrives in the forest and agrees to use the wheelchair. Vidal also expects his wife's death, telling the doctor to save his son rather than her. When Carmen is not sleeping or asking Ofelia to tell the unborn baby stories, she is bent over with blood. To be pregnant in the film is like waiting to die. The pregnant mother, like the pregnant toad, is only valued for the key-like object it hides inside. As it turns out, the baby is the key to the film's ending and Ofelia's fate. He is the central figure of the statue which is itself at the centre of the labyrinth. The statue depicts Ofelia holding her brother with the Faun behind them. As with the Book, this ambiguous image suggests that the future is already written, that it is literally set in stone. This is not true since Ofelia has a choice whether to hand over the baby or die to save him. The statue allows both possibilities.

Ofelia disobeys both figures of authority to protect her brother, first by stealing him from Vidal, then by keeping him from the Faun. The Faun implies that using the dagger will bring about Ofelia's transformation into Princess Moanna. He attempts to persuade Ofelia that he will not harm the baby since only a few drops of blood will be necessary to open the portal between the two worlds. The Faun becomes another version of the Pale Man demanding the sacrifice of innocents. Ofelia, perhaps remembering the paintings in the crypt where the same dagger had been used to murder, refuses to hand over her brother. This is the crucial choice in the film since once she has placed her brother's life before her own she cannot do anything to prevent Vidal taking him by force and shooting her. It is at this moment that the two worlds overlap as the Faun and Vidal occupy the same frame with Ofelia trapped between them. Ofelia dies to protect her brother in an act of self-sacrifice. However, in contrast to her mother's death in childbirth, hers is an affirmative act which rejects the rules of both Vidal's and the Faun's worlds. This is why del Toro places her literally between these two figures at the end of *Pan's Labyrinth* and figuratively throughout the film. She dies positioned between the real and underground worlds, leaning over the edge of the portal at the centre of the labyrinth. This ending makes sense of the first image of the film in which Ofelia is portrayed as a prostrated Christ. It is also in direct intertextual relationship with the scene of Isabel playing dead in *The Spirit of the Beehive* since the two girls share an almost exact posture. Isabel is dramatising her own death as a way of dealing with traumatic memories; Ofelia's death is a re-enactment of memories that have been submerged for decades. Both have their left arms extended, Isabel towards nothing and Ofelia towards the fountain/well that acts as portal to the Underground Realm.

Ofelia's unnecessary death, her sacrifice for her brother, is the exact opposite of what a civil war is all about. In this way, her act becomes a comment on the Spanish Civil War itself and its legacy for modern Spain. Her brother is the son of a fascist just as the new Spain emerging during the dictatorship and even today is born out of a fascist regime. But neither side wants to remember this, or if they do, nobody will admit it.

The punishment for standing up to totalitarianism is often to be killed and one's own dissent to be forgotten or misremembered. This is Ofelia's tragedy and that of the *maquis* who in the film appear victorious but in reality remain forgotten. To die is not the worst fate to befall characters in *Pan's Labyrinth*. It is to be forgotten. As the Faun warns Ofelia: 'Your spirit shall forever remain among the humans. You shall age like them, you shall die like them, and all memory of you shall fade in time. And we'll vanish along with it. You'll never see us again.' But this does not happen within the context of the film as Ofelia is shown to be reborn again as Princess Moanna in the Underground Realm where she rules alongside her father and mother for many centuries. In a clever self-reference, the King is played by Federico Lupi, who plays modern vampire Jesús Gris in *Cronos* and ghostly Casares in *The Devil's Backbone*. Ofelia is thus going down into the land of 'the unquiet dead', of those whose memories are suspended in time: 'something dead which still seems to be alive ... like an insect trapped in amber'.

Ofelia is appropriately dressed in red and yellow, both the colours of amber but also the colours of the Spanish flag. Is this an idyllic and sentimental vision of the restoration of the Spanish monarchy in post-Franco Spain? Such a fantasy ending is required by the genre of the fairytale and by the demands of audiences for a happy ending. The bright Underground Realm imagined by Ofelia corresponds to Princess Moanna's dreams about the human world 'of blue skies, soft breeze and sunshine'. At the beginning of the film, the underworld is shown as shrouded in darkness and dominated by grey stone and the world above ground is presented in the full glory of a bright day. Princess Moanna can only access the human world by obliterating herself and forgetting her past. The same happens in reverse at the end of the film to Ofelia as she leaves behind a dark human world. Both Moanna and Ofelia are in search of better lives and places, constructing fantasies about 'other' worlds above or below ground. The point is surely that neither of their escape routes is real or perfect just as there is no ideal way to remember the ending of the film or the Spanish Civil War. If one forgets the initial shot of Ofelia's dying body and the blood flowing backwards, it is similarly easy to forget the fact that Ofelia dies. The film ascends out of the labyrinth, past Ofelia's dead body and an inconsolable Mercedes weeping and ends with a sun-lit image of the tree below which the monstrous toad had earlier nested. The voiceover preserves the illusion that Ofelia has not died and that 'small traces of her time on earth' are 'visible only to those who know where to look'. Princess Moanna's story bookends Ofelia's tragedy in a way that attempts to make sense of unnecessary individual death and, by extension, provide an archetypal explanation for the Spanish Civil War and its aftermath. Like Princess Moanna, we have forgotten who we are and where we come from. Spanish citizens still live in a land of crypts full of child-eating monsters, forests of forgotten graves and wells that hide unspeakable secrets. Perhaps storytelling is the only way to begin the process of remembering how to remember, particularly in Spain where there have been so many decades of political and private pressure to remain silent.

NOTES

1   The gaze of the grandchildren no longer respects the pact of oblivion. While Spain's political class remains cautious about breaking the silence, a significant section of civil society is ready to remember the past and restless to tell and be told its almost-forgotten stories. Since the new millennium a series of civil pressure groups, most notably the Association for the Recovery of Historical Memory, has petitioned the government for financial assistance to locate and recover the bodies of all those who were killed by Franco's forces both during and after the Civil War.

2   For an excellent introduction to English literature on the Spanish Civil War see Paul Preston's 'Bibliographical Essay' (2006: 333–57)

3   'The Spirit of the Beehive is a seminal movie for me. I even modelled the girl in Cronos exactly on Ana Torrent. That movie, along with the films of Buñuel and the films of Hitchcock, is almost a part of my genetic make-up, buried deep in my DNA' (del Toro, cited in Wood 2006: 112). Released two years before Franco's death, The Spirit of the Beehive is located in a remote Spanish village around 1940. It concentrates on the experiences of two sisters, Ana and Isabel, and their detached parents, Fernando and Teresa. The film introduces both parents as inscrutable presences in their children's

lives. Each parent is shown hiding behind a literal and metaphorical disguise. Fernando conceals his gaze behind the protective armour of a beekeeper's suit. Teresa has her own form of hideaway. She spends most of the film writing letters to someone who may be a lover and is probably a fighter on one side or other. Like her husband, she keeps silent about her pre-Civil War life. He confides in a journal he quickly erases; she confides in her unknown correspondent who never receives her letters.

4   Thousands of Republican children were taken away from their parents and handed over to Francoist families for adoption or sent away to be re-educated in religious establishments. Amongst revelations that have only recently come to light is evidence that Franco's regime also shot pregnant women. One judge at the women's trial told the court: 'Imagine if I had to wait seven months for each woman who we have to mete out justice to ... it is impossible' (cited in Tremlett 2007: 74).

5   This is still unfortunately the case. In the last ever commemoration of the D-Day Landings in 2004, Spanish Republican veterans were not allowed to participate because Spain was judged to have been a belligerent nation during World War II.

6   For further information see Serrano 2001.

7   John Hooper (2005) charts the history of Spain from the Years of Hunger to the restoration and early years of democracy.

8   We would like to thank José Sánchez Trillo (b. 1941) and Ana Arce Sánchez (b. 1940) for sharing these memories with us.

9   José M. Sánchez (1987) is the key book on this subject. The Catholic Church is still not ready to accept the role it played in the conflict, preferring to highlight the plight of hundreds of priests and nuns who were killed by Republican sympathisers. As recently as 19 November 2007, 498 of these 'twentieth-century martyrs' were beatified in the Vatican in a provocative act held a few weeks after the Spanish parliament ratified the Law of Historical Memory on 31 October 2007.

WORKS CITED

Aguilar, P. (2002) *Memory and Amnesia: The Role of the Spanish Civil War in the Transition to Democracy*. New York and London: Berghahn Books.

____ and C. Humlebæk (2002) 'Collective Memory and National Identity in the Spanish Democracy: The Legacies of Francoism and the Civil War', *History & Memory*, 14, 1/2, 121–64.

Atkinson, M. (2007) 'Moral Horrors in Guillermo del Toro's *Pan's Labyrinth*', *Film Comment*, January/February, 50–3.

Balfour, S. (2002) *Deadly Embrace: Morocco and the Road to the Spanish Civil War*. Oxford: Oxford University Press.

Beever, A. (1999) *The Spanish Civil War*. London: Cassell.

Bradshaw, P. (2006) 'Monster Munch', *Guardian*, 24 November, 10.

Brooks, X. (2006) 'Pan's people' [Interview with Guillermo del Toro], *Guardian*, 17 November, 9.

Cook, P. (2005) *Screening the Past: Memory and Nostalgia in Cinema*. London and New York: Routledge.

French, P. (2006) 'A feast for the eyes', *The Observer*, 26 November, 14.

Graham, H. (2005) *The Spanish Civil War*. Oxford: Oxford University Press.

Hooper, J. (2005) *The New Spaniards*. London: Penguin.

Jensen, G. (2002) *Irrational Triumph. Cultural Despair, Military Nationalism and the Intellectual Origins of Franco's Spain*. Reno and Las Vegas: University of Nevada Press.

Preston, P. (2006) *The Spanish Civil War: Reaction, Revolution and Revenge*. London and New York: Harper Perennial.

Richards, M. (2002) 'From War Culture to Civil Society', *History & Memory*, 14, 1/2 (Fall), 93–120.

Ricoeur, P. (2004) *Memory, History, Forgetting*, trans. Kathleen Blamey and David Pellauer. Chicago: University of Chicago Press.

Sánchez, J. M. (1987) *The Spanish Civil War as a Religious Tragedy*. Notre Dame, IN: University of Notre Dame Press.

Serrano, S. (2001) *Maquis, historia de la guerrilla antifranquista*. Madrid: Temas de Hoy-Historia.

Smith, P. J. (2007) '*Pan's Labyrinth*', *Film Quarterly*, 60, 4, 4–9.

Tremlett, G. (2007) *Ghosts of Spain: Travels through a Country's Hidden Past*. London: Faber and Faber.

Varderi, A. (1996) *Severo Sarduy y Pedro Almodóvar: del barroco al kitsch en la narrativa y el cine postmodernos*. Madrid: Editorial Pliegos.

Wood, J. (2006) *The Faber Book of Mexican Cinema*. London: Faber and Faber.

10. REWIND: THE WILL TO REMEMBER, THE WILL TO FORGET IN MICHAEL HANEKE'S *CACHÉ* (2005)

JEHANNE-MARIE GAVARINI

Michael Haneke's *Caché* (2005) opens with an uneventful street scene in which the camera frames the Parisian home of Anne (Juliette Binoche) and Georges Laurent (Daniel Auteuil). The audience is caught unawares when the images they are watching on the screen fast forward, revealing that this scene comes from a videotape which in fact is being viewed by the Laurents. This tape was made and sent to the Laurents by an anonymous voyeur, and it is the first of a series delivered to their house. Not only is the couple being watched, but also the author of the video wants the Laurents to know that they are being watched. The anxiety provoked by the series of videos triggers flashbacks for Georges who has a well-kept childhood secret. Haneke creates ambiguity as to the origin of the tapes. Although the mystery of the actual person behind the video camera is never fully solved, evidence from images within the tapes lead to Majid (Maurice Bénichou), an Algerian man who shares a common past with Georges.[1] In the 1960s Majid was the child of Algerian immigrant workers employed by Georges' family. Majid's parents were victims of repression by the French police and killed in a massacre during the Algerian War of Independence. Soon after, Majid was framed and betrayed by young Georges who felt threatened by his own parents' desire to adopt the orphaned child.

Today, Georges' remembrances are neatly tucked away in the recesses of his memory. He has become a television icon and public figure with his literary programme that brings together French intellectuals. His wife, who works for a publishing company, contributes to the couple's image of social success. When he visits his mother, and she asks how he is doing, Georges does not talk about himself *per se*, he immediately shifts the conversation to his wife and son Pierrot: 'We are all very busy, that's it'. Georges conveniently hides behind the collective image of his picture-perfect nuclear family. Pierrot has already entered the competitive world of his parents; his success in swimming competitions is a great source of joy and pride for Anne and Georges. The family's accomplishments provide a screen for Georges' secretive past and validate him as a coherent subject. However, if Georges' success comes in part from his ability to deny memories from his childhood, his obsessive need to forget is offset by his compulsion to record. His living room is lined with shelves filled with books and videotapes of his television show, a personal archive and testimony to his brilliant career and accomplishments. In contrast, Majid lives in a poor part of the city in a small rundown apartment with his son (played by Walid Afkir). He is still haunted by the disappearance of his parents, and his life appears to be ruled by the memory of his childhood losses. Rebuilding his identity and finding a new sense of belonging have been a lifelong struggle for him.

After the initial surveillance of Georges and Anne's home, one of the videos features Georges' family farm where the betrayal of Majid took place. Haneke does not clarify the significance of this video. It is as if Georges' lies haunted Majid his entire life, leaving indelible marks in his mind. Is it possible that by fixing on tape the images of the *lieu*, the location where the events took place, Majid might clear his mind of his tormenting memories? Is he now using video, along with other scare tactics, to conjure up images from the past? Photography was used as a memory aide in the nineteenth and twentieth centuries; today, video has become another important tool for this process. Majid was deprived by his loss and never got to share photo albums with his parents as an act of family and cultural transmission. If indeed it is Majid who is creating the videos, then it appears that he is interested in something more personal than the simple threat of surveillance that video affords. Majid is on a private quest and his investigation seems to be driven by his need to clarify what really took place in his childhood.

The videos' mediated images trigger memories for Georges. One of the surveillance videotapes arrives wrapped in a drawing of a child with a bloody mouth. This brings back Georges' first recollection: a real child with a bloody mouth appears dimly-lit on the screen. A few minutes later, a short scene of the same child vomiting blood seems to come from a dream. But Haneke keeps the image unclear, leaving his audience wondering if the scene represents a dream, a memory, or possibly just a fleeting thought.

The use of the videotape in *Caché*'s opening scene brings to mind Heidegger's analysis of the modern age:

> The world picture does not change from an earlier medieval one into a modern one, but rather the fact that the world becomes picture at all is what distinguishes the essence of the modern age. (1996: 57)

And further:

> When, accordingly, the picture character of the world is made clear as the representedness of that which is, then in order fully to grasp the modern essence of representedness we must track out and expose the original naming power of the worn-out word and concept 'to represent' [*vorstellen*]: to set out before oneself and to set forth in relation to oneself. Through this, whatever is comes to a stand as object and in that way alone receives the seal of Being. That the world becomes picture is one and the same event with the event of man's becoming subiectum in the midst of that which is. (*Ibid.*: 58)

Cache, as do many of Haneke's films, provides a comment on the virtual space of the screen, the frame that 'separates two absolutely different spaces that somehow coexist' (Manovich 2001: 95). Like wallpaper, the large television screen in Anne and Georges' living room is a background to their daily

Fig. 29 The large television in Anne and George's living room.

activities. Whether the screen features the avian flu or bodies rushed on stretchers after a bomb attack, Anne and Georges do not get distracted; their life continues at its own pace. The news seems to merely serve as markers that punctuate the forward motion of time. However, in contrast, these characters also understand what is happening to them through mediated images.

In *Cache*'s opening scene, the audience is tricked by Haneke who shifts registers by imparting the act of viewing to the protagonists. He intentionally creates confusion between the director's camera and the diegetic video. The viewers become part of the surveillance system as witnesses or even possibly perpetrators of the act of surveillance itself. This makes the film's characters all the more present and real. As the film unfolds, Haneke's manipulation of the audience's position with regards to the surveillance operation resembles Majid's manipulation of Anne and Georges. In contrast to their usual lack of engagement with the news on television, Anne and Georges are unable to resist watching the videos that are delivered to them.

Each time the audience is presented with shots from Anne and Georges' house, tension rises. These shots create ambiguity as to who is watching what. They imply an unknown presence. Is the person holding the camera the same as the mysterious person who delivers the tapes to the couple's home? This person's intentions are unclear. Haneke's deliberate ambiguity as to the origin of the recorded images complicates the relationship of the viewers to the tapes.[2] How are viewers to trust what they see on the screen? Toward the end of the film, Haneke's manipulation of viewers' position increasingly involves them in Majid's gradual self-destruction. They remain powerless as they watch his sudden and violent suicide on the screen.

Although Haneke leaves room for questions and interpretation of his script, Majid is most likely the invisible man behind the video camera. But Haneke does not provide his viewers with clear answers regarding Majid's motivations. Majid's use of video as a device that puts Georges and Anne's environment into pictures is certainly a response to his childhood pain. However, viewers are left to wonder why he chooses surveillance and what he expects to accomplish with this. Is he seeking revenge? Is he expecting that Georges and Anne will fear an escalation of violence and that a gun might eventually replace the camera in future shots? Georges and Anne's intensification of fear and panic following the delivery of each new tape certainly leads the viewers to believe that the stalker might have ulterior motives. However, as the film develops, it becomes clear that the combination of videotapes and drawings triggers Georges' flashbacks. In this film, video gives access to repressed memories and the unconscious. The media and television are strong pillars that anchor Georges' life. He certainly knows the power of representation as he tirelessly sits in the editing room, carefully manipulating footage to construct his public image – along with that of his television show – for his audience. So it comes as no surprise that the mediated cinematic representation of his house and daily routine are so disturbing to him. Far from the narcissism that he is used to, watching his own image on television, this raw footage provides the inner eye of conscience that he is lacking. The act of representation itself could be Majid's – along with Haneke's – sole weapon. Majid's goal might be simply to unearth the past and initiate the work of memory.

Unable to confront Georges with words, Majid chooses the visual language of video and child-like drawings to reach out to him. These images are Majid's attempt to comprehend what happened in the past. They work on both characters at a pre-language level and reach into the individuals' unconscious. For Georges, while some of the images that surface are clearly memories from the past, others seem to be just constructs out of his imagination. Majid's use of images instead of words is a powerful technique that disturbs Georges and provokes reactions beyond the expected defensiveness of a habitual liar. Because both Majid and his son negate that they are the authors of the tapes, the images become authorless. Although Georges perceives this solely as Majid's revenge, instead, it might be Majid or his son's strategy to trigger Georges' self-examination. If Majid confronted him solely with words, Georges would shield himself by countering the accusations with lies, as he usually does. This would keep him in the present, and engaged with the mental constructions that have allowed him to remain in a complete state of denial throughout the years. However, images are harder to dismiss. They send Georges back to his past, shaking him on a profound level while penetrating his dreams and imagination. In one of the last scenes of *Caché*, Georges lies down on his bed to take a nap after Majid's son confronts him about his involvement in his father's death. Surprisingly, the blood Georges watched gushing out of Majid's throat is not what comes back to haunt him. Instead what surfaces is the original event that Georges witnessed as a child, the tenacious memory that persisted in spite of all his efforts to erase it. Although he has closed the curtains and hides under the blankets to block the outside light, Georges cannot escape his inner self. He revisits the dramatic childhood moment when a terrified Majid is resisting being taken away by two social workers as a result of Georges' lies and betrayal. It is interesting that Haneke has chosen to deliver this scene through Georges' memory, not Majid's.

Despite being unsettled by Majid's return to his life, Georges manages to still appear as a well-adjusted and successful man. In contrast, identity is clearly more problematic for Majid whose experience of the past has been repeatedly denied. Majid is haunted by what happened in his childhood and needs to revisit his history. As a child, he obeyed Georges' injunction – the white child's command – to kill the family rooster. But this was young Georges' way to create the image of an unstable and violent child in order to get rid of him. Georges also falsely reported having seen Majid spitting blood so that he would be sent away to a sanatorium. Georges lied so that Majid would not be adopted. Because it closely followed the loss of his parents, it is quite possible that – within the world of Haneke's cinematic fiction and in view of survivor's guilt – the violent act of killing the rooster became inscribed upon Majid's memory as the cause of his loss.[3]

The memory of blood is a tie that binds the two characters' lives. Ironically, despite Georges' original plan to annihilate all possible kinship with Majid, the blood of the rooster created a bond between the 'would-be-brothers'. Blood is central to the film's imagery: blood coming out of a child's mouth, blood from the rooster splattered all over Majid's face, bright red representations of blood on the drawings that accompany the video tapes. Finally, toward the end of the film, blood gushes out of Majid's throat that he slits in the presence of Georges. In *Caché*, the recurring appearance of blood is a reminder of the people who were sacrificed in the 17 October 1961 massacre that took the lives of Majid's parents.[4] It suggests the unhealed bleeding wound leftover from France's colonial past. Through his desperate act of suicide, Majid revives the blood bond with Georges and reminds French viewers of the complicated myths of brotherhood that the colonial powers established with colonised people. Although France is quite attached to its strong humanist image, it provided neither basic human rights, nor 'liberty, equality or fraternity' to its colonial subjects. Kinship only went as far as putting pressure on them to fight side by side with French troops whenever France went to war.

Following the rules and models established during the colonial era, Majid's disenfranchised life in a poor Paris suburb counters Georges' social success. Today, the two protagonists' positions have been solidified and seem inescapable. For Georges, the particular memories that Majid so desperately needs to bring back to the surface are far from being a source of pride. Pierre Nora explains the fundamental opposition between memory and history; he states that memory always fluctuates between remembering and forgetting;

History, on the other hand, is the reconstruction, always problematic and incomplete, of what is no longer. Memory is a perpetually actual phenomenon, a bond tying us to the eternal present; history is a representation of the past. Memory, insofar as it is affective and magical, only accommodates those facts that suit it; it nourishes recollections that may be out of focus or telescopic, global or detached, particular or symbolic – responsive to each avenue of conveyance or phenomenal screen, to every censorship or projection. History, because it is an intellectual and secular production, calls for analysis and criticism. Memory installs remembrance within the sacred; history, always prosaic, releases it again. Memory is blind to all but the group it binds – which is to say, as Maurice Halbwachs has said, that there are as many memories as there are groups, that memory is by nature multiple and yet specific; collective, plural and yet individual. History, on the other hand, belongs to everyone and to no one, whence its claim to universal authority. Memory takes root in the concrete, in spaces, gestures, images and objects; history binds itself strictly to temporal continuities, to progressions and to relations between things. Memory is absolute, while history can only conceive the relative. (1989: 8)

Georges and Majid incarnate that opposition. The former is remarkably French and unaware of his privilege. An intellectual and visible media celebrity, Georges represents power and authority; he is an active participant in the dissemination of French culture and ideology. As mentioned earlier, his compulsion to archive his life through the collection of videotapes of his television show turns him into his own historian.[5] Georges' drive to record the present is the means by which his past remains 'caché', hidden. Majid's memories are a nuisance to him. They threaten his sense of self-righteousness and his personal image that is strongly anchored in the social order. In the meantime, Majid is an emotional man; although the reason for the loss of his parents at an early age is denied by the official version of French history, it haunts him and constitutes the core of his identity. Majid lacks the anchoring critical for a child's healthy development, the type of security that is usually provided by family. Deprived of both parents and community, he did not receive the help necessary for a child to discover his sense of self. He was not afforded the kind of reminiscing and routine discussions critical to the construction of one's personal narrative and history. Jacques Hassoun states that cultural transmission accounts for both the past *and* the present. Further, he adds that a child's outlook on life, a positive or painless approach, is dependent on his or her parents passing on their history and talking about their daily lives.[6] Indeed, families hold a significant role in the formation of memory; the conversations that take place between parents and children, along with familiar objects, and personal memorabilia confirm in a child's mind what he or she remembers from the past. Memory itself contributes to one's sense of identity; it constitutes the bond between the past and the present that allows identity to take form. Memory provides unity of an individual's consciousness through time; it is the foundation of the sameness of a person that assures one's continuity between past present and future.[7]

Georges Perec, who lost both parents in World War II, describes his personal loss of childhood memory after being separated from his mother who was sent to a camp in the semi-autobiographical novel *W or the Memory of Childhood*. Through his character, Perec remembers that era as a time devoid of all landmarks. Perec's protagonist, who is sent to a mountain resort by the Red Cross, loses all sense of cultural belonging. He is cut off from his family and community and finds himself living in an immense void. Perec poignantly describes how memories cannot be fixed when a child has no place, people or objects to anchor them. Without this frame-work, Perec's character cannot develop a sense of chronology. For him, the present runs into the past. Events are not ordered according to any hierarchy. People, including aunts and other relatives, enter and exit this child's life but, deprived of intimacy, he cannot develop a sense of attachment to anyone. For this child, all these people remain faceless.

Perec's experience closely resembles Majid's. For both children, the loss of family and community is critical. This phenomenon is analysed by Maurice Halbwachs who explains the importance of community in the construction of one's memories. He also states that although we might not consciously remember the past, 'we can find in society all the necessary information for reconstructing certain parts of our past represented in an incomplete and indefinite manner, or even considered completely gone from memory' (1980: 71). However, no reconstruction or sharing of memories is possible for Majid who was raised in a French orphanage, away from his ethnic group and community. The disappearance of his parents positions him as an orphan deprived not only of his family but also of his ancestral lineage, and cultural heritage. For Majid, and other people of his generation, the silence of the French government and media about the 1961 massacre – a historical event that haunted their childhood – engenders a profoundly traumatic history. By becoming a ward of the state, Majid was separated from his own community, thus eliminating all possible sources of cultural transmission or any kind of social and collective memory. Obviously, for him, being French means erasing his own history; but Majid cannot forget and feels obligated to remember. Pierre Nora uses the term 'memory individuals' to describe people like Majid who compensate for the gradual erosion and disappearance of collective memory (1989: 16). Through individual means, these people feel it is their responsibility to recapture what is collectively lost.

Majid's will to remember is offset by Georges' will to forget which is implemented by his lies. Lying did not stop in childhood for Georges. It has become a well-established habit that he uses to cover up difficult truths. Impervious to his wife's anger and frustration, he keeps lying to her, pretending to be clueless as to the origin of the videotapes. Some of these scenes are almost unbearable to watch. After he witnesses Majid's suicide, Georges blocks out his emotions. He goes to a movie as a way to escape and deny that he has just been a participant-observer in this horrendous act of despair. Later, Georges finds refuge in his bedroom from which he calls Anne on the phone while she is entertaining in their living room. He instructs her to make up something, thus to lie to their friends, so that she can escape to join and comfort him. Georges tells her to lie and say that Pierrot, their son, is sick. Georges' lies are ingrained habits that seem acceptable to him. He does not appear limited in his capacity for deceit; and clearly, this has not impeded his social success. Pierrot's invented malady is a symptom of Georges' own illness.

Georges' lies mirror the lies of colonial and postcolonial France. His silence resembles France's denial of the 1961 massacre. The concealments and erasures on both sides illustrate the interpenetration of collective and individual memory.[8] For many years, the repression against Algerians that took place during and after the Algerian War of Independence was covered up. Benjamin Stora states:

> And you discover that forgetting about the Algerian War isn't due to lack of memory. This feeling of forgetting springs instead from truncated memories, incomplete and biased, from myths and stereotypes created out of fear of the truth. (1993: 97)

While France puts forth a secular politic of assimilation, it reinforces both judicially and culturally that all people living on French soil need to learn and adjust to French customs and cultural ways. This creates an appearance of a homogeneous culture and history. However, this is only possible through the erasure of shameful events. By denying the 1961 massacre, the French government not only deprived the families of the victims of the real environment of memory, which Pierre Nora calls *milieux de mémoire*, but also deprived the French nation of *lieux de mémoire* for this horrendous event.[9] Until recently, there were no anniversaries, no gestures of remembrance, no institutionalised memories, and no rituals. Stora adds:

It is in this reticence to see oneself in the other's suffering (and, to put it plainly, especially the part the French played in the drama lived out by the Algerian people) that there exists strong resistance to establishing an authentic memory – one that makes sense only by understanding the suffering that other groups have endured. In France we are not yet at that point. For the moment we can recall but not yet commemorate (which would imply acknowledging the notion of war). It's a question of seeing everything – history, horror, war with its ambiguities and contradictions – but not yet acknowledging a debt owed to the victims or admitting war crimes, or crimes against humanity, during the Algerian War. (*Ibid.*: 98)

It is precisely this lack of recognition of another person's suffering that Haneke so powerfully evokes in *Caché*. Georges personifies a country that denied its crimes while Majid's pain comes from the lack of recognition by another human being, as well as an entire nation, of what took place in his life in 1961. Majid's pain – and that of his whole generation – has been repeatedly dismissed and ignored. Re-visiting Leibniz's ideas about pain, Maurice Halbwachs explains:

The pain may not gradually diminish only because we can clearly represent its character and causation. Rather, by imagining that the pain can be experienced and understood by others (impossible were it a personal and hence unique impression), we seem to transfer some of its burden to others, who help us to bear it. The tragic character of pain – the fact that, beyond a certain point, it creates in us a desperate feeling of anxiety and powerlessness – results from our being unable to come to grips with an evil whose cause is within those regions of ourselves inaccessible to others. We are one with our pain, and pain cannot destroy itself. Hence we instinctively search out an intelligible explanation of our suffering; that is, we find an explanation agreeable to the members of our group. (1980: 97)

Majid's lifelong victimisation hopelessly leads him to seek understanding if not justice. He confronts Georges in a desperate attempt to ascertain the truth. Despite the plot's build-up, and contrary to the fact that Georges calls him a terrorist, Majid does not appear angry. He steers clear of accusatory confrontation and seems mostly preoccupied with Georges' state of denial. When led to Majid's front door by images from one of the videos, Georges, once again, uses his privilege and signifies that he does not recognise Majid

Fig. 30 Georges at Majid's door.

or forgot who he is altogether: 'Who are you?', he asks. His social class creates protection and distance. He does not feel that he has to take any responsibility. While Majid uses the informal *'tu'* as they both did in childhood, Georges uses the formal 'vous' to address him. By doing so, he signifies that he has completely forgotten Majid, who is now merely an anonymous figure for him. But the grief-stricken Majid is committed to his memory. He cannot escape Georges who invades his life, not only through memory but also through the popular French television programme he hoses. Majid needs to re-enter Georges' life and open up a dialogue; the videos appear like Majid's effort to reach out to Georges, and Majid's expectation could be that Georges' conscience will contribute the missing text to the silent tapes.

Using the power of images, the videos represent a last attempt to bring back to the surface the spectres of the bodies long-drowned in the Seine River. It is as if the opening of the iris of the anonymous camera could shed light on the lies of the past, unearth the memories and restore the dignity of the people whose lives were forever lost on 17 October 1961. If Georges acknowledged their shared experience, it would help Majid bear his pain and his burden might feel lighter. Stressing how groups are the repositories of memories, Halbwachs says that 'to be aided by others' memory, ours must not merely be provided testimony and evidence but must also remain in harmony with theirs. There must be enough points of contact so that any remembrance they recall to us can be reconstructed on a common foundation' (1980: 31). In *Caché*, Majid is unable to compare notes with Georges, who if he could admit his lies, would provide Majid with a sense of reconciliation with his past. But the court hearing that takes place in Majid's dingy apartment has a video camera for sole witness and does not bring reparations to him.

For Georges, the panic that surfaces with the videos is a symptom of his internal terror: if he were to start looking at his faults, it might make him crumble. Thus, he cannot admit what happened or did not happen, and the story that corresponds with Majid's sense of reality, memory and personal narrative is denied once again. This situation reflects the unbearable position of victims in need of reparations. Paul Ricoeur analyses the idea of forgiveness and the 'impossible commandment to love our enemies'; he addresses 'the invisible force that unites the two speech acts of admitting and forgiving' (2004: 481; 483). In *Caché*, Majid is indirectly inviting Georges to admit, but Georges is far from contrition. He does not even provide the plain acknowledgment that would confirm Majid's memory. His failure to admit comes from his unwillingness to repent and keeps Majid from the possibility of reconciliation.[10] Unable to arrive at a resolution, Majid can no longer live; suicide is his only option.[11] But again, Georges refuses to admit that he is accountable. Although he is disturbed by this horrendous act committed in his presence, his emotions are quite controlled. When Majid's son confronts him accusing him of having 'a man on his conscience', Georges says that he has nothing to hide and shows one more time that he clearly has no interest in repenting.

Georges feels no moral debt toward Majid. In fact, he upholds a guilt-less image, repeatedly bringing evidence of his innocence to himself and to the world. His unconscious corroborates with his lies. While watching one of the videos, a mental image of Majid spitting blood appears to him as if it were a real memory. This image is low-lit and very dark. It confirms his childhood lie as real and justifies his early selfish behaviour. Georges started his mental construction of Majid as a dangerously ill person and potential source of contagion to his family early in childhood. His self-righteousness is rooted in a belief system in which Majid represents otherness. Haneke gives evidence of this in several other scenes. For instance, Georges has a dream in which he sees Majid, his face covered with blood from the beheaded rooster, advancing toward horrified young Georges and brandishing the ax with which he has just chopped the head of the animal. When Georges lies down to take a nap after Majid's suicide he dreams (or is it just a memory?) of Majid's removal from the family domain by two social workers. Here, Haneke uses a long shot and still camera. The distance created by the camera's viewpoint reveals Georges' distance from his

Fig. 31 Majid (Malik Nait Djoudi), holding the ax with which he chops the rooster's head, is represented as a dark silhouette against a light background.

past and also his distance from Majid's experience. Georges has disconnected himself from the fact that his childhood lie made Majid's life take
a turn possibly as painful as that when his parents were killed in the massacre. This was the determining moment when, for the second time, Majid
was irreversibly branded as an orphan, the moment when his marginalised
position was fully established within the social framework. Concurrently,
Georges started the process of denial and lying. This process allowed him
not only to live his life without a conscience that gnaws at him with guilt,
but also to build a belief system in which he is able to repeatedly avoid the
repercussions of his lies and unethical behaviour. The distance of Haneke's
camera reveals the ranking order established by Georges throughout the
film, a hierarchy in which Majid's life is not as worthy as his own. While
Georges might not be an overt racist, his behaviour exemplifies covert
racism. Through this, he harbours negative images about Majid who is
both of a different class and different ethnic origin. From early on he has
constructed Majid as a threat to himself and his family, and he can only
perceive him as such. Georges' attitude and belief system represent the
power of the elite that upholds the dominant racial ideology. Examining
the evolution of the concept of racism, Etienne Balibar says:

> [Racism] had to be understood as a way of constructing and instituting
> communities, social formations, normative patterns of behaviour, and as a
> mode of thought, which combines intellectual, even sophisticated scientific
> or quasi-scientific hermeneutic models with affective complexes of sympa-
> thy and antipathy, therefore connects conscious or unconscious individual
> thinking with collective representations. (2005: 24)

Majid represents otherness for Georges. Their differing ethnic origins
and social status, as well as the long history of colonisation function as
entrenched separations between the two characters. These differences
explain Georges' unreasonable resistance to admitting his childhood
mistake. Rationally, the well-adjusted adult he has become should be able
to admit that his feelings as a child were immature and wrong. Indeed,
Georges is not a monster: when pressed by his wife who keeps asking what
he has done to Majid, he is finally able to confess to her. He also shows
that he is capable of apologising to her as he does several times during the
film both for losing his temper and for lying to her. However, he is not able
to do the same with Majid. Examining his childhood lie is threatening to

him because his belief system has clearly not changed very much. Georges' emotional block is telling; it shows that he still retains his privilege and reaps the benefits of Majid's exclusion. Revisiting theories of Otherness developed by Edward Said, Balibar examines the construction of the *essential Other* as an 'active "subject" of threats'. He also points out that 'the construction of the Other is the construction of an alienated Self' and adds, 'an uncanny double, the Other is not really or not purely exterior. It is also interior, constitutive of oneself. Without this "otherness", there would be no possibility of civilising oneself' (*Ibid.*: 30). Balibar examines the progression of the concept of racism and highlights the idea that exclusion – particularly what he calls 'internal exclusion' – is one of the foundations of today's world. He demonstrates that exclusion is internal because globalisation has, at least in principle, no exterior. He speaks of the exclusion of

> those who, from inside, are deemed to be impossible and unnecessary to include, or in the end those whose exclusion is deemed necessary for the inclusion of all others to take place and become effective. As we know, this is the problem and the crux of inclusions, integrations, assimilations: that they apparently are possible only at the cost and under the condition of admitting of a reverse side, most of the time a dark side, the side of exclusion. Just as sameness is possible only at the cost of discarding difference, and selfhood at the cost of projecting otherness. (*Ibid.*: 32)

As discussed earlier, *Caché*'s narrative is constructed around the contrast between its two central characters. Haneke uses the dialectic of Otherness to create this opposition and to build up the tensions between Georges and Majid. The film reflects the postcolonial framework and the conditions under which people of Algerian origin live in France. It indirectly incriminates the system of exclusion that allowed France to deny its crimes during and after the Algerian War of Independence. *Caché* underlines the inextricable entanglement of power, class, race, exclusion and alienation and reveals how the dominant class depends on the oppression of marginalised people. *Caché* is an allegory for the guilt of France whose denial and concealments so closely resemble that of Georges. Moreover, the film meditates on the conditions of all those who live selfishly in today's global world, a world where it is easy to ignore other people's exclusion, alienation and suffering; but Haneke also makes it clear that we all share that world. Transforming his viewers into direct witnesses, Haneke uses his cinematic form to implicate them and make them feel that, just like Georges, they can be held accountable. *Caché* implies that revisiting memories is difficult and painful for everyone. Admitting one's mistakes means that a person is willing to undergo self-examination and take the necessary steps to change. For individuals, as for nations, it is hard to apologise because apologies are a gift from one to another. They are offerings that disrupt the established hierarchies and, as a result, level out differences. As evidenced in Haneke's film, for both France and Georges, changing would mean examining and disrupting a system of privilege and power that is hard to renounce. This is the reason why Georges feels that Majid is a terrorist. In the same way, this is the reason why people who are kept out of official versions of history, are always perceived as threats. Just as France is well aware of its past errors, Georges absolutely knows the truth of the past but conveniently and consistently forgets. The fear of eroding his own feeling of entitlement to social status and power is what dictates his compulsive amnesia.

NOTES

1 However, throughout the film, both Majid and his son deny being involved with the videos.

2 In terms of whether Majid or his son is meant to be the author of the videos, as cleverly pointed out by Catherine Wheatley (2006): 'ultimately the person responsible for the tapes is Haneke himself'.

3 Following Freud's revelations on the role of imagination and phantasy on the unconscious, Maurice Halbwachs points out the discrepancies in what we believe happened in our past: 'how many of the remembrances that we believe genuine, with an identity beyond doubt, are almost entirely forged from false recognitions, in accordance with others' testimony and stories'! Halbwachs talks about a certain 'chiaroscuro effect in the mind' and underlines how childhood memories change through time and are based on immaturity, inexperience and inattention. He says that, because children are ignorant of certain facts and circumstances that are controlled by adults, their remembrances are a mix of clarity and darkness (1980: 71–3).

4 During the Algerian War of Independence, the Head of French police established a discriminatory curfew directed solely against Muslims of Algerian origin. As a response, the Algerian National Liberation Front (FLN) called for a demonstration. On 17 October 1961 French police violently attacked the demonstrators, many of whom were killed. Numerous bodies were found floating in the Seine River; and to this day, the exact number of victims remains unknown due to the cover up of the event by both the French government and media.

5 Jacques Derrida talks about *le mal d'archive* or 'archive fever'. He says: 'But the point must be stressed, this archiviolithic force leaves nothing of its own behind. ... Because the archive, if this word or this figure can be stabilised so as to take on a signification,

will never be either memory or anamnesis as spontaneous, alive and internal experience. On the contrary: the archive takes place at the place of originary and structural breakdown of the said memory' (1996: 11).

6 'Aussi devons-nous entendre la transmission comme ce qui rend compte du passé et du présent. Dans ces conditions, elle permet à l'enfant d'aborder l'existence qui va être la sienne d'autant moins douloureusement qu'il entendra ses parents parler de leur histoire et de leur quotidien' (Hassoun 2002: 17).

7 Investigating the nature of the self, James Booth talks about the limitations of the physical person when it comes to moral responsibility. He adheres to what he calls 'the best known of the psychological theories of identity: Locke's argument that "the identity of a (forensic) person resides entirely in memory"'. Booth states: 'This view ... is bound up with [*Locke's*] certainty that while a materialist account may, in Locke's distinction, explain the identity of a man (i.e. as a natural kind), it cannot express the duration of the person as an accountable moral agent. For that purpose, what is needed is the unity through time of our consciousness. And what does the work of binding together past and present states into moments of the consciousness of one being is, Locke contends, memory' (2006: 10).

8 In *The Collective Memory*, Maurice Halbwachs introduces the idea of the difference between collective and historical memory and stresses that there is no universal memory. He talks about the multiplicity of collective memories as they represent the various groups that constitute one's belonging. In the case of *Caché*, although Georges himself is part of different groups, his belonging in the dominant French class creates a direct correlation between his country's official history and his own construction of the past.

9 Nora states: 'There are *lieux de mémoire*, sites of memory, because there are no longer *milieux de mémoire*, real environments of memory' (1989: 7). He adds: 'The moment of *lieux de mémoire* occurs at the same time that an immense and intimate fund of memory disappears, surviving only as a reconstituted object beneath the gaze of critical history' (*Ibid.*: 12).

10 James Booth talks about the ethical dimension of memory. He writes: 'Memory weaves narratives and judges, calls to mind both the good and the shameful, and allows us to weigh them. The person who willfully chooses amnesia about wrongs for which he is responsible, or whose recollection of them is unable to discern their evil, is a person whose memory has failed, not necessarily in the sense of being factually in error but rather as having failed morally. We judge a person in part by what and how he remembers, and we call those shameless who consider irrelevant their past bad conduct. Memory makes us whole by (among its manifold forms of presence) binding us in judging remembrance with our past and is thus itself the subject of ethical strictures, of a duty to remember. It is a way in which we secure our persistence through time, not as materially identical beings but as self-conscious, active moral agents with an accountability arrayed across time. Memory is, in brief, deeply bound up with our ethical life: it is part of the persistence of the person as agent; it casts judgment (or fails to), awakens shame (or is shameless), and responds (or not) to the imperative to remember' (2006: 11).

11 Etienne Balibar explains that in today's global world 'you cannot have external places of Otherness, you can only have ubiquitous "limbos" where those who are neither assimilated and integrated nor immediately eliminated, are forced to remain' (2005: 31). Here Haneke implies that in view of Georges' and France's denial, Majid is forever stuck in oblivion. His suicide is the only way to put an end to his exclusion.

WORKS CITED

Balibar, E. (2005) 'Difference, Otherness, Exclusion', *Parallax*, 11, 1, 19–34.

Booth, J. (2006) *Communities of Memory on Witness, Identity, and Justice.* Ithaca: Cornell University Press.

Derrida, J. (1996) *Archive Fever*, trans. E. Prenowitz. Chicago: University of Chicago Press.

Halbwachs, M. (1980) *The Collective Memory.* New York: Harper and Row.

Hassoun, J. (2002) *Les Contrebandiers de la mémoire.* Paris: La Découverte.

Heidegger, M. (1996) 'The Age of the World Picture', in T. Druckrey (ed.) *Electronic Culture.* New York: Aperture, 47–61.

Manovich, L (2001) *The Language of New Media.* Cambridge: MIT Press.

Nora, P. (1989) 'Between Memory and History: *Les Lieux de Mémoire*', trans. M. Roudebush, *Representations*, 26, 8, 7–25.

Perec, G. (1988) *W or the Memory of Childhood*, trans. David Bellos. Boston: D. R. Godine.

Ricoeur, P. (2004) *Memory, History, Forgetting.* Chicago: University of Chicago Press.

Stora, B. (1993) 'France and the Algerian War: Memory Regained? An Interview with Benjamin Stora', trans. D. Cianfarini, *Journal of Maghrebi Studies*, 1, 2, 95–102.

Wheatley, C. (2006) 'Secrets Lies and Videotape', *Sight and Sound*, February. Online. Available at: http://www.bfi.org.uk/sightandsound/feature/49266 (accessed 23 December 2007).

11. MEMORY, NOSTALGIA AND THE FEMININE: *IN THE MOOD FOR LOVE* AND THOSE *QIPAOS*

LYNDA CHAPPLE

A preoccupation with the past has emerged as one of the surprising trends of recent cinematic history. In a world that often appears cemented in the present tense, we have become obsessed with the past, both as a temporal and a spatial phenomenon. If modernity seems to have produced a longing for past time, and post-modernity a longing for vanished spaces, then, in its own attempt to make sense of the present, the turn of the millennium appears to be desperately negotiating the tensions between the two, producing an intensified form of mourning for something lost. Yet our access to history is always mediated through the unreliable processes of memory, and often represented in highly nostalgic terms. Nostalgia is a desire for the past, a longing 'not for the past the ways it was, but for the past the ways it could have been' (Boym 2001: 351), and in this sense it involves both memory *and* forgetting. As Pam Cook points out, nostalgia is even more unreliable than memory, and is usually derided as such (2005: 3). However, this does not seem to have prevented a recent proliferation of films which engage nostalgically with memory and its processes. Cinema has a particularly interesting relationship to memory and nostalgia given that its representations exist simultaneously in both the present and past tenses: present, in that each screening is an immediate experience of a given moment; past, in that the object represented by the image has long vanished. In a sense, cinema itself is memory recuperated in images; time and space cohere in a very present tense experience of the past. Perhaps it is not surprising, then, that cinema often has a comfortable relationship with nostalgia. Wong Kar-wai's *In the Mood for Love*[1] (2000) exemplifies this, indulging as it does in a celebration of its own nostalgia for a particular place and time, at a very particular moment in history.

In the Mood for Love is a beautiful film; it is also a disturbing film. Its beauty resides in its rich visual and aural textures and its evocative sense of longing and desire. It is a film rendered through the lens of subjective memory, self-consciously imbued with nostalgia for a long-vanished past. As an elegy to another time and place – Hong Kong, 1962 – and an exploration of repressed emotion, there is an oneiric quality to the film, which is informed by the haunting music, the obsessive recreation of place, the minute details of the *mise-en-scène* and the broader thematic concern with temporal displacement. The textures of memory and repetition, enhanced by the grainy quality of the film stock and the slow motion panning of the camera, create an extraordinarily poetic and lyrical vision of longing, presence and absence. Repetition is central to the film's structure and enacts an almost desperate attempt to secure the past as enduring present – sequences, dialogue and the insistent use of Shigeru Umebayashi's 'Yumenji's Theme'recurring as nostalgic refrains throughout. Yet, as the concluding epilogue suggests, the past represented by the film is long gone, blurred and irrecoverable, as if looked at through a dusty window pane; both spectators and characters are forever divided from it. Like the main temple of Angkor Watt in the final sequence, the film stands as an extraordinary monument to this vanished and inaccessible era.

Fig. 33 Sartorial Nostalgia. Li-zhen (Maggie Cheung Man-yuk) in one of many qipaos.

It is a beautiful film; yet within this extraordinary and highly evocative beauty resides a potentially disturbing resonance. Nostalgia is linked through the excessive representation of the *qipao* – the central costume worn by the female protagonist, Su Li-zhen (Maggie Cheung Man-yuk) – to the female body in troubling, often highly fetishised ways. Li-zhen is the central object of the film's nostalgia; the camera continually caresses her image, often focusing only on parts of her body – torso, hips, spine – in ways that have little relevance to the narrative, so that at times the character seems not to be subjectively present at all. She is the object of the gaze, but, as a character, is denied a reciprocal power: we rarely see her looking back. Often the frame contains only half her figure, or parts of her body, which is emphasised by and in the *qipao*, so much so that the garment itself becomes as much a fetish as an object of nostalgia. The *qipaos* therefore provide the central link between the film's enunciation of the feminine and its nostalgia: they are highly gendered relics from the past, intimately related to the female body.[2] They are overinscribed in a way that little else is within the film, the excess resulting in a gendering of the past and an eroticisation of the female body that is both seductive and troubling.

This essay investigates the workings of nostalgia in the film, particularly as it is enunciated by the costume. In attempting to account for the excessive representation of the *qipao*, it will examine the relationship of nostalgia to the feminine as it is invested in the garment in socio-historical and psychoanalytic terms, arguing that in its visual excess the dress enacts a fundamental nostalgia for the female body and a tactile relationship to the experience of it, an experience that is denied in the cinematic emphasis on the visual. While much conventional cinematic and feminist theory might see this as yet another example

Fig. 34 Dress as constraining spectacle.

of the objectification of the female body through the inscription of a male gaze, I will argue that in its evocation of, and mourning for, the more fully sensuous experience of touch, the film challenges the visual paradigms upon which the objectification of the feminine rests; in doing so it shifts the locus of subjectivity to the embodied spectator.

SHE DRESSES LIKE THAT TO GO OUT FOR NOODLES?

The narrative begins in Hong Kong in 1962. The two protagonists, Su Li-zhen and Chow Mo-wan (Tony Leung Chiu-wai) and their respective spouses move into rented rooms in adjoining apartments owned by Shanghainese immigrants. Li-zhen and Mo-wan slowly become aware that their spouses are having an affair and, in an effort to try to understand and cope with their emotional responses to this, they together begin to rehearse the circumstances under which the affair might have begun. Although the two increasingly spend more time together, they resist the growing attraction for each other by insisting that they will not 'be like them'. As the title suggests, the film is a 'mood' piece. Little really happens in terms of plot; importantly rather, it is a film where things do not happen. It is a film of coincidences and missed opportunities, of unrequited desire and regret.

As the two central characters struggle with their illicit attraction to each other, what remains unexpressed – the repressed and constrained – provides the emotional content of the film.

As a homage to the past, much of the film's nostalgia exists in the details and daily objects of a vanished era. As Rey Chow comments, 'Wong offers glimpses of a Hong Kong that no longer exists' (2002: 646).[3] The accumulated details of daily life from the time – the seasonal food, the new rice cooker, Shanghainese singer Zhou Xuan's song 'Huangyang de Nianhua', the radiogram, the martial arts stories – anchor the film both temporally and spatially in a very specific historical context. However, it is Li-zhen's extensive wardrobe of *qipaos* that stands apart. Designed by William Chang, and made by a traditional Shanghainese tailor in Hong Kong, the dresses are an undeniable force in the film. In their shape, colours, patterns and sheen they announce themselves in ways that little else does. Lit for emphasis and juxtaposed with the muted palette of the rest of the *mise-en-scène*, the coloured and textured dresses frequently constitute a visual disruption to the narrative. The film itself acknowledges this when Mrs Suen, the landlady, comments wryly of Li-zhen's clothing, 'She dresses up like that to go out for noodles?' The comment marks both Li-zhen and the *qipaos* out as central, the self-reflexivity pointing ironically to the excessive nature of the representation, and endowing the dress with an iconic status. Certainly, as part of an almost obsessive recreation of the period, the costumes lend the kind of historical verisimilitude often aspired to by period films. The *qipao*, in particular, is invested with very specific cultural and historical associations, and they contribute both familiarity and exoticism to the portrayal of the past.[4] They are traditional garments, no longer a part of the daily wardrobes of modern Chinese women, and so acquire the glamour and fascination of the foreign, yet they are connected in the cultural imagination of Hong Kong with a generation that has past, but can still be remembered.

The historical influence of the Chinese diaspora on Hong Kong cinematic imagination has been well documented.[5] Shanghai is central to the film's construction of nostalgia, and the historical positioning of the story and the film itself are both significant to an understanding of the *qipao*'s role in the film. In the 1950s and early 1960s, the Shanghainese diaspora arriving in Hong Kong were fleeing the austerities that had been imposed by the Communist regime subsequent to its 1949 victory over the Kuomintang. The date of the film itself, three years subsequent to the return of Hong

Kong sovereignty to China, is also relevant here. In 1962 (the date the film's narrative commences), Chinese immigrants looked to Hong Kong as a place of refuge, although not home; by the time the film was made, the post-colonial context had problematised the notions of refuge, home and ethnic/racial identification. Many Hong Kong people had emigrated in the wake of the Sino-British Joint Declaration on Hong Kong in 1984; and, while many also subsequently returned, it was not without a good deal of circumspection and anxiety about the future relationship of Hong Kong to 'mainland' China. Where was home now? Chow (2002) argues that the nostalgic impulses in this film are representative of a desire for a return journey; and, as part of a national narrative, the *qipao*'s association with Shanghai can easily be read as signifying the prodigal return of Hong Kong to the larger maternal body of China.

As has been argued elsewhere, given this very specific historical context the garment can also be understood as embodying the feminised relationship of Hong Kong in relation to colonial and national traditions (see Marchetti 2002; Yue 2003). Until its revival as an object of retro-chic in the 1990s the *qipao* was considered by many Hong Kong women as an outmoded, traditional dress that had little role in the modern and fashionable world of contemporary Hong Kong; it was considered an old-fashioned and parochial sartorial *oeuvre*. Yet, as a quintessentially Chinese garment, it was also invested with a form of nationalistic sentiment which rested upon identification with the notion of 'Chineseness', however that may be defined.[6] Three years after the reunification of Hong Kong and China (the date of the film's release), there had emerged a much stronger and more stable sense of national pride and patriotism. The nostalgia associated with the dress is, therefore, necessarily inflected by Hong Kong' complex relationship to its own ethnic, national and global identity, and it incorporates mourning for time, place and an elusive form of racial subjectivity.

However, while this goes some way toward explaining the object mourning in the film, it does not adequately account for the excess in the representation of the dress, or the melancholy textures of its nostalgia. The *qipaos* link history and memory in complex ways, and they function as markers of both historic and cinematic time. The tension between the editing, which suggests a rather static sense of time, and the changing *qipaos* effectively evokes the temporal ambivalence that is central to the film. In the sequences between Mo-wan and Li-zhen, the passing of time is often only indicated by the change in pattern of the dress she is wearing.

Fig. 35 Competing colours, patterns and textures: Li-zhen in the hotel room.

In the processes of repetition and variation – repetition of the dress as a form, variation of the patterns, colours and textures of the fabric – the past is secured; it is the variation, in a sense, that ensures the repetition, and becomes a way of holding onto the past by excessively representing it. The cinematic image is always a memory, so in many ways this excess is not so much a strategy for remembering but one that signals despair at the ever-present potential for forgetting, and the object of nostalgia is not just a time or a place but something both specifically cinematic and, I will argue, specifically feminine.

GENDERED MELANCHOLY?

Nostalgia is an escape to a stable, yet often imagined, and irrecoverable past. It incorporates a strong sense of loss, a good deal of melancholy. Freud makes a useful distinction between mourning and melancholia in his explanation of nostalgia. Nostalgia is imbued with a particular form of mourning for a lost object; melancholia, however, is a more excessive kind of mourning for something that is lost to the ego. It is more narcissistic because it conflates the object of desire with an unconscious need within the self (see Freud 1984). Melancholy is, therefore, a projection rather than a reflection; it is about the subject, not the object of nostalgia, and the lack is within the self. It is also often inscribed in excessive terms.[7] In discussing the textures of memory that reside in this film, such a distinction is productive. Wong's films are centrally concerned with time and with memory, but the emphasis on nostalgia and the subjectivity of memory in this film transcends any of his others. It weaves a texture from the competing tensions of mourning and melancholy, past and present, absence and presence, memory and forgetting and the visual and the tactile, and this texture is materialised in the excessive representation of the *qipaos*.

The tension between the physical restraint imposed on Li-zhen by the shape and style of the dress and the excesses of the prints and numbers of the dress reflects some fundamental stresses in the film's nostalgic desires. Peter Brunette has argued that Li-zhen's dresses represent a realisation of opposing sexual forces, being form-fitting and tightly wound, they are highly sexual, but represent repression of that sexuality (2005: 91). However, there is clearly an over-investment in the representation of the *qipao* which transcends any diegetic need; the sheer number of garments – at least twenty – and elaborate designs of the fabric attest as much,[8] and, given her socio-economic status, it is unlikely that Li-zhen would have been able to afford such an expensive or extensive wardrobe. At times, the dresses seem to have more materiality than the character who wears them; indeed she is often shot from behind or in partial profile, so it is the dress and not the character which is the centre of attention. The *qipao* is, therefore, fetishised in the film, and this masks an underlying absence at the centre of its signifying power. A fetish disguises an irrecoverable sense of lack and, according to Freud, this lack should be understood in terms of castration anxiety and disavowal. Inevitably the fetish comes to replace the female body as a sexual object: the fetish is present, the body itself absent (see Freud 1977).[9] Such is partly the case with the *qipaos*. Many of the sequences which privilege the dress are almost expressionistic in design, the gendered body becoming a stylised pastiche of surface images and body parts. In a sense, Li-zhen becomes a mannequin for the display of the outfit, reduced to an insubstantial image; and as a subjective presence she is often not actually there. The dress is the real presence, it is the woman herself who is absent, the *qipao* instead a metonymic replacement.

Millennium debates about subjectivity have produced a good deal of anxiety about the gendered body. Feminists have maintained considerable ambivalence in their attitudes to the sexed body, many continuing to resist the essentialism implicit in the masculine/feminine binary, with others continuing to argue for a sexually specific understanding of the practices of gender (see Grosz, 1994; Grosz & Probyn, 1995). Foucauldian constructionist analysis has led to an increasing scrutiny of the concept of gender and its complex interaction with the body. Theorists such as Judith Butler (1990, 1993) have comprehensively deconstructed the categories of sex and gender, and queer has emerged as a powerful challenge to normative heterosexual constructs. We now recognise gender as a performance, a narrative that will transmute over time, and cannot be circumscribed by the immobilising forces of easy definition. In a sense, the sexed/gendered body has become a memory, rather than a presence. Yet, despite the increase in more complex awareness and discussions of masculinity (see Buchbinder 1998; Savran & Adams 2002), the feminine continues to be highly marked: it both is and is not a material reality. In this context, we need to see the *qipao* as also reflecting a kind of desperation about, and a melancholic desire for, the female body; in a sense, the dress is a remnant, a leftover scrap of the fabric of the feminine, a material memory of a vanished idea. By dominating her body, the *qipaos* contribute to an erasure of Li-zhen, and in this sense, the costumes signify a specific corporeal absence. Rather than articulating her physical presence, they evoke only the memory of embodiment. In these terms, the lack represented in the excessive inscriptions of the dress is for the female body itself.[10]

In the Mood for Love employs a melancholic substitution. The film is centrally concerned with nostalgia, both historically and psychically, and in a world of increasingly unstable and traumatised identities, the *qipao*, I would argue, attempts to stabilise the feminine. In the context of the increasingly ambiguous and fluid nature of identity, the *qipao* corsets, shapes and makes visible the female body in a melancholic attempt to solidify gender. The film represents the female body as a highly stylised and nostalgic artefact. The *qipao* signifies the memory of the feminine, and mourns its loss. The costume does not simply represent the body, or some idealised notion of it, nor does it just inscribe the body as a nostalgic remnant of the past; it actually replaces the absent, lost body of the woman/mother. Clothing in this film becomes a sartorial substitute for the displaced notion of the feminine. Yet, paradoxically, this desire for the stabilisation of gender results in a displacement of subjectivity, at least at the level of representation. However, to see this simply as an expression of castration anxiety is to accept unproblematically the masculine bias of Freud's model, and to undermine the extraordinary affective impact of the dresses for the spectator. Nor does it adequately account for what I want to argue is a much more feminine kind of mourning. If the dress is fetishised, we must see this as far more implicated with the question of texture, a more sensuous quality, than a psychoanalytic reading allows. In erasing the character, the excess shifts the locus of subjectivity to the spectator; at a spectatorial level it produces the most extraordinary affective impact, a form of plenitude that cannot be accounted for in the limited terms of Freud's model.

FEMININE TEXTURES

In narrative terms this is a film of unrequited desire; there is a good deal of longing, but almost no pleasure, which is not to deny a kind of pleasure in longing itself. Look, it seems to say, but don't touch. This lack of consummation at a narrative level both belies and reflects the extraordinary, affective impact of the dresses at a spectatorial level, an impact that is an equal mix of pleasure and melancholy and operates at another level of significance. The pleasure is produced through the textures created in the frisson between the excessive colours, patterns and forms of the *qipaos* and their juxtaposition to the muted tones of the rest of the *mise-en-scène* and the narrative frustrations of the characters. It is a visual pleasure certainly, at least in the first instance. However, in the weave produced by the multiple threads and layers of presence and absence, past and present, mourning and melancholy, Shanghai and Hong Kong, fetish and body there exists another textural resonance that recalls a different kind of absent pleasure. These tensions reflect a greater division between materiality and representation, between the tactile and the visual.

Of the textures of the film, Rey Chow argues that 'the material fullness of the sounds and images becomes ... a screen for fundamental lack' (2002: 649). This lack is a peculiarly cinematic one, involving a particular form of melancholic pleasure; however, it cannot be accommodated within the specular, masculine model articulated by Freud and his successors. What psychoanalytic accounts of excess, nostalgia and lack foreclose is a consideration of the materiality of the body; in psychoanalytic theory, as in the cinematic experience itself, the body remains an image, an abstraction of the corporeality of flesh. Within such paradigms pleasure remains profoundly specular. Yet the textures embodied by the *qipaos* suggest a much more tactile form of nostalgia, a different kind of lack. Touch is one of three senses excluded directly from the cinematic experience. Yet, given this is a cinematic experience, these textures are experienced primarily, at least, as visual; we may see them, but we cannot actually feel them. In a film as concerned as it is with memory, it would seem that the memory here is touch itself.[11] To account for the affect produced by the excessive and nostalgic textures of the dress, we need to focus on the relationship of the film to a more fully sensuous and embodied experience of tactility, as both a memory and a presence.[12]

Luce Irigaray is one of very few theorists to recognise the close association between the feminine and the tactile. She develops the idea of feminine specificity in her formulation of the 'two lips':

> As for woman, she touches herself ... all the time, and moreover no one can forbid her to do so, for her genitals are formed of two lips in continuous contact. Thus within herself, she is already two – but not divisible into one(s) – that caress each other. (1985: 24)

For Irigaray, the feminine is corporeal and is characterised in and through touch, a sense she opposes to sight which she sees as complicit with the patriarchal objectification and annihilation of the feminine, *'the horror of nothing to see'* (*Ibid.*: 26, empahsis in original). Her stress on the continuous nature of feminine touch, the reflexivity of the experience of it and the indivisible multiplicity of selves this entails has productive implications here. Touch, as she describes it, is a specifically feminine sense and related to specifically feminine pleasures, including erotic pleasures. It exists in a different realm to vision.

> The visible and the tactile do not obey the same laws of the flesh. And if I can no doubt unite their powers, I cannot reduce one to the other. I cannot situate the visible and the tangible in a chiasmus. Perhaps the visible needs the tangible but this need is not reciprocal. (1993: 162)[13]

She links touch explicitly to the feminine, and specifically to the tactile relationship to the maternal body, and it is this alternative way of apprehending and experiencing the world, a variation on the visual, that is of interest here. In this film, if the female body is in some ways a melancholic artefact, the experience of touch is similarly recalled yet absent.

Yet touch remains elusive. Cinema's present resides in image and sound; the experience of touch is always a memory, it belongs to the past, although it can be relived viscerally through the processes of affect. Like Li-zhen's and Mo-wan's spouses, absence is registered through a continual presence that is hinted at, sometimes glimpsed, often felt. The textural presence of the dresses mourns the absence of the materiality and tactile pleasures of the female body. The *qipao*'s proximity to the female body recalls its materiality and the haptic pleasures of silk on skin. The excessive nature of its representation does represent a lack and enunciates a cinematic form of mourning for the lost plentitudes of touch. The tensions in the film between presence and absence, between the present and the past, between the visual and tactile reflect a melancholic relationship to the female body. This inheres in the affective quality of the textures of the *qipao*, which in their profoundly visual excess mourn a tactile plenitude, feminine in nature, which is forever lost to us in the cinematic experience itself.

NOTES

1   In Mandarin Chinese, as rendered in Pinyin, the title is *Huayang nianhua*, which trans-lates as: *When flowers were in full bloom*. Rendered according to the Cantonese tonal pronunciation, the title is *Fa yeung nin wa*.

2   It is specifically the *qipaos* worn by Li-zhen to which this essay speaks. Although the dress is also worn by other characters in the film, Mrs Suen (Rebecca Pan) for example, it is those worn by Li-zhen which are marked by a nostalgic significance that is over-invested and which requires explanation.

3   Ironically, or perhaps appositely, the film was actually shot in Thailand because it offered more extant historical sites than contemporary Hong Kong.

4   The dress emerged in northern China in the seventeenth century, and is associated from then with the rule of the Qing dynasty (1609–1911). Although it was originally worn by Manchu women, it became the standard form of dress for both men and women, enforced by sumptuary codes from the middle of the seventeenth century. Originally a loose fitting outer garment that covered the body from neck to foot, worn with trousers underneath, the modern version of the tightly-fitted female dress was developed and popularised in Shanghai in the early twentieth century. For a discussion of the histori-cal evolution of the dress see Jackson 2005.

5   For a discussion of pre-war, post-war and post-revolution Shanghainese diasporic influences in Hong Kong cinema see Tan 2004.

6   See Chu 2004 for a discussion of some of the complexities related to post-colonial identity in Hong Kong cinema.

7   Pam Cook also notes the essentially melancholic nature of nostalgia (2005: 9).

8   It is worth noting that although the patterns and fabrics appear excessive in the context of the film's much more muted *mise-en-scène*, they are a reasonably authentic reflec-tion of those worn by Chinese women in the 1950s and 1960s.

9   Here I will confine my comments to a discussion of psychic rather than commodity fetishism. For a discussion of the latter see Yue 2003.

10 This is well illustrated by another of Wong's films, one intimately related to *In the Mood for Love*: the short film *The Hand* (2004). The narrative centres on the unrequited relationship between a prostitute, Ms Hua (Gong Li), and her tailor, Xiao Zhang (Chang Chen). As her tailor, Xiao comes to know her body intimately through the measure-ments and fittings required for the production of her *qipaos*, and his meticulous work in tailoring the garments for her clearly becomes an act of love. Ms Hua is a prostitute, yet, like Li-zhen for Mo-wan, she too is inaccessible. In an extraordinary and telling scene, after overhearing Ms Hua having sex with a customer, Xiao Zhang is shown desperately fondling the dresses she has given back to him as payment for a debt. His hands move slowly up from the hem of the dress, along the slits at the sides, until his whole forearm is inside the garment, which he kisses and cries over, all the time gasping for breath. In other words, he makes love to the dress. Here, the dress is an

erotic metonym for the absent woman; the *qipao* replaces Ms Hua herself.

11 *The Hand* also emphasises the importance of tactility to the knowledge of the feminine in both narrative and affective ways. Ms Hua initially warns Xiao that he cannot become a tailor without having touched a woman, and it is through her touch that he learns this: as he later says to her, he has become a tailor because of what he learned through and about touch from her. Her sexuality is linked through tactility to the dresses she wears. His knowledge of her body is similarly inflected. He does not need to take her measurements, 'I'll just use my hands', because he knows her body intimately through his memory of the tactile relationship to the garments.

12 Here I intend affect to be understood as a felt response; it happens in a split second before it is possible to interpret and control it; it is registered extroceptively as a shudder, a tingle down the spine, a shiver of the skin, and introceptively as a visceral force. It occurs with the shock of the unexpected, the joy of surprise and the excessive pleasure of adrenalin. It is not cognitive, for once it resolves itself into thought or emotion it dissipates (see Massumi 1995). In its non-mediated immediacy it is not easily containable, and cannot be controlled.

13 Irigaray's comment here is in response to Merleau-Ponty's formulation of the chiasmus. His argument is a highly complex response to the de-corporealised, disembodied subject of psychoanalysis, and the binaries implicit in the mind/body distinction this embraces. He attempts to argue for a reciprocal relationship between the visible and the tangible in his formulation of the chiasmus. There is, he argues, a reversibility in the subject's relationship to the world, which can be characterised in terms of torsion: 'There is a circle of the touched and the touching, the touched takes hold of the touching; there is a circle of the visible and seeing, the seeing is not without visible existence'; he goes so far as to extend this reciprocity to the relationship between the visible and the tangible: 'there is even an inscription of the touching in the visible, of the seeing in the tangible' (1968: 143), a process which he articulates in his notion of the 'flesh'. However, in a cinematic context this kind of interface between the visual and the tactile is simply not possible. It is the (im)possibility of linking the visual and the tactile in such a comfortable, symbiotic relationship that is precisely what the film mourns.

WORKS CITED

Boym, S. (2001) *The Future of Nostalgia*. New York: Basic Books.

Brunette, P. (2005) *Wong Kar-wai*. Urbana: University of Illinois Press.

Buchbinder, D. (1998) *Performance Anxieties: Re-producing Masculinity*. St. Leonards, N.S.W.: Allen & Unwin.

Butler, J. (1990) *Gender Trouble: Feminism and the Subversion of Identity*. New York: Routledge.

_____ (1993) *Bodies That Matter: On the Discursive Limits of "Sex"*. New York: Routledge.

Chow, R. (2002) *Sentimental Returns: On the Uses of the Everyday in the Recent Films of Zhang Yimou and Wong Kar-wai*. New Literary History, 33, 4, 639–54.

Chu, Y.-W. (2004) 'Who am I?: Postcolonial Hong Kong Cinema in the Age of Global Capitalism', in E. M.K. Cheung & Chu Y.-W. (eds) *Between Home and World: A Reader in Hong Kong Cinema*. Hong Kong: Oxford University Press, 39–58.

Cook, P. (2005) *Screening the Past: Memory and Nostalgia in Cinema*. London and New York: Routledge.

Freud, S. (1977) 'Fetishism (1927)', in *On Sexuality, Vol. 7*, trans. J. Strachey. London: Penguin, 351–57.

_____ (1984) 'Mourning and Melancholia (1917)', in *On Metapsychology: The Theory of Psychoanalysis, Vol. 11*, trans. J. Strachey. London: Penguin, 245–68.

Grosz, E. (1994) *Volatile Bodies: Toward a Corporeal Feminism*. Bloomington and Indianapolis: Indiana University Press.

Grosz, E. & E. Probyn (1995) *Sexy Bodies: The Strange Carnalities of Feminism*. London; New York: Routledge.

Irigaray, L. (1985) *This Sex Which Is Not One*, trans. C. Porter. Ithaca, NY: Cornell University Press.

_____ (1993) *An Ethics of Sexual Difference*. Ithaca, NY: Cornell University Press.

Jackson, B. (2005) *Shanghai Girl Gets All Dressed Up*. Berkeley: Ten Speed Press.

Marchetti, G. (2002) Hong Kong in the 1960's. *In the Mood for Love (DVD)*: USA Home Entertainment.

Massumi, B. (1995) 'The Autonomy of Affect', *Cultural Critique*, 31, Fall, 83–109.

Merleau-Ponty, M. (1968) *The Visible and the Invisible: Followed by Working Notes*, trans. A. Lingis. Evanston. Il: Northwestern University Press.

Savran, D. & R. Adams (2002) *The Masculinity Studies Reader*. Malden, MA; Oxford: Blackwell.

Tan, S.-K. (2004) 'Chinese Diasporic Imaginations in Hong Kong Films: Sinicist Belligerence and Melancholia', in E. M.K. Cheung & Chu Y.-W. (eds) *Between Home and World: A Reader in Hong Kong Cinema*. Hong Kong: Oxford University Press, 147–76.

Yue, A. (2003) '*In the Mood for Love*: Intersections of Hong Kong Modernity' in C. Berry (ed.) *Chinese Films in Focus: 25 New Takes*. London: BFI, 128–36.

12. MEMORY AS CULTURAL BATTLEGROUND IN PARK CHAN-WOOK'S *OLDBOY*

TERENCE McSWEENEY

I

> What exactly is this 'past'? Is it what has passed? And what does 'passed'
> mean for a person when for each of us the past is the bearer of all that is
> constant in the reality of the present, of each current moment? In a certain
> sense the past is far more real, or at any rate more stable, more resilient than
> the present. The present slips and vanishes like sand between the fingers,
> acquiring material weight only in its recollection.
>
> — Andrei Tarkovsky (1986: 58)

Oldboy (Park Chan-wook, 2004) is arguably the defining film of what many
have described as the 'New Wave' of South Korean cinema. On winning the
Grand Jury Prize at the Cannes Film Festival in 2004 it immediately became
an international cause célèbre. Described by many as setting 'an ideal for
contemporary Korean cinema with the successful combination between
commercialism and artistic experiment' (Lee 2006: 191), it has cemented
Park Chan-wook's reputation as one of Korea's most important directors
and provided the burgeoning movement with both international acclaim
and box-office success. The film's hyper-stylised cinematic aesthetic,
sustained graphic violence and repeated transgressing of social taboos has
been the focus of much criticism and debate. Its controversial status was
shockingly reinforced in April 2007 after being implicated in the massacre
at Virginia Polytechnic Institute in which 32 people were killed and many
more injured. Cho Seung-hui, a native of South Korea, prepared a 'multi
media' manifesto which several sources claimed recreated scenes from
Oldboy in photographic form.[1] Yet to focus predominantly on the violence
in *Oldboy* is to deny its contemporary relevance and subtlety, for it is also
a sensitive mediation on memory, trauma and social alienation on the
divided peninsula. This essay intends to read *Oldboy* as a visceral cultural
artifact, a film which encapsulates the turbulence of a post-colonial climate
on screen, so much so that Liese Spencer suggests that 'it is tempting to see

Oldboy as representing the return of the repressed on a national as well as a universal level: an acting out of fantasies that was impossible under the old regime' (2004: 18).

The Korean film industry has almost as vivid and tumultuous a history as the country itself. The national traumas experienced by Korea in the twentieth century are almost too many to list, encompassing colonisation and civil war, assassinations and decades-long states of civil unrest. Its situation is unique in world geopolitics and it has been an object of colonial interest for much of its history: Britain, Russia, France and the US have all attempted to influence Korean affairs. Shortly after it was brutally annexed by Japan from 1910 until the defeat of the Axis forces in 1945,[2] the United Nations took the momentous decision to divide a racially and culturally homogeneous country into two separate states along an almost arbitrary line known as the 38th parallel, an action that was vigorously opposed by the vast majority of Koreans. It could be argued that, in this regard, the country itself inhabits a permanent state of post-memory as the result of the collective trauma persisting in South Korea more than six decades after the civil war. Even those who have not lived through the chaotic political and historical events themselves experience the trauma as inherited from the generations which preceded them; through their memories, their narratives and their very experience.[3]

These events, of course, have had and continue to have a significant impact on the South Korean film industry and the films produced. However, for a long time many of these issues went unrepresented on screen:

> Until the late 1980s Korea had one of the most highly regulated and heavily censored cinema industries outside the Communist bloc. This trend is a deliberate reaction to the previous genres in the country's cinema. Before the 1990s, Korean directors imposed a system of virtual self-censorship to be able to continue filmmaking. Heavily restricted by government censors, directors took refuge in predictable/formulaic genre films with 'safe' topics. (Jackson 2005: 14)

In the last few years South Korea has undeniably experienced a cinematic renaissance. Many films from this New Wave are marked by an urge to explore the impact of the past on contemporary Korean life and identity in provocative fashions, and they frequently revel in a new found freedom of expression. One might suggest that art, and particularly film, is the perfect stage for this cultural battleground, given the symbiotic relationship between memory and cinema. Andrei Tarkovsky, perhaps the director of cinematic memory *sui generis*, whose quotation opens this chapter, suggests that film is capable of directly recording a living 'matrix of time' on screen. For Tarkovsky, this recording process is akin to memory as both are intensely subjective and both are able to be returned to again and again. Cinema's capacity for presenting and interrogating memories of the past even led D. N. Rodowick to describe film as 'a time machine' in his book *Gilles Deleuze's Time Machine* (1997).

Adapted from a Japanese Manga comic by Minegishi Nobuaki and Garon Tsuchiya, *Oldboy* is one such exploratory text, dealing as it does with memory, the relationship of the past to the present and the fragile nature of identity.[4] It is the second part of Park's revenge triptych which began with *Sympathy for Mr Vengeance* (2001) and concluded with *Sympathy for Lady Vengeance* (2006). *Oldboy* borrows as much from Alexandre Dumas and Mary Shelly as it does from Alfred Hitchcock and Jacobean drama. It revolves around a seemingly innocuous middle-aged 'salary man' called Oh Dae-su (Choi Min-sik), who is abducted and placed in solitary confinement by an unknown kidnapper for fifteen years without explanation. When he is finally released he faces a choice: live the life that has been denied to him for so long, or search for revenge. For Dae-su the burden of the past is too great to leave behind and he sets out to find the person responsible for his incarceration, and even more importantly for him, the reason why he was held. Dae-su's experience and trauma are connected to memory, its fallibility and the violent struggle for identity. His quest is one that will take him deep into his own memories, force him to relive them as if they were present, and compel him to face truths about his identity that he would perhaps rather forget.

II

I don't understand why other film directors do not make vengeance stories, because they are so dramatic and attractive. As people are becoming more educated and society more developed, venting one's anger has become a social taboo. But that doesn't mean that the anger itself has disappeared completely. I believe that people live in a state where anger still exists, but an exit for the anger has been blocked ... So the inner hostility is growing within.

– Park Chan-wook (in Salibury 2005: 61)

The credits sequence im-
mediately makes the themes
of the film clear; at its heart
Oldboy is concerned with the
chaotic tapestry of memory
and temporality. Park
himself has suggested that
Oldboy is 'a film about the
flow of time, the irreversible nature of time'.[5] On the
screen a series of animated
clocks and watches emerge

Fig. 36 Oh Dae-su wields a hammer in his quest for revenge and identity.

in a frightening array of muted reds and blacks, self-consciously reminiscent of Saul Bass's award-winning designs for the Alfred Hitchcock films
Vertigo (1958) and *North by Northwest* (1959), themselves tales of identities in crisis. Park has stated on numerous occasions, 'Hitchcock was the
biggest influence on me during my college years. I decided to become a
filmmaker after watching *Vertigo*' (2006: 27). The credits conclude with the
twisted hands of a clock distorting and collapsing, evoking the fragmentary
and fleeting nature of memory, before finally revealing the title of the film,
the significance of which will not be made clear until much later in the
narrative. Park's representation of temporality is not a Proustian 'Time
Regained' (although he will later explore the concept); but rather a tale of
time irretrievably lost.

The film reveals that Dae-su was kidnapped on his daughter's birthday.
Locked in a room without human contact, he has no idea who has imprisoned him or why he has been put there. As the days progress, he hears
that his wife has been murdered and that he is the prime suspect. Dae-su
becomes effectively paralysed by his Kafkaesque situation and has a psychological breakdown, his anguished features symbolically juxtaposed with
the painting of a hideous face which hangs on his prison wall, based on the
work of the expressionist painter James Ensor.[6] In a sequence reminiscent
of David Fincher's satire of consumerism and pre-millennial masculinity
in crisis, *Fight Club* (1999), the frame of the screen shakes off its axis, as
if the film itself cannot contain Dae-su's suffering.[7] He hallucinates ants
crawling under his skin in a Dali-like vision of alienation and temporal
dislocation and proceeds to attempt suicide on three separate occasions.
Even death eludes him, as each time he is revived and treated by unseen

guards; whoever put him in this prison has no intention of letting him die so easily.

The room in which he is incarcerated is no ordinary prison cell, but rather is reminiscent of an anonymous hotel room. Dae-su is not physically mistreated; in fact he is fed regularly, his hair is cut, he is shaved and even given a television, but he has had his freedom removed and is powerless to prevent it.[8] On the decision to have the prison look like a hotel room, Park comments, 'When you first enter a hotel room it feels comfortable and nice, but spend a few days there and it becomes the most claustrophobic space imaginable' (quoted in Spencer 2004: 20). There is a strong sense that with *Oldboy* Park is comparing contemporary capitalist life in Seoul to a somnambulistic, self-made prison. David Scott states that this is a common theme in contemporary South Korean films; the Westernisation of South Korea has not produced the liberation that was once expected and these films often depict the 'isolation experienced by emotionally starved Seoul-ites trapped in the tenement prisons of a Westernised, post-industrial wastescape' (2000: 76). The link to unrestrained capitalism is further compounded when we discover that the prison facility is actually a profitable business run by a Mr. Park, who offers an expensive kidnapping service to clients. *Oldboy* shows capitalism taken to what some might suggest is its logical extreme, human beings becoming a commodity.[9] In this way *Oldboy* seems to offer a critique of the unbounded promise of capitalism and Westernisation which was supposed to heal the cultural traumas after South Korea's turbulent twentieth century. In a further twist, every room has video surveillance, so the clients can watch live feed of their captive in a perverse extension of the new millennial obsession with voyeuristic reality television which now spans the globe.

In one of the most striking images of the film, Dae-su records time as it passes by etching a single black line on his hand for every year he is detained, an ironic twist on how prisoners usually mark their walls to record the length of their prison sentence. For Dae-su this process is more personal, a rejection of his anonymous status as a prisoner and the fact that he has had his identity removed from him, his body itself is the site of this cultural battleground. Thus, he is never able to forget his suffering, much as the protagonists of *Memento* (Christopher Nolan, 2000) and *Eastern Promises* (David Cronenberg, 2007) ink reminders of their life and memory trauma onto their skin, creating a virtual map of their identity.

Dae-su's only connection to the outside world is the television. In voiceover he suggests, 'Make friends with the television, it is both clock and calendar. It is your school, home, church friend and lover.' As he watches the screen endlessly, an expertly composed montage sequence condenses fifteen years of his imprisonment into less than a few minutes of screen time. The montage reveals the cultural events which occur during the period he is incarcerated: from 1988 to 2003, depicting events that many of us, like him, only experience vicariously through our television and yet have become the defining moments of our lives. Park Chan-wook takes care to expand the associations beyond Korea's borders by including international events as well as domestic ones; we see the hand over of Hong Kong, the World Cup in South Korea and Japan, the death of Princess Diana, the approval of IMF funds, the historic visit of President Kim Dae-jung to North Korea and the 9/11 attacks on the Twin Towers. Park Chan-wook accentuates Dae-su's dislocation from real experience and compares him to contemporary South Koreans by showing how these recorded events have become part of the collective memory of South Korea, even though most have not directly experienced them.[10]

Dae-su also fills these empty days with a rigorous regimen of physical training, which consists of repetitively striking the brick walls of his room and shadow boxing invisible opponents. In an attempt to regain his identity he reconstructs his body from that of an overweight middle-aged man into a taut and smoothly muscled boxer and martial artist. This is the first step of Park's elaborately constructed revenge fantasy, which will encompass Dae-su's transformation from an ineffectual drunk to a heroic protagonist in search of his arch-nemesis and one who embarks on an affair with a beautiful young virgin.[11] Yet one must distinguish Park's film from other simplistic revenge fantasy films personified by the likes of *Death Wish* (Michael Winner, 1974) and *Kill Bill* (Quentin Tarantino, *Vol. 1*, 2003; *Vol. 2*, 2004) in that Park considers the psychological impact of violent conflict and revenge on the psyche of those involved. In a culture where the population has been frequently defined by their powerlessness and inability to play an active role in the history of their country, Dae-su's decisive actions are perhaps what many have fantasised about.

Dae-su is also provided with empty notebooks, in which he at first refuses to write. He cannot bring himself to acknowledge the bearing the past has on the present; so obsessed is he with revenge he is unable to reflect on his experiences and perhaps his own complicity in the events which have led him to being incarcerated. As time passes, however, he begins work on what becomes his autobiography, surprising himself by filling note-book after notebook with accounts of his misdeeds and the people he has wronged. He is revealed to be a resolutely unsympathetic protagonist; a heavy drinker, a notorious womaniser and a bad parent. Dae-su becomes surprised at the weight of his past: 'I thought I had lived a normal life, but there was so much wrongdoing.' He concludes that, before being impris-oned he hadn't really lived, content to have almost sleepwalked through his existence. Writing an autobiography is often considered a cathartic act, an embrace of and reconciliation with memory, but for Dae-su it is nothing but torment. Ironically, his copious volumes of completed notebooks ulti-mately prove worthless, as we later discover that the events which caused him to be imprisoned were at the time so insignificant to him that he had completely forgotten about them.

III

I think flashbacks lend films the surreal quality of dreams. When people remember things in films you always wonder 'Is that true?', and there's always this ambiguity in the flashbacks in my films.

— Park Chan-wook (in Spencer 2004: 19)

When Dae-su is finally released after fifteen years, as abruptly as he was kidnapped and equally without explanation, he sets out for revenge. Later, when he makes contact with the individual responsible, Lee Woo-jin (Ji-tae Yu), the man will continue to taunt him by paraphrasing the Horace proverb (later popularised by the Ella Wilcox poem *Solitude*[12]), which was inscribed under the Ensor painting in his prison cell; 'Laugh and the world laughs with you, weep and you weep alone.' His captor will quixotically continue; 'How is life in a bigger prison Oh Dae-su?'

Dae-su soon enters into a fragile relationship with a young woman called Mido (Kang Hye-jeong). Initially distrustful of each other, they share a common bond of loneliness; both are alienated from so-ciety and have no family, and the implication is that Mido too has had a troubled and

Fig. 37 Oh Dae-su and Mido form a tragic partners

eventful past. She initially refuses Dae-su's aggressive attempts at seduction, but they embark on a sexual relationship with one another, despite the age difference: Dae-su is old enough to be her father.

Even when Dae-su learns the name of the person who ordered his abduction and that they had been to school together, it still sheds no light on the mystery as to why he was imprisoned. Here the title of the film is given its relevance: Lee Woo-jin and Oh Dae-su are old boys, that is alumni of Sangnok Catholic High School. The old boys are also known as the Evergreens; for a film which is a meditation on memory and the impact of the past upon the present the title is apt, and when we see the youthful Lee Woo-jin for the first time the title will become even more relevant.

After further investigation Dae-su finds out that Lee Woo-jin's sister, Lee Soo-ah, committed suicide after rumors circulated the school about her having an incestuous relationship with her brother. Oh Dae-su had accidentally come upon the two of them having sex and told his friend, but he had no idea they were siblings. Dae-su left school soon after to join the army and the rumour accidentally spread around the entire school, all believing Dae-su to be its original source. Etiologically, it is ironic then, that the crime for which Dae-su has been punished, is the one of which he is largely innocent of, and an event so insignificant to him he barely remembered it.

This description of how Dae-su finds out why he was imprisoned does not do justice to the way it is presented in the film, failing to take into account the multiple planes of temporality presented in the narrative. *Oldboy* deviates substantially from mainstream depictions of memory, which have historically used flashbacks to render reflections of the past onscreen. Flashbacks generally tend to follow a similar pattern, a memory is introduced, which is significantly demarcated stylistically and temporally from the present, which then usually goes on to reveal an essential and uncontested truth about that present before being concluded, thus allowing the contemporary narrative to continue. For many this is indicative of how culture generally regards time: as a firmly chronological process continuing along a fixed line of 'nows'.

Gilles Deleuze described flashbacks as 'a precisely closed circuit which goes from the present to the past, then leads us back to the present' (1989: 48). In *Oldboy* the flashbacks are not so clearly signposted; they often seem involuntary, as if Dae-su has no control over whether he wants to remember or not, he is as powerless over his memories as he is over his own life.

This idea of involuntary memory has become a significant aspect of contemporary postmodernism; the recent novel by Brett Easton Ellis, *Lunar Park* (2005), a narrative also about loss, identity, memory and broken families, uses it frequently. The narrator (Ellis himself) ironically misremembers the Proustian concept itself:

> 'God what are you wearing?' I murmured. 'That smell, it takes me back.' 'To where?' I was licking her mouth. 'Just, like, back. The past. I'm experiencing my whole adolescence.' 'Just with lip gloss.' 'Yeah,' I sighed 'It's like those tangerines in Proust.' 'You mean madeleines.' 'Yeah those little tangerines.' (2006: 121)

For Proust an image or even a smell could conjure up a concomitant association in the mind and emotionally transport a person back to that original moment of experience. Proust's dual-layered approach takes on the experience of his characters' involuntary memories and the involuntary memories of the reader inspired by the novel itself. In Proust, temporality is an equivocal construct, as through the 'Sensuous Sign' memory is able to eradicate the conventional passage of time by recreating the sensual impression with all the dynamism of the original experience. The past is always alive, hidden somewhere within us and may be discovered and recreated through mediating sensory perceptions.

The medium of film, with its broad range of cinematic properties encompassing imagery, sound (both music and otherwise), theme and characterisation, can perform the same function perhaps even more strikingly than literature. This type of associational memory occurs several times throughout *Oldboy*, where events, even tastes and sounds, trigger Dae-su's memories, leading to experiences not codified *just* as a memory, but as real and as vivid as the current moment or the moment they were first experienced, what might be termed a 'living memory'. The sequence set in Dae-su's school is one such 'involuntary memory' and is the most powerful and literal manifestation of memory in the whole film. The trigger that literally takes him back to the past is the sound of a doorbell and the sight of the bare knees of a teenage girl; this immediately transports him into his memory, as he remembers the bell on the bicycle that Lee Woo-jin's sister rode and *her* bare knees.

As Dae-su remembers his time at the school, the sequences break with traditional representation of memory in film by, rather than simply recalling the event, Dae-su takes an active part in the sequence itself, locating him *within* the memory. Often in mainstream films, memories are presented as if they have recorded the past as fact by some sort of surveillance camera, but *Oldboy* shows an active remembering process, where new meanings are constantly created and the past is relived as if it is a contemporary event. We see the young Dae-su look through the window at Lee Woo-jin and his sister having sex; the couple hear a noise at the window and turn to look towards it, only to see the older Oh Dae-su in his younger self's place.

This imbrication of an 'actual' and a 'virtual' is Deleuzian in its approach and has far-reaching implications. For the representation of memory, the 'actual' is the one we are experiencing at any given moment (a time that passes), and the 'virtual' is a memory of an event that has already occurred (a preserved time). Cinema has traditionally demarcated these two concepts, preserving the notion that memory is 'just' a fragment of the past. However, it is the interaction of these concepts that provides the key to a more provocative perception of temporality, one which challenges the idea that time is a linear construct.[13] This temporal dislocation is also reflected in the spatial dislocation of the *mise-en-scène* of the sequence, as the older Dae-su chases his younger self through a series of incongruous stairways, self-consciously reminiscent of an Escher etching. For Dae-su the struggle to remember something which he had previously forgotten becomes the defining event in his life.

IV

I try not to express onscreen violence as something that is beautiful to look at or something that is playful or fun or that relieves the stress, I try to convey a feeling of pain in both the tormentor and the victim.

— Park Chan-wook (in Salisbury 2005: 60)

Before Dae-su discovers that Lee Woo-jin is the man responsible for his incarceration, the audience has already been introduced to him. We see his luxurious penthouse apartment, a stark contrast to Dae-su's prison cell, which seems to stretch across an entire floor of a downtown skyscraper overlooking Seoul, radiating affluence and power. One corner is filled with a collection of antique cameras and a wall of photographs of his dead sister, captured moments of the past. The image Lee Woo-jin focuses on is of his sister just moments before she fell to her death. In the film, photographs are a metaphor for attempting to reclaim the past. However Lee Woo-jin's memories of his sister are revealed through the unfreezing of photographic images as they come to life, transporting him back in time. Like in the school sequence with Dae-su, the memory comes alive for Lee Woo-jin. Here D. N. Rodowick's description of film as a 'time machine' is revealed to be strikingly apt, just as memory is able to store events and replay them, transporting the viewer into the past, so is film. Lee Woo-jin's fetishisation of his sister's image presents his longing for an impossible restoration of the past, memory and family unity. In the photograph she is recorded as an object, forever frozen in time, but for Lee Woo-jin, as Catherine Keenan's work has suggested (1998), the photographs become more real than the events themselves. Lee Woo-jin's use of the photographic image to record his personal pain and defining moment of his life also recalls Siegfried Kracauer's influential work on photography, in particular his essay on the subject from 1927 where he suggests that a photograph is much more than the reproduction of an image, but an interpretation of all the subjective experience of that particular moment in time from the perspective of the photographer.

The film implies that a large part of Lee Woo-jin died with his sister on that day. He is as obsessed with the past and desirous of revenge as Dae-su. His emotional immaturity is reflected in the crude metaphor of his heart problem and the fact that he has become a passive observer of life only using his energy to orchestrate his decades-long revenge over the one person he believed caused his sister's death.

Fig. 38 Oh Dae-su comes face to face with his nemesis Lee Woo-jin.

Despite being roughly the same age as Dae-su he looks preternaturally young, perhaps even twenty years younger, as if he is a living version of Oscar Wilde's Dorian Gray.

Lee Woo-jin's apartment is dominated by water, a reccurring theme and motif throughout the film. Park suggests that he uses 'a lot of water as in the giant mural of a tsunami – water is usually used to symbolise creation but here it signifies death because his sister drowned' (in Spencer 2004: 20).

The mural is the famous *The Great Wave off Kanagawa* (1832) by Katsushita Hokusei. Just as the Ensor painting was juxtaposed with Dae-su revealing his mental deterioration, the tsunami shows him for what he is, as inexorable as a force of nature, driven only by one thing, revenge.

It is this revenge that connects both characters, both are consumed by the past and are in many ways each other's double. Park underlines their emotional connection by manipulating *mise-en-scène* and using split screen editing techniques to connect their faces or by having them frequently adopt the same body position within the shot. While it is always ambiguous as to what Lee Woo-jin wants, it appears he needs Dae-su to experience the same pain he has, so his elaborate plan is to become the architect of Dae-su's life. However, he is much more aware of their predicament than the mercurial Dae-su; Lee Woo-jin knows that the quest for revenge is ultimately futile, despite claiming that 'seeking revenge is the best cure for someone who has been hurt,' he continues: 'What comes after?' In this respect Dae-su is a monster that not just Lee Woo-jin but Korean culture has created; akin to the Godzilla of Japanese disaster films, the mutated fish-like monster which emerges from the Han river in Seoul in Bong Jun-ho's *The Host* (2006) and of course the archetypal Frankenstein's Monster from the novel by Mary Shelly. Park even shows a clip of *Frankenstein* (James Whale, 1931) on screen while Dae-su is in captivity to underline the point.[14]

Park also confirms that the working title for the film was *The Beast*, referring to Dae-su's animalistic behavior and a line which reoccurs throughout the film, 'Even though I am a beast do I not deserve to live?' Shortly after this sequence he enters a Sushi restaurant where his wish is to eat something alive. The 'Sannakji' sequence is one that has caused most offence to Western viewers, as Choi Min-sik, as Dae-su, proceeds to eat a live octopus on camera, largely in a single take, leaving no doubt that the octopus is real.[15] Dae-su's desire to eat something alive is to prove to himself that *he* is still alive.

V

Revenge is a taboo in modern society: everyone has a strong desire for it, but it's prohibited. Incest too is a suppressed desire in all of us – it appears in old tales from all over the world, long before Freud.

– Park Chan-wook (in Spencer 2004: 19)

The climax of the film sees Dae-su confront Lee Woo-jin in the luxurious tower block apartment. Dae-su has learned what he believes to be the true reason he was imprisoned; that Lee Woo-jin blames Dae-su for spreading the rumour which lead to his sister's death. Yet Lee Woo-jin merely shrugs off this explosive revelation, telling Dae-su that his incarceration was merely the first part of an elaborate revenge plan. It transpires that Lee Woo-jin raised Dae-su's daughter in secret over the years and orchestrated the meeting of father and daughter through post-hypnotic suggestions given to them both at Lee Woo-jin's orders. Lee Woo-jin points at a beautifully ornate purple box, inside is a family album. Through photographs the past once again comes alive, as the images flick from one to another we see a baby grow into a girl, then into a young woman. Dae-su's daughter is revealed to be none other than Mido, with whom Dae-su is now in love and having a sexual relationship.

With the revelation of incest many other elements begin to retroactively slot into place, the sound of the name Oh Dae-su and its proximity to Oedipus, the use of the tongue as motif and metaphor which has recurred throughout the film. Park says:

> I didn't particularly have Sophocles in mind when I was working on the script. But I couldn't avoid the association when the idea of incest appeared. Then I gradually came to think of a way to insert a scene in the film that would parallel Oedipus poking his own eyes. My original plan was for Oh Dae-su to cut off his own penis after he found out he had sex with his own daughter. (2006: 33)

Park here register's his distress at the collapse of the traditional Korean family unit through father/daughter incest, an act which destroys both past, present and future.

On realising what he has done Dae-su begs for forgiveness and implores Lee Woo-jin not to reveal the secret to Mido; he cuts off his own tongue as a gesture of his sincerity. Having gained his revenge over Dae-su, Lee Woo-jin agrees not to tell Mido, though even then his motivation is ambiguous. He states 'We knew what we were doing and we still loved each other; will you and Mido be the same?' Just as he predicted, revenge has brought no relief for either of them. Lee Woo-jin steps into the lift and looks down to see his sister's hand reaching into the frame, crossing the bounds of temporality, memory and reality, as two temporal planes momentarily become one. Like Dae-su's return to the past in his visit to the school, Lee Woo-jin returns to the most important moment of his life, an event so powerful it has become more real to him than reality. Like the previous sequence featuring both young and old Dae-su, here Park cuts between the young and the old Lee Woo-jin until his sister lets go of his hand, revealing the truth about her death, she had killed herself, distraught about the rumours and the possibility she might be pregnant with her brother's child, and Lee Woo-jin had tried to stop her. At the moment of her death he too commits suicide by shooting himself with a pistol; leaving his gun shot and sister's last words echoing together, 'Please remember me.'

Oldboy concludes with an ambiguous epilogue, which takes place after the events described. In a snowy landscape, Dae-su is revealed as a broken man, physically and psychologically ravaged; he now completely resembles the Ensor painting which hung on the wall of the room in which he was incarcerated. He has contacted the Japanese hypnotist who originally gave him post-hypnotic suggestions at the request of Lee Woo-jin. His request to her is to rid himself of the traumatic memories and the knowledge that Mido is his daughter. With this Park challenges the audience one final time: why does Dae-su choose to remove his memory? Is it so he can resume his incestuous relationship with his daughter in ignorance? Or is he planning to become a father to her without the pain of the knowledge of their past together? After the treatment, the camera stays on Dae-su, his pained expression ambiguous testimony to whether the hypnotic suggestion has been successful or not.

When Dae-su chooses to erase his memory rather than confront and live with the truth, like the protagonists of *Eternal Sunshine of the Spotless Mind* (Michel Gondry, 2004), he learns that it is impossible. Memory, and frequently the trauma it contains, is an integral part of individual, or indeed national, identity. Oh Dae-su's experience is manifested in his appearance and defines him whether he likes it or not. Memory lives on in him as it lives on in the divided peninsula; in its very geography, its narratives and its people, in a bewildering tapestry of nation-state history. Not content to relegate memory to an historical abstract, the films of the Korean New Wave explore forms of recollection which are as 'real' as contemporary events. What had previously been 'the past' is acknowledged as still alive and as present as the here and now, with all the paradoxes and implications this entails. *Oldboy* is just one of the many contemporary films both in South Korea or outside to represent such a 'living past' on screen. Many of these films deal with the fallibility and fidelity of human memory, they choose to tackle apparent truths, themselves notoriously subjective, as a way of reconciling the self with experience of the past. It is this interrogation of stereotypical representations of memory which makes *Oldboy*, and films like it, such valuable texts.

NOTES

1 Despite assertions about a connection between Cho Seung-hui and *Oldboy* no confirmed link has been established by the police. Stephen Hunter's 'Cinematic Clues to Understand the Slaughter' in the *Washington Post* of 20 April 2007 is characteristic of the largely hysterical media frenzy that circulated the purported connection in the days after the Virginia Tech massacre: '*Oldboy* must feature prominently in the discussion, even if no one has yet confirmed that Cho saw it. On the surface, it seems a natural fit, at least in the way it can be presumed that Cho's hyper-fervid brain worked. It's a Korean story – he would have passed on the subtitles and listened to it in his native language – of unjust persecution and bloody revenge.'

2 Under the Japanese occupation Koreans were harshly mistreated physically and psychologically; sections of the populous were forced into slavery and those that weren't were severely taxed, speaking the Korean language was outlawed and Koreans were forced to adopt Japanese names.

3 While 'postmemory' was initially related to the experience of subsequent generations of holocaust survivors by Marian Hirsch in *Family Frames: Photography, Narrative and Postmemory* (1997) one can see its relevance in other conflicts too. This is further compounded by the fact that the Korean War has never officially ended and no peace treaty has ever been signed.

4 Until recently the fact that a film was adapted from a comic book might have been cause for concern but films like *Road to Perdition* (Sam Mendes, 2002), *A History of Violence* (David Cronenberg, 2005), *American Splendor* (Shari Springer Berman & Robert Pulcini, 2003) and to a lesser extent *V for Vendetta* (James McTiegue, 2005), *Sin City* (Robert Rodriguez, 2004) and *Watchmen* (Zack Snyder, 2009) have shown that graphic novels can be fertile source material.

5 Park Chan-wook on *Oldboy* DVD. Tartan Video, 2005.

6 The Belgian expressionist painter James Ensor (1860–1949) frequently depicted the more monstrous elements of humanity and heavily influenced Edvard Munch. The picture in *Oldboy* is based on the painting *The Man of Sorrows* (1892).

7 There are some interesting parallels between *Fight Club* and *Oldboy*. Both challenge stereotypical representations of masculinity, feature a 'double' motif, both can be read as satires of consumerism and conformity. Yet arguably *Fight Club* renounces its anti-capitalist message in favour of a romantic dénouement where the hero is reintroduced into society. *Oldboy* offers no such simplistic resolution.

8 Several modern films like *Children of Men* (Alfonso Cuarón, 2006), *Babel* (Alejandro Gonzalez Iñárritu, 2006), *28 Weeks Later* (Juan Carlos Fresnadillo, 2007), and *Hostel* (Eli Roth, 2005) have explored unlawful incarceration themes with conscious or unconscious allusions to Guantánamo Bay and the 'War on Terror'.

9 The first film in the trilogy, *Sympathy For Lady Vengeance*, explored a similarly cannibalistic extension of capitalism. The protagonist is deceived by a company which

steals people's kidneys and other vital organs, and sells them on the South Korean black market.

10 The inclusion of the Princess Diana footage is interesting; Diana's death has been frequently evoked as a culturally significant moment in not only *Oldboy* but in films as diverse as *Amelie* (Jean-Pierre Jeunet, 2001) and *The Queen* (Stephen Frears, 2006). In each of these three films the death of Diana is also related to the functions of memory and the memorial process.

11 If there is any connection between the Virginia State killings and the film *Oldboy* and there has been no officially stated link, it might be this element of the narrative which attracted an alienated and disturbed young man; a passive outsider chooses to take what he perceives is an active role in his own life and take revenge on an individual he believes has persecuted him. Yet this interpretation of the film fails to take into account the fact that it portrays the ugly realities of the aftermath of revenge, as *Oldboy* offers no consolation for either the perpetrator or the victims.

12 See R. LaGalliane (ed.) (1935) The *La Gallienne Book of English and American Poetry Vols. 1 & 2*. New York: Garden City Publishing, 244.

13 The school could be regarded as a locus of lived experience or a *lieux de mémoire* as Pierre Nora suggests, which connects experiential memory to a 'physical and tangible location'. See Nora 1989.

14 Dae-su's internet user name is revealed to be 'monster' and Lee Woo-jin agrees: 'Yes you are the monster that I created.' In the director's commentary Park discusses his initial desire to intercut scenes from the *Bride of Frankenstein* while Dae-su is destroying Lee Woo-jin's apartment but he omitted it for pacing reasons.

15 The actor Choi Min-sik is a Buddhist and offered a prayer for the three separate animals devoured over the three takes required for this scene. The rare Korean delicacy of 'Sannakji' and this consumption of a live animal has seemed to be perhaps the most shocking part of the film for Western audiences. This is indicative of how culturally specific the nature of taboo is, as the same sequence is considerably less shocking for a Korean audience. However, one might ask how different this is to eating oysters or the boiling of live lobsters which is still relatively common in the West.

WORKS CITED

Deleuze, G. (1989) *Cinema Two: The Time-Image*, trans. H. Tomlinson and R. Galeta. Minneapolis: University of Minnesota Press.

Easton Ellis, B. (2006) *Lunar Park*. London: Picador/Pan MacMillan.

Hirsch, M. (1997) *Family Frames: Photography, Narrative and Postmemory*. Cambridge: Harvard University Press.

Hunter, S. (2007) 'Cinematic Clues to Understand the Slaughter', *Washington Post*, 20 April, C01.

Jackson, A. D. (2005) 'Korea's New Cinematic Language', *Osian's Cinemaya: The Asian Film Quarterly*, 1, 2, 13–16.

Keenan, C. (1998) 'On the Relationship between Personal Photographs and Individual Memory', *History of Photography*, 22, 1, 60–4.

Kracauer, S. (1995) 'Photography (1927)', in T. Y. Levin (ed.) *The Mass Ornament: Weimar Essays*. Cambridge: Cambridge University Press, 47–64.

Lee, Hyang-jin (2006) 'South Korean Film on a Global stage', in A. T. Ciecko (ed.) *Contemporary Asian Cinema*, New York: Berg, 182–92.

Nora, P. (1989) 'Between Memory and History: *Les Lieux de Mémoire*', *Representations* 26, 7–25.

Park, Chan-wook (2006) *Park Chan-wook: Saviour of Violence*, ed. Lim Youn-hi, trans. Park Soo-Mee. Seoul: Korean Film Council Seoul.

Rodowick, D. N. (1997) *Gilles Deleuze's Time Machine.* Durham: Duke University Press.

Salisbury, M. (2005) 'The Oldboy network', *Fangoria*, 240, Feburary, 58–61.

Scott, D. (2000) 'Seoul as cinematic cityscape: Shiri and the Political Aesthetics of Invisibility', *Asian Cinema*, 11, 2, 76–91.

Spencer, L. (2004) 'Revenger's Tragedy', *Sight and Sound*, 14, 19, 18–21.

Tarkovsky, A. (1986) *Sculpting in Time: Reflections on the Cinema*, trans. K. Hunter-Blair. London: Faber and Faber.

LaGalliane, R. (ed.) (1935) *The La Gallienne Book of English and American Poetry V1&2*, Garden City Publishing: New York.

INDEX

J-n Erihsen
& Stjernfelt   Den Amtrlutus ?
Multulturla

M. Kuntzel Ichul & Tew-Mstel.